THE BLOODY CROWN

THE STORY OF THE LIVES, LOVES AND BATTLES OF THE KINGS OF ENGLAND
1066 TO 1485

James Keys

DEDICATED TO THE MEMORY OF

Private Jason Burt and Private Ian Scrivens
3rd Battalion The Parachute Regiment

Mount Longdon, The Falklands
June 12th 1982

And the Officers and Men of
The Paras

Proper Soldiers

CONTENTS

Introduction

At a little after 7 0 clock on the morning of 14th October 1066.Harold Godwinson, King of England stood in the centre of the Saxon shield wall of red and yellow beneath his personal banner of the Fighting Man and the Golden Dragon of Wessex. Facing him was a Norman army of around 9000 men led by William the Bastard, Duke of Normandy. The next few hours would decide the future of the English throne.

The outcome of the battle altered the course of English history. The bloody wars of the next 400 years can trace their origins to this event. In this book I have set out to tell the stories of the struggles, battles and tribulations of the Kings of England, not just as a catalogue of facts (although all events and dates listed are accurate) but to show them as human beings, their quirks, tempers, weaknesses, strengths and, in some cases, their humour.

My thanks to The Anglo Saxon Chronicle, Wace, Dudo, Orderic Vitalis, William of Malmesbury, Mathew Paris, Froissart, Hollinshead and many other long dead chroniclers for their help in the compiling of this book.

Forward

This is a book about the medieval Kings of England, that strange island of which so much has been written. The many invasions that it has suffered and its ability to assimilate them all. Where did the name begin? The Celts knew it as Albion, being their name for white, the colour of the south eastern cliffs that would have first confronted them. The Greek navigator Pytheas on his visits to the tin mines of what is now Cornwall knew it as Pretannike, the land of the painted people, the Romans later translated this to Pretannia, which eventually became Britannia. The Angles and Saxons drove the Celts to the fringes of the islands (and to the edges of western France) and the land became that of the Anglo Saxons or Anglo-lond in their tongue. By the tenth century England was united under one King, its laws, customs, courts and government divided into Shires Hundreds and boroughs were highly developed with a national language, national tax system and military command These were no ignorant savages that met William of Normandy on that October morning.

To understand the motivations and actions of medieval man we need to examine his view of the world

His life was short, often brutal and riddled with fear, disease and superstition. His universe was flat and little known beyond his own immediate locality; the edges of the world were peopled by monsters, dragons and exotic beasts that lived in these dark fringes where no man went. His own world was full of fears of witches and devils, every graveyard, every crossroads; every ring of stones was the haunt of the devil's creatures. His only protection was prayer, calling on the name of Jesus or making the sign of the Cross. The church was at the centre of life and prayer worked, Christian saints were renowned for their powers of miracles and pilgrimages were seen as a major way to expiate sins and to visit the holy places and pray in these sacred places and to touch the

3

holy relics could cure all this world's ills. The Church fed on these fears and grew rich.

By 638 the armies of Islam had wrested the holy land from the rulers of Byzantium. They were surprisingly tolerant of the Christians wishing to visit Jerusalem and even the former citizens preferred the tolerance of the new rulers to the high taxes and narrow rules of Byzantium. This situation lasted until 1071 when the Seljuk Turks from the north invaded the Empire from eastern Turkey. As they tightened their hold on the conquered lands, the pilgrim routes were closed. It was still possible to reach the holy land by sea, but many pirates operated in the Mediterranean making the journey perilous.

The Empire of Byzantium became increasingly weakened by the relentless attacks from the Turks culminating in the disastrous battle of Manzikert when the Byzantine army was virtually destroyed. The Emperor did not attempt to appeal directly to the Christians of Europe for help, he appealed to the Pope in Rome to help rescue the Christians of the east from the tyranny of the Moslem hordes. It was intolerable that the holy places of the Christian faith should be trampled under the foot of the infidels.

His words, designed to inflame, had the desired effect. Pope Urban called a Council of Bishops at Clermont and after the business of the church was attended to, he detailed the Emperor's plea. Urban was a great orator and his words struck a chord in all who heard him. His bishops went back to their lands and preached the justness of a crusade to drive the infidel from the birthplace of Jesus. The cry echoed around the western world, "Dieu le Volt!" God wills it! Here was a chance to wipe out a man's sins by fighting God's holy war, the chance to kill infidels, an act not considered sinful, and to earn a place in heaven. Not to mention the opportunities for looting etc.

The mind of medieval man was rooted in his belief in the power of God. With Him on your side you would prevail no matter what the obstacle, a belief that drove warrior Kings such as Henry V to face forces many times the size of his own in the sure knowledge that, if your cause was just, God would grant victory. This balancing of the lust for power and the fear of God explains much about the power wielded by the church

4

throughout the turbulent events described. It alone had the power to grant absolution of sins and thus the path to God's grace.

This then is the story of the lives of those kings from William's invasion in 1066 to the death of Richard on Bosworth Field in 1485.

Chapter One

William 1.

To understand the reasons for William's invasion of England in 1066 and his subsequent victory at Hastings, we need to go back over one hundred years to 911 when Charles the Simple of France granted a part of Northern France to the Norse Viking Rollo at a treaty signed at St Claire-sur-Epte. The treaty granted the Viking full ownership of the land although it is recorded that both Rollo and later his son William Longsword did full homage to the Frankish King indicating their acceptance of French sovereignty.

Charles was known as "The Simple", not through feeble mindedness, but because he was reckoned to be plain and straight in his dealings with others. The writer Dudo records that Charles also gave his daughter Gisella to Rollo as wife, but there is no confirmation of this although it would not have been seen as unusual as a way of solving territorial problems.

This grant was maybe not as generous as first seen. Charles knew that Vikings were a fact of life and, rather than forever having to defend against them, it would be better to have them as allies and also use them as a buffer against the always aggressive Dukes of this western edge of the Carolingian empire. This empire, loosely based on the original Roman, was founded in 800 with the coronation of Charlemagne, but by the 9th century had proved too cumbersome and had divided into roughly the areas now known as Germany France and the Middle Kingdom (the areas of Lorraine, Burgundy and Lombardy) and by the 10th century had fragmented into principalities under the control of Dukes, Viscounts and Counts constantly seeking to extend their own power at the expense of their neighbours.

Charles, in addition, faced constant troubles from the Scandinavians in the North, the Bretons in the West and the Muslims in the South, who, following their defeat by Charles Martel in 732 at Poitiers had retreated over the Pyrenees but still harried southern France. He also knew that he had the option to invade and retrieve Normandy if he

6

wished and that there was no guarantee that the Vikings could hold the land against the many warring factions of the time and they could perhaps be thrown out by any of them...

The arrangement also suited Rollo, a true Viking, who gained a foothold on the coast of Europe, much closer to the rich pickings of the south and convenient for raids on England. Rollo adopted the title Count of Rouen as did his son William, but William's son Richard 1st, after forging an alliance with Brittany by marrying the Duke's daughter Judith, styled himself Marquis of the Normans or Northmen.

In 1015, his son Richard 2nd took upon himself the title of Duke asserting his rights to control the church, a most important distinction as it gave him the right to appoint Bishops and to appoint Counts under him with all the attendant rewards. To strengthen his dynastic ambitions he betrothed his son Robert to the daughter of the Dane Cnut, but Robert died in Asia Minor returning from pilgrimage, the proposed alliance dying with him

Charles' strategy worked. The Vikings, now referred to by their Frankish neighbours as Normans or Northmen, and after a period of ravaging from this new more southern base and establishing a thriving trade in slaves, were gradually assimilated, converting to Christianity by the year 1000. Many spread southward and by 1050 had established control of large parts of Southern Italy, plus Sicily and Malta in addition to Normandy.

William was born in Caen in 1027,the illegitimate son of Robert Duke of Normandy and a peasant girl from Falais named Harlotte or Herleve, the daughter of Fulbert, a local Tanner. She was subsequently married off to Herluin of Conteville and bore him two sons, Odo and Robert, both of whom would join William in his invasion of 1066.
In 1034, Robert, in a fit of devotion, decided to go on a pilgrimage to the Jerusalem to seek forgiveness for the sins in this life and, as a further penance, would make the journey on foot. His Barons protested, arguing that the journey was risky and should he die, who would rule in his absence? Robert replied," I will not leave you without a Lord, "I give you my son William, I know he will grow to

be a gallant man, receive him as your Lord for I make him my heir and give him from this time forth my whole Duchy". Robert never returned from his pilgrimage and William became effectively the Duke of Normandy from the age of 7.

William grew up under the notional protection of his feudal lord King Henry and his Aunt's stepson Count Baldwin of Flanders. During the next 12 years William survived the murder of three of his guardians, the last one, Osbern, being killed in the very room in which William slept. It must be presumed that such a childhood endowed William with a fairly cynical view of the world and the power of violence. He grew to be 5'10" tall, with red hair, close cropped in the Norman fashion and was noted for his strength. It was said that he could easily carry another man's armour as well as his own.

In 1047, commanding for the first time and with the help of Henry, he put down the last of the rebellions by the Norman barons at the battle of Val-et-Dunes, establishing himself, at the age of 20, as the most powerful force in the country. His life, however, was not to be an easy one. He was an energetic and clever ruler, growing to be a fierce warrior and the civil wars that racked the Duchy showed him to be very cruel to his enemies. He once ordered that 32 of the citizens of Alencon have their hands and feet cut off because they jeered his illegitimacy. His policy of laying waste to the lands of his enemies caused far more deaths through starvation than the actual fighting

His father had given refuge to the English claimant to the throne, Edward, during the years of England's occupation by the Danes which does much to explain Edward's pro Norman choice of his successor. Edward the Confessor was born in 1019,the son of Ethelred the Unready =Unraed (meaning "bad counsel) and Emma of Normandy, he spent the first 25 years of his life in Normandy and became King following the death of the ferocious Harthacanute, son of Cnut and Emma of Normandy, ex wife of the Confessor. Harthacanute died in Lambeth at the age of 25 while attending a wedding. It is said that he died 'standing at his drink and he suddenly fell to the ground with fearful convulsions and those nearby caught him and he spoke no word afterwards'. Harthacanute was a healthy young man and to die in such a way would indicate poisoning, which begs the question of who would benefit from his death other than Edward?

Having spent so much of his life in France, Edward had no power base to consolidate his rule in England and needed friends. Step forward Godwin Earl of Mercia with his five sons. Godwin was related through marriage to the King of Denmark and had spent much of his life fighting in Denmark's struggles with Norway.
Edward, who's upbringing had made him more Norman in outlook than Anglo Saxon had reputedly supported William to succeed him to the English throne, even sending Robert, Archbishop of Canterbury to Normandy to assure William of his support. This was to be the first part of William's determination to rule England. It was also said that, in 1064, Harold, son of Earl Godwin of Wessex was shipwrecked off Ponthieu and captured by William. Although being treated as a guest he was not allowed to leave until he had agreed to support William in his claim to the English throne.

Harold eventually gave his word, but later learned that the oath had been given over a hidden holy relic, giving his pledge much more power. This gave William further justification to his claim for the throne. We must ask why Edward was so keen to hand the country over to William, but the only explanations available to us were written by people with vested interests in the affair. With no clear succession and with Saxon, Norman and Scandinavian contenders, it is more likely that Edward was playing a placating game by playing off one against the other.

Edward married Editha the daughter of Earl Godwin the most powerful of his subjects, ruling most of Southern England. Godwin's assistance to Edward had been rewarded by the gift of Earldoms to his sons Sweyn who had been given Herefordshire and Harold given East Anglia. Further lands were granted later in his reign and by 1066 a third of England was under the control of the Godwins. The relationship between the two men was not an easy one however and by 1051 had quarrelled to such an extent, mainly over the increasing Norman influence in England, particularly the appointment of a

Norman, Robert of Jumiages to the important position of Archbishop of Canterbury.

Things were made worse by a fight that broke out in Dover between some of Godwin's followers and Eustace of Boulogne's men. Eustace was the brother in law of King Edward and complained to him of Godwin's actions. The King summoned Godwin and his sons to trial, but the Earl and his sons fled to exile. Godwin fled to Bruges with three of his sons, Sweyn, Tostig and Gyrth, while two other sons Harold and Leofrine went to Ireland. Being free of his Saxon father in law enabled Edward to bring over many more Norman knights and clergy causing much resentment among the English.

In 1052 Llewelyn of Wales invaded Herefordshire and during this diversion Harold sailed from Ireland to raid the south coast. He was joined by his father and the two fleets sailed up the Thames to threaten Edward who was forced to accept defeat with his forces refusing to fight the popular Harold and to return Godwin and his sons to their power. The Norman Archbishop was replaced by the Saxon Sigand. Godwin did not live long however, in 1053 while at dinner with Edward in Winchester, he died, apparently of a stroke in circumstances similar to Harthacanute, thus removing the second of Edward's enemies. Edward's half brother Edmond Ironsides had a son who could also be considered a natural heir to the throne and in 1057 was brought to England from Hungary where he had lived most of his life. He did not long survive in England and although little is known of him it is said that he met a 'miserable fate' his death removing a third rival for the throne.

He too had a son, Edgar (the Atheling), who, as grandson of Edmund and Great Grandson of Ethelred, could also lay rightful claim to be Edward's successor.
History views Edward, with his white hair and pale skin as a saintly man mainly due to his passion for collecting relics and for his many gifts to churches and monasteries, contemporaries describe him however as 'very slothful and having an unsteady attention to duty and being devoid of sound judgement' He founded the great Abbey of St Peter at Westminster a burial place for many of the future Kings of

England and spent the latter part of his life in overseeing his creation, allowing Harold Godwinson to attend to affairs of State This work continued under his direction for a further 14 years and it was consecrated in 18th December 1065 shortly before Edwards death on 5th January 1066.

His nearest surviving heir was Edgar the Atheling (meaning "Related to Royals") who was however, a minor. Harold had some advantages over his rivals, being the most powerful man in England he had been in command of the Army for some 13 years and was known as 'subregius'' or 'Underking' and was, at that time, the only one capable of withstanding the invasion threats of Normandy and Norway. He was much experienced, having fought in Ireland and on the continent. He invaded Wales in 1063 and so crushingly defeated King Llewelyn that it is said that the remnants of the Welsh army brought Llewelyn's head to Harold in a bag as tribute. Now, in England, he was "the man on the spot"; he would not miss this chance.

Edward's funeral was held the following day. Harold had gone to the Witan, the Saxon council, immediately after Edwards death to claim the throne, but he was told that he could not legally be crowned until his predecessor was buried, thus the reason for haste. By ancient custom, Eldred the Primate of Northumbria asked the consent of the people and Harold, last of the Saxon Kings was crowned. It is recorded that William, on hearing the news, stood unable to speak in his wordless fury,"constantly tying and untying his cloak".

Harold' short reign was a violent one. 1066 was the year of Halley's Comet. It appeared first on 24th April and was seen throughout England. Men reckoned it a great omen and called it the long haired star. It shone in the night sky for seven nights.

Within a short time of his coronation Harold Hardrada (meaning ruthless), King of Norway and Denmark together with Harold's brother Tostig invaded the north. Tostig had raided the Humber estuary earlier, but had been defeated by Earl Edwin of Northumbria Tostig's men deserted him and he sailed for Norway in 12 small ships.

King Harold of Norway met him and Tostig bowed to him and became his man. It is known that, shortly after his coronation, Harold journeyed to the north, probably to talk to Earls Edwin and Morcar and to reassure them that Tostig would not be allowed back to England.

There is also some evidence that Harold did, at this time, marry Edwin and Morcar's sister Alditha to seal the loyalty of the men in the north. Harold Hardrada's claim to the throne as a kinsman of the family of King Cnut was only as strong as his daring could make it, although there was an agreement allegedly made in 1040 between Magnus of Norway and Harthacanute that promised the English throne to the Dane. Standing 6'6" tall Hardrada was a giant of his time and had fought for many years as commander of the famous Varangarian Guard of Byzantium throughout Europe.

After ravaging Cleveland and capturing Scarborough they defeated the northern Fyrd under Edwin Earl of Northumbria at Fulford near York on 20th September. Harold, ever ready for a fight, rode with his Housecarls up the Roman road gathering his Midland levies as he went, arriving in York on 25th September. He pushed on a further 7 miles to Stamford Bridge were he surprised Hardrada in his camp. The Norwegians and Danes knew nothing of the attack until they saw through the mist the English armour 'glistening like ice'. It is recorded that Harold met with his brother Tostig briefly before the battle and promised him a third of the kingdom if he would change sides and support Harold. Tostig asked "and what will you give Hadrada?" Harold replied "I will give him 6 feet of English earth or 7 because he is so tall".

Tostig declined the offer, a decision that was to cost him his life. Hardrada retreated across the Derwent to the high ground and formed his shield wall. He also sent word to his lieutenant Eystein Orre who was guarding the Viking ships at Ricall to bring reinforcements. To gain time one berserk, so called because he fought 'bare-sark' i.e. without armour, stood on the narrow bridge defending the passage with his war axe. He was able to halt Harold's advance until one of the English soldiers rowed out beneath the bridge until he was beneath the Viking and slew him with an upward thrust of his spear. The

English then rushed the bridge and fell on the Viking shield wall. The arrival of the reinforcements from Ricall did not help as they were too exhausted from the march to sway the battle.

The battle lasted for several hours and ended only when Hardrada was killed beneath his World Ravager banner. Tostig was also killed and it is said that of the 300 ships that brought the invaders to England, only 24 were needed to carry the survivors to safety. The Anglo Saxon Chronicle tells of the Norwegian shield wall breaking and the English chasing and slaughtering the Norwegians back to the shore. In the 'Heimskringla', (the lives of the Norse Kings) Snorri records that Harold's soldiers were mounted and used bows in the battle, how different might Hastings have been if Harold's forces had used the same tactics there! Harold made terms with Olaf, Hardrada's son who swore that he would ever hold peace and friendship with this land.

Harold had no time to rejoice in his victory; on 2nd October he learned that William, sailing on his ship "Mora", with his fleet, had landed at Pevensey on 28th September. This was particularly galling to Harold as he had had his fleet patrolling the channel throughout August and had also mobilised the Kentish Fyrd to guard the beaches in anticipation of a Norman attack. With the worsening autumn weather, Harold had decided that the threat was over until the following year and had sent his fleet back to the Thames to re-provision on the 8th September and dismissed the Fyrd to go home to bring in the harvest. Under the Anglo Saxon system, every freeman was expected to serve in the Fyrd in times of national emergency, although normally only in their own shires. The "Common Burden" of service in the Fyrd was imposed on all freemen by English kings since the 8th century. Military service was also due from those who had been granted "Bookland" that is, land granted in perpetuity, not loaned. How much service depended on the size of the estates; it was understood that, using the measurement of hides (an area of land reckoned to be capable of supporting one family) every 5 hides should supply 1 soldier or sailor for the Fyrd. Further, any churl, theign or noble, killed while fighting in his Lord's service, was exempt from payment of death duty.

Harold road fast for London, covering the 190 odd miles in 6 days, arriving on October 6th. He summoned the Southern Fyrd to him and prepared for battle. Although he had achieved a great victory at Stamford Bridge, his force had been much weakened and only those with mounts could travel south with him. Harold was counselled to wait for reinforcements, but knew that any delay would only strengthen William's position and Harold was not a patient man.

William had not as yet moved far from his ships, cautious as ever, he had spent some days securing his bridgehead, he knew he had but one chance to defeat Harold and wanted to fight close to his ships. He had sent his archers ashore first to cover the landing of his knights and then built strong entrenchments with materials brought with him from Normandy. He dragged his ships up on the shore and unstepped the masts as a precaution against a surprise attack from the English fleet which had sailed from the Thames to harass his supply lines. Once secure, he moved on to Hastings and erected a Motte and Bailey castle on the site of an old Roman fortification, his soldiers ranging the surrounding countryside looting provisions for the army and destroying everything in their path to intimidate the local people and force Harold ,who held these lands as the king, to battle.

Harold left London on 11th October for the 60 mile journey to Hastings gathering more shire levies as he went and arrived just north of Hastings by 13th. The army camped for the night on a ridge known as Senlac Hill where the great forest thinned out into open country. Senlac Hill was the centre of a number of paths and track ways. The Anglo Saxon Chronicle reports that Harold met William by the "hoar apple tree" suggesting that on this ridge was an ancient landmark and was probably a traditional meeting place for the Sussex Fyrdmen

Harold chose the site also because it was a good defensive position, with ravines and deep woods behind him and a marshy valley in front to hinder the heavy Norman cavalry.

Williams's scouts warned William of the Saxon's arrival and, fearing a night attack, he made his men stand to their arms though the night. Early next morning he led his men towards the Saxon host, a knight named Vital, a vassal of Bishop Odo reported that he had sighted the English positions. Shortly after, as recorded in the Bayeaux Tapestry, Harold's scouted reported sight of the enemy. William halted to enable his knights to don their full armour, William's servants, helping him into his chainmail chanced to start putting it on back to front, a very bad omen, William passed the incident off as a jest saying that it signified that he would soon be changed' from a Duke to a King.'

William's army was composed of between 8,000 and 9,000 men, of these, some 3,000 were mailed knights. The rest on foot and armed with bows, slings, javelins, spears and swords. The short French bow was only pulled back to the chest, but could still penetrate chain armour.

William divided his army into divisions based on nationality, the right wing being led by Eustace of Boloigne and Robert of Mongomery commanding Flemish, French and Picards.

In the centre stood William with his Normans under the Leopard Banner and the Papal gonfalon sent by the Pope to bless William' quest. This holy banner was reckoned a powerful omen and was given by the Pope to mark William's return to grace following a threat of excommunication due to him having married his cousin and resolved by William's promise to build two churches as expiation. William wore a necklace of holy relics to signify his moral right to the English crown Harold was also considered an oath breaker due to his previous promise to William. With him stood his half brothers the warlike Bishop Odo and the Robert, Count of Mortain. On William's left stood the Men of Brittany under Count Alan Fergeant.

The standard Norman tactics of the day depended on the shock charge of Mailed cavalry, the Normans had mastered the art of fighting on horseback with the use of stirrups plus the high pommel and cantle of their saddles, giving them great stability in battle, foot soldiers were often used to open up gaps in the enemy lines for the cavalry to exploit. William drew up his divisions in three lines containing archers, slingers and spearmen and bodies of mounted knight. William positioned himself in the centre of the Norman cavalry ready to exploit any gaps in the Saxon shield wall

Harold's army was arrayed in a simpler formation, his line of troops, perhaps 1,000 yards long, locked behind the the yellow and red wall of shields with the house carls and thegnes in the centre and the shire levies on the flanks, Harold's army probably numbered more than the French and were armed primarily with the terrible battleaxe that could cleave armour, man and horse with one blow. Harold, after the Saxon fashion, fought on foot beneath the Golden Dragon of Wessex and his own banner, the Fighting Man.

William's army began to march towards Harold's position fanning out to cover the ground, the chronicler Wace records that Williams centre came up late to fill in the gap between the two wings, they halted about 500 yards from the English line.

With a blare of trumpets and horns, plus the shouts of Dex Aie! (Gods Aid) from their leaders, the Normans advanced, their archers running forward to fire at the English line. Most of the arrows passed over the heads of the defenders and some smacking into the limewood shields of the wall. William knew that unless he could break up the Saxon wall, he could not deploy his cavalry, he ordered his spearmen to attack and they advanced to within 40 yards when they were met by hails of arrows, axes and stones. Stung by the missiles, the Normans closed on the line of defenders, stabbing and cutting against the shield wall, the Saxons fighting back "each man according to his own strength". Within the struggle the noise was deafening, the cries of the wounded, the shouts of triumph and the clash of weapons adding to the din...

The shield wall did not break, following the attack of the spearmen, many of the Norman Knights eager to get into the fight threw away their lances and drew their swords and charged up the slope towards the English line. The sloping ground, plus the presence of their own infantry reduced the impact of their charge and disintegrated into individual knights hacking at the English line. The mailed hauberks and conical helmets of the attackers giving little protection from the terrible Saxon war axes that could dismember man and horse with a blow. You can see this depicted in the Bayeaux Tapestry as the axemen hack limbs off their enemy.

The Breton soldiers of the left wing of William's army had advanced easily up the gentler slope ,but faced with the ferocity of the Saxons, began to waver and fall back showing little stomach for the bloodbath that the battle had become. They panicked and broke running down the hill and scattering the cavalry around them, the horses reared and bucked, throwing their riders and galloped back down the hill to the marshy bottomland. Many of the Saxons, their blood up and raging, ran down the hill and hacked at the dismounted Knights causing much slaughter.

Seeing their left flank exposed, the Norman infantry in the centre began to fall back, the right wing also began to pull back, the rumour of William's death was shouted by the retreating troops and a growing panic ensued. Upon seeing this, William spurred forward, pulling off his helmet and standing up in his saddle so that all could recognise him. Shouting to make himself heard, he barked, "Look at me well, I am still alive and by the grace of God I shall yet be the victor" William was a violent man and much feared by his men, seeing him bearing down on them swinging his mace ,the Normans with a great shout fell again upon the English line,

Bishop Odo and Eustace of Boloigne led a cavalry charge against the English who had rashly broken rank to chase the fleeing Normans, the Bayeaux Tapestry shows a scene of some of the English axemen with their heavy moustaches making a stand on a small hillock, but they stood little chance against the armoured horsemen.

If Harold had been mounted he may have been able to ride along the line to steady his men against breaking ranks, but he had sent his horse to the rear at the start of the battle to show his troops that there would be no retreat for him. William now signalled for his main body of cavalry to advance up the slope over the mounds of corpses strewn on the ground, the English stood their ground with their shouts of "out, out", the bodies of the dead held up by the press of the living. Slowly the cavalry began to force gaps in the shield wall; William threw in his small cavalry reserve to widen them. Time after time the English managed to close the gaps inflicting terrible casualties on William's men. On several occasions, the attackers fell back under the weight of the fierce English defence and, despite their earlier bloody lesson, the English again followed the retreating Normans down the hill, slashing and hacking and hurling shouts and insults at their enemy.

Some Norman historians say that the withdrawals were a feignt planned by William to draw the English from their line, but it is more likely that the partial retreat was to enable the cavalry to regroup under their leaders.

The battle wore on throughout that grey afternoon, the Normans, again and again hurling their cavalry up the slope, but the shield wall would not break, the English closing their ranks to fill the gaps left by the dead... As twilight came the sheer strain of the day began to tell on the defenders and the Autumn cold began to seep into their bones, some of the fyrdmen began to slip away, slowly the shield wall contracted into a hollow circle around the royal standard, the weary theignes and house carls were quieter now and one chronicler recorded that the movements of the wounded on the ground were greater than those still standing.

Harold rallied his tired troops with his battle cry "Holy Rood, Holy Rood" the Norman cavalry beginning to move in from the sides now as well as the front. William had to finish this quickly, with night approaching, Harold's army could slip away to fight another day with reinforcements from Mercia and Northumbria, he had already had two horses killed under him. He called forward his archers again, but this time had them fire high. Guy, the Bishop of Amiens records that William ordered them to "aim at the faces of the English" The English still engaged in their desperate hand to hand fighting could not properly protect themselves from this new threat from above by holding their shields aloft and many were hit. History says that it was at this time that Harold was hit in the eye, the Bayeaux Tapestry shows about 24% of the English arrow wounds are to the head, so Harold's wound would not be uncommon, but there is no contempory confirmation for this. Furthermore, it is known that the Tapestry has been altered and repaired a number of times in its history. In 1729 an artist called Benoir carried out a full scale tracing to help in creating a set of engravings, another survey was carried out one hundred years later by the Englishman Charles Stothard and later still in 1872 the Victoria and Albert museum made a photographic record of the work. When these three records are compared there are approximately 379 differences, one of the main changes being the arrow in Harold's eye, firstly being depicted as a lance, then feathers are added to make it a large arrow and finally the angle of the arrow is shifted downwards and points directly to the King's eye, It is recorded that Harold was slain by a sword cut and the Bayeaux Tapestry would seem to confirm this, another contempory description of Harold's death states that "four knights finally got close to the English King, the first blow cleaving his breast through his shield with his point, drenching the earth with a gushing torrent of blood", the second smote off his head below the helmet and the third pierced his inwards with a lance, the fourth, a Norman knight from Ponthieu called Ivo tried to hack off

Harold's leg as a trophy, a needless mutilation. It was not unusual for the victors to mutilate the bodies of their dead foes and it is thought that the Chronicle was being a little delicate regarding Harold's leg; it was more likely that Ivo castrated Harold's body, a much commoner mutilation. William saw no honour in this and later stripped Ivo of his knighthood for the act. With the King's brothers Gurth and Leofwine already killed, many of the English theigns began to scatter, leaving a dogged few to make a last stand

Most of the fugitives escaped into the woods, some rallied in ambush behind a steep valley known as the 'Malfosse' intersected with ditches and the tired Normans on their weary horses and ignorant of the area came crashing to the ground. It is recorded that Eustace of Boloigne turned from the pursuit and met William heading for the ravine; he urged him to withdraw and, while pleading, was struck a violent blow in the back "so hard that the blood gushed from his mouth", which indicates how dangerous was the area at that moment. William attacked however and with the few troops with him, overcame this stoical rearguard

The battle was over, Norman soldiers, by the light of torches were stripping and plundering the dead. Next morning they were joined by relatives of the dead seeking to bury the corpses before the wolves came. According to the Norman account Harold was found near the bodies of his two brothers and could only be identified by the tattoo marks on his throat and right wrist. The Normans are said to have cruelly buried him on the seashore that he had failed to defend... A Saxon version however states that two monks from Waltham, a church founded by the Saxon Kings, came to William offering 10 gold pieces for permission to give Harold proper burial. Permission was given, but they could not identify the dead King among the press of bodies., it is said that Harold's betrothed ,Edith Swaneshalls " Edith the swan necked" eventually identified Harold and the body was taken, first to Battle Bridge and then to Waltham which was to become an Abbey in 1177. William ordered that the corpses of the remainder of the Saxon army should not be buried but left to rot or be eaten by wolves

In Palgrave's "History of the Anglo Saxons" he tells of years later when men toiled under the yoke of Norman rule and Hastings was but a memory, there was a decrepit anchorite who inhabited a cell near the

Abbey of St John in Chester. This recluse, deeply scarred and blinded in one eye lived in strict penance and seclusion. Henry 1st once visited the hermit and had long discussion with him. On his deathbed he declared to the attendant monks that he was indeed Harold. He had been secretly conveyed from the battle to Dover Castle.

After the battle, the remainder of Harold's family fled to Europe. His daughter married and bore a son named Harold who became Prince of Kiev, This Prince Harold had a daughter Ingborg who married King Vladimir of Denmark and from these roots, the royal houses of Denmark and England are descended.

William expected the surviving English leaders to submit to him and waited for 5 days to receive their submission. When no word was received he marched north east along the coast securing ports and placing garrisons at strategic points to secure his communications. He occupied Dover and was joined there by reinforcements from Normandy. He marched with his host first to Canterbury en route for London, burning and destroying farms and villages as he went. The army was halted for a time due to an outbreak of dysentery, but eventually arrived at Southwark. The English had not entirely lost their taste for resistance and Londoners led by Edgar the Atheling one of the few remaining claimants to the English throne fought with the Normans but without either side gaining a victory. This did have the effect however of making William think twice about attacking London, he burned Southwark and moved westwards and began to receive submissions from the Anglo Saxons who were beginning to believe that Duke William would become King of England.

Local opposition began to fall apart when Archbishop Stigand met William at Wallingford and pledged allegiance to him. Edward the Confessor's widow Edith gave up the royal treasure at Winchester, a tacit acceptance that William was now the ipso facto Ruler of England. William moved on and made camp at Berkhamsted...With William's forces controlling all the main routs to and now facing isolation and famine, London surrendered while at Berkhamsted William received the submission of Archbishop Aldred,the Earls of Mercia and Northumbria and, most importantly, Edgar the Atheling.

In addition to replacing the defeated Saxon leaders with Norman knights, William had sent for his Norman bishop Lanfranc to organise the replacing of English bishops with his own. Lanfranc was most efficient in this task and became a great strength and support for William. An early miracle was recorded around this time at the tomb of Edward the Confessor. Lanfranc had summoned Wulstan, Bishop of Worcester to give up his ring and staff of office.Wulstan refused saying that he had been appointed by a holy king and he then appealed to Edward's tomb to take away his staff or leave it with him "on his judgement" He then thrust the staff into the stone of the tomb where it stuck fast, Lanfranc ordered Gundolf, Bishop of Rochester to remove it, but it could not be moved, others tried but with no avail.

The new King was summoned and went with Lanfranc to the tomb.Wulstan now asked the Confessor to return the staff to him if he thought it was right, the staff came away in Wulstan's hand "as if it were stuck in clay" The King and Lanfranc knelt and asked Wulstan's forgiveness. Wulstan was the only Saxon Bishop at William's coronation.

William was crowned on Christmas day 1066.It was the custom at that time for nobles to signify their approval of the anointing by shouts of assent and William's guards, hearing the noise and thinking it an attack, rushed out and slaughtered many townspeople.

William now began to consolidate his hold on the country. He forbade his men further pillaging, a little late considering the desolation already caused and offered pardon to all Saxons who had not fought at Hastings. In response, many of the northern thegnes came to William's base at Barking to submit to him including Edwin and Morcar the Earls of Mercia and Northumbria. It is said that William received them cordially and even offered his daughter to Edwin as a bride, In truth the Earls were captive guests and when William returned to Normandy in the spring of 1067, he took them with him, together with Archbishop Stigand and Edgar the Atheling .

William's return to Normandy became a royal progress, first to Rouen and the monastery of Fecamp where he gave many splendid plundered treasures to the monastery. He then travelled to Jumieges to consecrate a new abbey and give the church the gift of Hayling Island. Chroniclers record the wonder and amazement of the people at the huge quantities of gold, silver, fine clothes and precious ornaments that William had brought back from England.

William had left his half brother Odo in charge of southern England and had given him the title Earl of Kent in addition to all the lands settled on him after Hastings. Odo was reckoned to be the richest landowner after the King himself and revelled in luxury despite his title of bishop. All land north of the Thames was to be in the charge of William Fitz Osbern who was given the title Earl of Hereford. During William's absence there was an uprising in Hereford and at the same time the men of Kent had allied with the Norman Count Eustace and besieged Dover Castle, Eustace felt that he had not been properly rewarded for his services at Hastings, but quickly lost his nerve and deserted the English. By the time William returned in December 1067, these uprisings had been quashed and early in the New Year he marched deep into Wessex. Harold's mother and bastard sons had found refuge in Exeter with the English thegnes who had not been at Hastings due to the speed of Harold's journey southward. William laid siege to Exeter with his army which, for the first time contained Saxons and Normans fighting side by side. The city surrendered after 18 days, but Harold's family escaped to cause further unrest during the next two years with raids on the west coast.

After the fall of Exeter, the rest of the West Country submitted and at Whitsun William returned to London only to learn of another uprising in the North. Three of his hostages had escaped captivity, Edwin and Morcar were raising armies in Mercia and Northumberland and Gospatric (a Saxon to whom William had sold the Kingdom of Bernicia on the Scottish border) was proclaiming Edgar the Atheling as the true King. These uprisings failed to unite the people and, at Williams approach, they

Faded away with the Thegnes returning to their homes and the leaders seeking refuge with King Malcolm Canmore of Scotland.

William was an astute politician as well as a ruthless soldier. He recognised that there was still some residual loyalty to the old regime in England and did not want to create martyrs who would serve as a focal point in any future uprising. He therefore made a public show of granting pardons to Edwin and Morcar while at the same time instigated the building of many Norman castles throughout the land with forced labour and put French and Norman commanders in charge of them. The Tower of London and Windsor Castle were both commissioned in this time. Feeling safer now that he had faced down any opposition, William brought his diminutive Queen Matilda over from Normandy and had her crowned as his Queen at Winchester. William had thus fought and triumphed over his enemies in his second year as King, 1069 however was to be a far more dangerous year.

A northern revolt began when the people of Northumbria, outraged at the indiscriminate slaughter and destruction that took place under the Northern Commander Robert of Commines, attacked the Norman camp at Durham and slaughtered the troops in their beds, burning down the Bishop's house and murdering Robert.William again marched north with a large army, the Northumbrians besieged Durham Castle, the rebels were taken by surprise at William's approach and the revolt melted away. Later that year the King Sven of Denmark who had been negotiating secretly with the northern rebels sailed into the Humber estuary with a fleet said to have consisted of 240 ships. There he met with Edgar the Atheling and a number of previously pro Norman thegnes. With their numbers growing each day the force marched on York and by September the town had been destroyed together with many of the castles built by William, any Normans captured alive were imprisoned on the Danish ships. News of this uprising inspired rebels in the South West and fearing a general revolt, William marched north, leaving the Southwest to his subordinates

The rebels had retreated to the Humber, but the revolt was gathering momentum, leaving his half brother Robert to protect his flank he marched into Mercia and defeated the rebels at Stafford. On his way back he learned that more of the Anglo Danish force was returning to York. William raced to reach the city first, but the rebels destroyed the bridges over the River Aire causing William some delays while searching for a fording place.

Using the same cruel strategy as he had around London, William circled York and destroyed everything in his path devastating the region and isolating the the city. Realising that they could not withstand a long siege, the defenders sued for peace and once again William was generous, granting pardon to the leaders and allowing Edgar the Atheling to once again escape to Scotland, and allowing the Danish fleet to winter in the Humber.

William was determined however that he would not suffer any further uprising in the north and throughout November and December showed his ruthlessness and cruelty by ordering his soldiers to set about the destruction of villages, hamlets and farms between York and Durham, killing everyone and everything before them leaving a desert where nothing survived for a generation. Every male over 12 years old was killed, leaving the women and children to starve. After Christmas they continued with the slaughter and destruction throughout Stafford Derby and Chester in the episode described as "the harrying of the north"

Even in these cruel times William's treatment of the North was considered barbaric. The writer Simeon of Durham records much detail of these raids and describes the desolation and the rotting and putrefying corpses that littered the waysides of England and "no stone left standing upon another".

A great strength of William's rule was his use of family in positions of authority; he had used this system in his duchy before the conquest. Further, he was very loyal to those who showed true support, one such being William Fitzosbern, the son of Osbern the Duke's seneschal who was killed during William's minority. Fitzsosbern was William's steward and had been given vast estates in the Welsh Marches after the conquest. Even with all the rebellions facing William he had time to aid his friends. In 1071 Fitzsosbern was sent to Flanders to aid the Regent Richildis and her son Anulf (Williams's nephew) against Robert le Frison, Anulf's uncle who was attempting to usurp his nephews claim. Fitzsosbern was successful in this, but was killed at Cassel in February 1071

The last of the uprisings broke out in East Anglia. William appointed an ally. Turold of Fecamp to the post of Abbot at Peterborough, Turold was a soldier in addition to his clerical leanings and was tasked by William to suppress the area. The locals. objecting to this appointment, called in the Danes to help their resistance and they were led through the fens by a man who has become legend, Earl Hereward,known as " the Wake" because of his ever watchful guard against the Normans. It is interesting to note that Hereward was banished from his estates in Lincolnshire by a petition from his father in Edward the Confessor's time, as a troublemaker and was thus already an outlaw before the Norman invasion. His lands were distributed among the Normans following William's victory. The Danes, led by Sweyn, remaining true to type, merely stripped the

Abbey of its treasure and left. Hereward and his followers now isolated retreated to the Isle of Ely. William again took charge of the assault on the rebels going so far as to build wooden paths over the fens for his army and by 1071 the revolt was over. Hereward was eventually reconciled with William, but was later murdered by other Frenchmen to prevent him claiming back any of his old lands. Hereward vanished into history, but romanticised tales of his exploits soon began to appear, his deeds being recorded in Ely, Peterborough and in Gaimar's "Histoire de Engleis"painting him as a figurehead of English resistance. By 1140,fenlanders were naming their sons after him.

The only threat remaining to William was that posed by Malcolm of Scotland, he had married the sister of Edgar the Atheling thus ensuring that his offspring could have some claim to the old Saxon royal line. After some threats and mutual posturing the two Kings concluded a treaty at Abernathy on the Tay. William gave Malcolm some estates in northern England and Malcolm gave William his son Duncan as hostage and agreed to expel Edgar the Atheling. William again showed a surprisingly generous streak when he forgave Edgar, even granting him a pension. William must have been aware that Edgar had never been more than a puppet in the northern uprisings and was not well enough known in England to be a rallying point although he appears in many plots and uprisings until his death in 1135.

William now turned his mind to government and taxation. The Domesday Book (from the Old English "Dom" meaning assessment) was compiled to measure the rents and fees due from every landholder and also to check that none of his barons had unlawfully seized lands. Controlled by his rapacious treasurer Ranulph, of whom more later, his men were sent all over England measuring and recording, the completed work summing up the total value of his conquest. It is interesting to note that by this time; only 5% of the land was still in the hands of Saxons. This book was to be the means of levying the proposed new, heavier land tax on the population, but William died before it could be implemented.

By 1072 the English were relatively passive with the Old Saxon estates divided up among William's comrades in arms and the clergy firmly in Norman hands under Lanfranc. The feudal system imposed by William tied the peasants to the land much as had the old manorial system, but many Saxons were allowed to keep their old positions of Reeves and Foremen on the new Norman estates. Many farms and hamlets were destroyed by William and the new Lords to clear the land for the creation of hunting areas, the largest being the New Forest in Hampshire and many of the old Saxon laws were swept away. William spent much of his time in Normandy leaving England in the hands of his Regents, he did not attempt to extend his Kingdom to Wales, Scotland or Ireland although suffering much provocation from raids in the border regions. Bishop Odo led a campaign into Scotland in response to Scots incursions and reached Falkirk, but no systematic conquest was attempted.

William gained much weight in his later years and it is related that King Phillip of France once jested as to "when he expected to lie in". William was enraged and swore that, at his churching (a service for women after childbirth) he would pay a visit to the French King with "10,000 lances instead of tapers and set all France ablaze"

The remainder of William's reign was disrupted by rebellions in France and further troubles in England. The Norman borders were threatened by attacks from Anjou, Maine and Flanders while in England a revolt by Roger of Hereford and Ralph of Norfolk flared up with some promised help from the Danes. The plot collapsed however and both men were tried for treason and imprisoned for life while a Saxon supporter of the revolt, Earl Waltheof was executed, thus according to his supporters, becoming the first Saxon to be martyred by the Normans. It could be said however that Waltheof had it coming. He had been pardoned twice before for rebellion, once after Hastings and again after the rising of 1069/1070. With a Danish father and as a supporter of the attempted Danish invasion of 1069, his fight was more likely against William as an English King rather than a Norman usurper. He was beheaded at dawn to prevent the English rescuing "so noble a companion" This marked the end of William's attempts to court the Old Saxon nobility and thereafter he installed French or Normans in all regional positions of power.

With the French constantly raiding his Norman borders William marched on Paris and it was on this venture that he met his end. Having attacked and destroyed the town of Mantes, his men were pillaging and looting .William was riding through the burning town when his horse reared in fright from a blazing timber and "threw its ponderous rider against the iron of his saddle." William collapsed in violent pain and the army was halted. He had received a severe injury from which he was to die. It is thought that he suffered a ruptured urethra, such a blow causing urine to leak into the tissue when trying to pass water and blood to appear in the small amount of urine that he was able to pass... It is recorded that, physicians who examined William's urine pronounced death to be inevitable due to a "bursting of the bowels" The leaking of urine into the tissues has dreadful consequences as the tissue becomes necrotic and gangrenous and, these effects must have been noted by his doctors. William lingered on for a further 10 days. He asked to be taken to St Gervais Priory in Rouen where the Physicians were noted for their skills, but they could do nothing. William remained lucid and was able to attend to his affairs but became progressively weaker. In increasing pain, it was obvious to him that he was dying; finally he passed into terminal renal failure with the resultant uraemia and died.

The writer Orderic Vitalis wrote an account of the dying King, concerned over his salvation and the future of his domains. William confessed himself to be "too fond of war" and his life was stained "with rivers of blood". In his hope for salvation William bequeathed that his treasure in Rouen should be given to churches and the poor.

The division of his lands was more difficult. His eldest son Robert had often been in open rebellion with his father and had, in fact, been with the French armies at the time of William's death. As the eldest son he would however succeed to the title of Duke of Normandy. William's second son Richard, having been killed in a hunting accident in 1075, left the English throne to his third son William Rufus. It is said that William gave Rufus a letter to pass to Archbishop Lanfranc confirming his succession and Rufus, without waiting for his father to die, rushed to England to confirm his inheritance before Robert could make a claim. His fourth son Henry was given the sum of £5000 in silver, he was not happy with his inheritance, but also rushed to claim it, not waiting for his father to die.

William died on Thursday 9th September 1087, saying at the last "I commend myself to Mary, the Holy Mother of God, my heavenly mistress, that by her blessed intercession I may be reconciled to her beloved son our Lord Jesus Christ" Those about him feared the outbreak of lawlessness following his death and they all left in great haste to protect their property. His servants then plundered the bedchamber, taking furniture, linen, arms, silver and vestments, leaving William's body naked on the floor. There was panic throughout Rouen at the news of his death.

The Archbishop of Rouen gave orders that William was to be taken to St Stephen's monastery in Caen, but nobody remained to carry out the move. It is recorded that a Norman gentleman called Herluin arranged for the body to be taken by boat down the Seine to Caen where it was met by many mourners and carried in procession. It is reported that a great fire broke out in the city and the mourners rushed away to fight the flames, leaving a scant few to continue the journey to St Stephen's.

A service was held for William, conducted by the Bishop of Lisieux also attended by Henry recently returned from England and the body was about to be lowered into the grave. At this point a knight called Ascelin of Caen rose and argued that, due to the fact that William had built the church on land taken by force from the father of Ascelin, he forbade the burial on ground consecrated after such a happening. With some consternation,Ascelin and others were questioned and all upheld that the land had been taken by force. After much consultation it was agreed that Henry would pay Ascelin 60 shillings for the grave and promised to repay the full price of his father's estate. Ascelin accepted and the burial continued. William's swollen state over the last months would have continued after his death particularly in the lower regions and it was found that the stone coffin was not big enough to receive the King's body. His body was forced into the coffin, bursting in the process and filling the church with the stench of corruption, so much so that the service was concluded in great haste.

William's coffin was enclosed in a beautiful shrine commissioned by Rufus from a famous goldsmith named Otto. William remained undisturbed for nearly 500 years when the Pope authorised it to be opened and the remains examined. The body was found to be in a good state of preservation and was reverently reinterred. In 1562 the Calvinists invaded the church and rifled the tomb scattering all but one thighbone. This relic was reburied under a new structure and lasted until the revolution of 1783 when it was demolished. Now only a simple stone slab marks the supposed final resting place of William, first Norman King of England.

William had shewn himself to be a cruel and violent man during his lifetime, but had consolidated his hold over the country following his victory at Hastings. He had established the French feudal system, regularised the English churches' relationship with the Pope and imposed strong laws throughout the land. He had also implemented the act of Scutage whereby a noble could commute the act of military service by payment of a "shield Tax", thus enabling William to employ full time professional soldiers. This was a significant change and greatly aided William in his suppression of rebellion. It was said of him that "he had made the good peace in this land so that a man may go the the length and breadth of the Kingdom with his pockets full of gold and no man durst slay another"

The Conquest, in retrospect, was much more than a mere change of dynasties. England now had a new royal family and ruling class. Before 1066 there were over 4000 thegns, yet just 20 years later, just two English lords remained in a land ruled by fewer than 200 Normans from their garrison fortresses.

It is not really known what become of his last remains, locals say it is buried beneath the stone slab, others think it was destroyed in the 1944 fighting to liberate Normandy. A thighbone which the French authorities claim to be genuine was discovered in the old tomb and was reburied under a new tomb on 9th September 1987, on the 900th anniversary of his death.

William 11

William 2nd known as Rufus due to his red hair and ruddy complexion was born in Caen in 1060, the 3rd son of William the Conqueror and Mathilda of Flanders.

He was described by his contemparies as a ruthless sadistic homosexual and an atheist, but was William's favourite son, probably due to his undoubted abilities as a soldier and his support for his father against his brothers in their many disputes, even sustaining wounds at the battle of Gerboroi in 1079 fighting for his father against his elder brother Robert. He was not a popular King however and imposed harsh rule on England, outlawing many of the old customs and enclosing much of the land for Royal hunting. In addition and with the aid of his chancellor Ranulph, nicknamed Flambard due to his fiery temper and mischief making ,he imposed draconian taxes on his barons and withheld monies from the church by refusing to appoint clergy to vacant properties and renting out the land to farm or, in the words of the chronicler Peter of Blois 'to usurious Jews' In addition to retaining the income of the see of Canterbury, vacant due to his having exiled Archbishop Anselm, Rufus held the revenue from 11 abbeys and 4 bishoprics, Ranulph kept the see of Durham for himself.

Following the conqueror's death in 1087, his eldest son Robert became Duke of Normandy. It would be normal in those times for the eldest son to inherit the presumably greater prize of the throne of England, but it is thought that William was to some extent punishing Robert for all the years that he had opposed William and had frequently been in open rebellion against him.

William's second son, Richard of Bernay had been killed by a stag while out hunting in the New Forest some years before and William therefore decided to pass the English crown to Rufus and on his deathbed put these wishes in writing for Rufus to take to Archbishop Lanfranc. Rufus, not waiting for his father to breathe his last, hurried to England to claim his inheritance and received the kingdom and the blessing from Archbishop Lanfranc three days before Michaelmas. Rufus armed with his new authority travelled to Winchester to claim his fathers treasure, sharing it out as his father had bade for the salvation of William's soul, to each monastery in the land giving 10 Marks to each monastery and 60 pence to each country church. Each shire was given 100 pounds to share out for the poor. William's will also requested that all men imprisoned under his rule should be released and this was done, including the Kings half brother Odo.

William Rufus' accession caused much dissent in England and, with the aid of Robert of Normandy who's eyes were ever on the English throne, Earl Robert of Shrewsbury, Bishop Gosfrith of Durham and William's half brother Odo who had been reluctantly released by the conqueror on his deathbed, rose against Rufus in an attempt to unite the Anglo Norman lands and install Robert as king. These rebellions were to continue throughout his reign, Robert finally giving up his claim to the throne at the Treaty of Alton in 1101. It must be remembered that many barons held land both in England and in Normandy and in view of Rufus' harsh government, favoured the more popular Robert as King.

In 1088 Durham castle was besieged by the rebels and a number of other royal castles were captured, notably Bristol, which fell to Bishop Geoffrey of Coutances and his cousin Robert, Earl of Northumberland .Rufus enjoyed a high reputation as a soldier and was successful in suppressing these uprisings .He appealed to all Englishmen to help him destroy the rebels, promising that he would restore their woods and their hunting, cancel all unjust taxes and promised them the 'best laws in the land'. Once the fighting was over however, Rufus reneged on these promises as he was to do on many other occasions.

Surprisingly, the English flocked to the aid of the King and Rufus, with his army marched on Rochester castle were Odo was believed to be, but he had travelled on to Pevensey. Rufus besieged Pevensey castle for 6 weeks until the defenders were starved into submission and Odo, surrendering, swore that he would leave England and never return unless Rufus sent after him... Odo also promised to give up his stronghold of Rochester and went with the King's men to hand it over. His garrison however, did not accept the surrender and took Odo and the King's men captive. When Rufus learned this he again appealed to the English and French freeman to join him and marched on Rochester, starving the garrison into surrender.

Bishop Odo was sent 'over the sea' never to return. Again, Rufus reneged on his promises of reward.

The last remaining rebel was the Bishop of Durham; Rufus sent forces to the castle and forced its surrender, the Bishop and his followers being banished. The King could now concentrate on his brother Robert who throughout this time had been aiding rebellion in England as well as attempting an invasion of his own. In 1091 he took a force to Normandy, in the words of the Anglo Saxon Chronicle 'to do his brother damage 'A reconciliation was made between them however and after combining their forces to oust their brother Henry from Cotentin which he had bought with his inheritance money, Robert agreed to give up the towns of Fecamp, Eu and Cherbourg which had been taken from Rufus earlier. Furthermore, Robert was to leave unmolested, the garrisons that Rufus had placed in the castles of St Valery and Aumale which he had maintained as footholds in the Duchy .In return Rufus promised to return to Robert the territory of Maine which had been won by the Conquerer, but which had been taken from Robert during their many squabbles. He also promised to restore lands to the English earl's who had supported Robert in his claim to the English throne. Finally they promised that, should either die without a son by legal marriage, the other would inherit all. This pact was to be the cause of much bloodshed in years to come.

While Rufus was engaged in these arrangements, King Malcolm of Scotland raided the borders causing much damage. Rufus returned to England together with his brother and they went north in force, but Malcolm wisely withdrew to Lothian. It is reported in the chronicle that Robert and Edgar the Atheling, who, in view of his being the only remaining Saxon contender for the English throne, appeared to have a charmed life, went between the two Kings and made reconciliation and Malcolm knelt and did homage to Rufus as his vassal. This homage was to be the basis of many subsequent English claims Lordship over Scotland. In reality, Malcolm had little choice, his eldest son Duncan was hostage in London against his good behaviour and his raids had tried Rufus to the limit.

Whatever promises may have been made, Rufus was cynical enough to know that, given an opportunity, Malcolm would attack northern England whenever possible and accordingly, Rufus built a great castle at Durham with a large English garrison. As a further buffer he sent many ordinary people from the south to settle in the area and cultivate the land as had his father before him.

In 1093 Rufus was taken ill and it was rumoured everywhere that he was dead. In his sickness he made many promises to God, vowing to lead a better life. During his reign he had taken to himself many monasteries and churches refusing to appoint clergy to them and keeping the revenues for himself. This included Canterbury itself, which, following the death of Lanfranc in 1089 had been left vacant with all revenues going to Rufus. Now, believing he was dying, he gave Canterbury to Bishop Anselm, Lincoln to Bishop Robert and also made many grants of land to the church... It was perhaps typical of Rufus that, following his recovery, he reneged on most of these promises. The year ended with another bad harvest and much starvation. In April of the next year there came a great meteor storm with many falling stars' so many that they may not be counted'. Men reckoned this a bad omen and there was much disquiet. Contempory writers tried to demonise Rufus and attribute all ills to his reign. Peter of Blois writes,' Thunders terrifying the earth ,lightning's and thunderbolts most frequent, deluging showers without number, winds of astonishing violence that shook the towers of churches and levelled them with the ground. On the earth there were fountains flowing with blood and the Devil himself walked in the forest'

To add to his troubles, Rufus was faced with yet another Scottish invasion. Malcolm had demanded that the promises of land made to him at their previous reconciliation, be made good. A meeting arranged in Gloucester ended in much acrimony and Malcolm returned to Scotland to raise his forces to once again ravage northern England.Rufus'response was to annexe Cumbria and to send his northern Barons against Malcolm. The Scottish force was met by the Earl of Northumberland and in the ensuing battle; both Malcolm and his son Edward were killed. When the Scots heard of the death of their King they rose up and threw out all the English in their lands and proclaimed Malcolm's brother Dufenal as King. It will be remembered that Duncan, the eldest of Malcolm's sons was in England as a hostage and hearing of Dufenal's usurpation, he begged Rufus to allow him a force to reclaim his kingdom. Rufus agreed and Duncan led an English and French force into Scotland and overthrew Dufenal. Not all of

33

the Scots wanted Duncan however and the subsequent uprising defeated Duncan who managed to escape with a few of his followers.

The Scots were eventually reconciled with Duncan on condition that he 'never lodges English or French in the land again.' Within a few months however, the Scots had killed Duncan and reinstated Dufenal. They also received the French back in to their country who continued their old game of creating friction between the two nations to further their own ends.

The reign of Rufus was not an easy one with constant uprisings in Scotland and Wales as well as the many raids on his domains in France. Robert of Northumberland rose against the King in 1095. He had been summoned to attend the King at Winchester but had refused. Rufus sent messengers to insist that Robert attend the court at Pentecost, but again Robert refused. Rufus marched on Northumbria and, following a siege, captured the Earl's brother and his castle of Tynemouth. He then marched on to Bamburgh. Seeing the strength of this castle, Rufus ordered the construction of a new castle to be built close to Bamburgh. He called the castle Maluesin meaning in old English "Evil Neighbour". It stood on the site of the modern Newcastle. When Robert eventually left the safety of Bamburgh castle he was wounded and captured by the English. Rufus, displaying his Norman cruelty, ordered Robert to be taken to the outskirts of Bamburgh castle still held by Robert's wife and his kinsmen. The garrison were told that Robert would have his eyes put out if they did nor surrender and in the face of this, the gates were opened.

Rufus returned south to Windsor and then to Salisbury. While there a knight named Gosfrai Bainard accused William of Eu, kinsmen of the King of treachery and plotting with others to offer the English throne to Robert of Normandy. Gosfrai offered the traitor trial by combat. Gosfrai defeated him and this was reckoned as proof of his guilt. He was castrated and had his eyes put out... Others involved in the plot were taken to London and executed cruelly.

In 1095, Pope Urban had announced the First Crusade and Robert of Normandy was resolved to go. He offered to mortgage the Duchy to Rufus for 10,000 marks for a period of 3 years and Rufus assumed the Dukedom, thus uniting the two lands as in the time of his father. The money was raised by a tax of 4 shillings on every hide of land, a very harsh levy which caused further resentment to his rule. In all this he was ably assisted by Ranulf Flambard,"fiery,flamboyant" his royal extortion who travelled the land on the King's business issuing writs, administering vacant dioces,settling land and title disputes as well as setting revenue rates for property. He loved the finer things of life and was not above siphoning royal monies for himself and his family. William of Malmesbury called him "a torch of iniquity", and Archbishop Anselm called him "the Prince of publicans due to his siphoning off royal revenues." Today he would be known as an asset stripper. His administration of vacant clergy estates made him wealthy in his own right, Ramsey, New Minster, Winchester, Canterbury and Worcester as well as Durham came under his control. Records show that between 1096 and 1099 he was making £300 per year from Durham alone, finally purchasing the living outright for £1000.For all his power and style, his fall was rapid following the death of his master Rufus in 1100, within 2 weeks he was arrested and imprisoned in the Tower of London, becoming the first political prisoner to be held there.

Ever the expansionist he fought to make good his father's claim to the Vexin 1097/8 and Maine in 1098/9 Rufus had his eyes on yet more territory and particularly coveted the riches of Aquitaine, a contempory notes that when Rufus was once asked where he would spend Christmas, the King replied "Poiters" It was rumoured that he even aspired to the French throne. He was in the process of arranging an agreement with the Count of Poitiers to annexe Aquitaine in return for the costs of the departing Count's crusade, but died before this could be completed.

One positive legacy that Rufus left was the building of Westminster Hall. He was directly responsible for the construction of this fine edifice measuring some 240 feet long and 68 feet wide and for the next 1,000 years has witnessed many scenes of royal splendour. Rufus once boasted that the hall was "merely a bedchamber" compared with the palace he intended to build beside it He also ordered the construction of the first stone bridge to span the Thames. He died before he could begin his grand vision.

The death of Rufus remains a mystery although there are many extant but conflicting reports... William of Malmesbury wrote of the King's death.

Rufus was apparently out hunting in the New Forest with just one companion a knight called Walter Tyrel

"Thinking to bring down another stag which chanced to pass by, the headstrong and reckless Walter Tyrel pierced the royal bosom with a fatal arrow. The smitten King uttered no sound but, breaking off as much of the shaft as stuck out of his body, forthwith fell on his wound and so hastened his deathMathew Parish records that when a great stag passed close by,"the king shouted to his companion Walter Tyrel "shoot damn you The"shaft fled and, glancing off a tree, pierced the King full in the heart. Walter Tyrel had no obvious reason for seeking the death of Rufus, as the Lord of Poix he was a rich man and Castellan of Pontoise in the strategically important Vexin on the Norman borders. He was also related by marriage to the powerful Clare family and was a close friend of Rufus

It must be remembered that many of the Anglo Norman barons hated Rufus and would rather see Robert or Henry on the throne. The chronicler Eadmer notes that the court of Rufus was filled with 'effeminate young men with long hair, mincing walks and flirtatious glances' and William of Malmesbury writes some years later of the King 'wearing garish shoes and tight fitting clothes' The reference to long hair can be traced back to 1077 when William of Poitiers wrote of the Norman astonishment of the English habit of long hair. Homosexuality was considered a mortal sin but nobody dared accuse the King during his lifetime, although, when Anslem proposed to call a council in 1094 to condemn sodomy,

 the King refused. Further, none felt that they had been properly rewarded for their support in the many rebellions of the time and Henry who knew of the pact that Rufus and Robert had made regarding succession, knew that he had to choose the right moment to move against Rufus without Robert being able to claim the throne Furthermore, Robert was a popular figure and an ally of the King of France, Henry would have to act with caution. The attitude of Rufus to the church and his insistence on keeping the authority to nominate clergy to himself had also made him very unpopular with the clergy and with Rome. Archbishop's Anselm's preaching's against Rufus' homosexual lifestyle had resulted in Anselm being banished and Rufus had, as usual confiscated the revenues. The fact that Rufus was apparently hunting with just one companion can only be described as unusual. Further more, his brother Henry was in the vicinity with the main hunting party so could claim a solid alibi, yet still be close by when the deed was done. The King's body was reputedly found by a charcoal burner called Purkiss, who took it on a handcart to Winchester. Purkiss was subsequently gifted a small parcel of land as his reward. Henry wasted no time in rushing to Winchester to claim the crown. The monks at Winchester buried Rufus with little ceremony and much haste beneath one of the church towers which collapsed some years later, convincing everyone that it was the judgement of God showing his displeasure that such a wicked man was buried there...

It is interesting to note that a man called Sererius , the Abbot of a St Denis who was a contempory and friend of Walter Tyrel wrote years later that "He often heard Tyrel affirm upon oath that he neither came that day into any part or side of the forest where the King hunted, nor ever saw him there" It is reasonable to assume that Rufus was murdered by supporters of his brother and Henry's dash to claim the crown would seem to support this view. Did Tyrel murder William? And if so, why? Tyrel was a member of the powerful and favoured Clare family and thus was a supporter to William. He certainly received no obvious reward for the deed. It is possible that he was "set up" and saw no other course than to run for his life, although apart from his talks with Serenius, he never attempted to set the record straight

The life of Rufus should be seen in the context of the age in which he lived. The ruling classes were only scant generations away from the barbarians who ravaged Europe after the Romans left. War or hunting was the only fit occupation for a warrior and each grabbed what he could during a short and brutal life. A more dispassionate view of Rufus could be that he did that which was required of a good leader, namely to establish his leadership, quell rebellion and bring peace to the land. It was said of Rufus that "he cared little for his fellow man and for God, not at all" Further, William of Malmesbury describes him as a' short, pot bellied, red faced braggart with long combed hair and wearing the latest fashion'. There is no doubt that Rufus was all these things, but could also command loyalty and be decisive. . He was impetuous, ambitious and ever aggressive. It is said that, while dining at Brockenhurst in July 1099, he learned of a French attack on his garrison at Le Mans.He immediately set off for France and, despite the distance and conditions, arrived in France the next morning to raise an army. This immediate response to an enemy was typical of him and he was ruthless in his dealings with those who opposed him

There is little doubt that he saw England as a place to be plundered and as a means of raising revenue for his endless quest to expand his dominion. With the aid of the very able but hated Ranulf he taxed the barons through his manipulation of the Shire Courts and feudal laws. Confiscations and forfeitures were harshly enforced and exorbitant inheritance taxes were imposed. Small wonder that most of the Anglo Norman barons favoured Robert, who, had he been a more decisive leader and organiser, could have taken the crown from Rufus. In the event, Henry was in the right place at the right time when Rufus died and seized his chance.

Today there is a grave in Winchester Cathedral marked with the King's name on a plain tomb. This was opened in 1968 and the bones were found in a reasonable state along with the shaft of an arrow. The bones were replaced and the tomb resealed. Behind the altar screen however are a number of reliquary chests removed from the Abbey that once stood on the site. One of the coffins bears the inscription "In this chest and in the one opposite are the remains of Cnut and Rufus Kings, of Emma Queen and Wina and Alwyn Bishops".

Henry 1st.

Henry was born in July 1068 the third of William the Conqueror's sons. He is described as a strong muscular man with thick black hair, a cruel temper and, as Henry of Huntingdon relates 'ruthless, violent and vicious.' His life combined all the virtues of military success, wisdom, diplomacy and wealth with the Norman streak of greed, cruelty and lust. He was said to have fathered 29 illegitimate sons and 11 illegitimate daughters in addition to his 3 children by his wife Matilda. As the youngest son, he would almost certainly be expected to become a bishop and received a somewhat better education than was normal for a young noble of the time.

On the death of his father, his brother Rufus was given the English crown, Robert had the Duchy of Normandy and Henry was given £5000 in silver with which he purchased land on the Cotentin peninsula, but later driven out by an alliance of Rufus and Robert, making a new base in Domfront.

Henry is known in history as 'Beauclerc' due to him having had some education, but this soubriquet was first mentioned some hundred years after his death. It is not known if he could actually read and write, but it is recorded that he learned some Latin in 'snatches' and we can presume that he was at least semi literate. He was also the first Norman to king to speak fluent English. He once remarked that "an unlettered King is a crowned Ass"

He had no expectation of Kingship, but had spent many of his early years battling with his brothers for territory, playing them off one against the other to his own advantage. During the 1090s he gained much experience of intrigue, war and diplomacy in the never ending rivalries of territorial disputes and border conflicts that were endemic in Normandy due in some part to the weakness of Robert who lacked the steel to impose firm rule on the Duchy. When the Duchy was mortgaged to Rufus, Henry was given Coutance and Bayeaux to keep him loyal. He finally sided fully with Rufus and became a trusted member of the court, a decision that placed him in an ideal position to claim the throne on the death of Rufus. On hearing of the Kings death, Henry galloped immediately to Winchester to demand the keys to the Treasury. Some of Rufus' supporters tried to stop him but he drew his sword and swore he was the heir and would challenge any man who said otherwise. He then raced on to London and, not waiting for the return of Anselm from exile or even for Thomas of York to officiate, had Maurice, Bishop of London anoint him King just three days after the death of Rufus. He now needed to win over the baronage and church in anticipation of a challenge from Robert. He immediately issued a manifesto, later called the Coronation Charter in which he promised not to tax vacant churches, to avoid arbitrary changes to rules governing baronial inheritance and marriages and to exempt lesser royalty from the geld and other non military levies. He retained and strengthened royal rights over the forests however and, in a number of significant clauses, he instructed the barons to treat their tenants as he treated them and warned that anyone guilty of disseisin during the interregnum (2nd to 5th August) was liable to pay a penalty to the King regardless of wether the land taken was royal or not, this being a common crime in medieval times. Further, he re established the laws of his father, recalled Anselm from exile and repealed the laws of Rufus

These measures were designed to curry favour with those who had suffered under Rufus while at the same time, reassuring the royal administration and its guarantees of the liberties of all royal tenants and sub tenants. The Charter was used as a model by the framers of the Magna Carta one hundred years later. Ever the politician, Henry had Rufus' hated chancellor Ranulf Flambard arrested and imprisoned in the Tower, but retained the services of William Giffard, Rufus' Treasurer. The changes were reckoned to cost Henry up to one third of his income, but were no doubt thought to be worth the price of political support from the barons and church at that time.

In November 1100, he married Edith, daughter of King Malcolm 111 of Scotland, a symbolic and a practical move. Edith changed her name to Matilda after her marriage in a move to placate some of the king's Norman nobles who were unhappy at this alliance with Scotland. Being unmarried and childless at his coronation, Henry needed the security of clear succession as soon as possible. Further, by marrying Matilda who was the great granddaughter of Edmund Ironsides and great great neice of Edward the Confessor himself, he pleased the Anglo Saxons by uniting the new dynasty with the old and also solved the problem of controlling the north, which Henry visited only once in 1122. Some of the grander Anglo Norman barons were less impressed, contemptuously referring to the King and Queen as 'Godfric and Godifru', no better than yokels.

The marriage produced three children, Matilda, William and Richard. His sexual appetite was however, huge. He took care to prey on female members of the lesser nobility and not on the wives and daughters of his barons (unlike the later King John).

He did not want to risk his relationship with the people who could bring him down.

Henry was as energetic and driven as Rufus but much more suspicious. He trusted few men, suffering from anxiety and fear of his enemies. He had nightmares and greatly feared being murdered in his bed. His life was full of contradictions making it difficult to decide wether he was a great King or a tyrant. He certainly had the cruelty and mood swings of his father and brothers, his treatment of some enemies (blinding etc) set against the more lenient imprisonment of his brother, his harsh taxation, his attitude to the church etc reveal the many facets of his personality. He retained a large number of doctors including the famous Spaniard Pedro Alfonso. He had an enquiring mind, ever seeking to understand the intricacies of law and, in particular, how they could help him consolidate his position He was interested in the natural world and established a menagerie of exotic animals at Woodstock. He could be jovial although it is said that men feared him more when he jested. His driving ambition after gaining control of England was to unite his father's old possessions. He needed money to finance his aims and taxed Lay and Clergy with ferocity. Furthermore his brother Robert now firmly re established in his old Duchy was still fomenting trouble between Henry and the Anglo Norman barons to strengthen his hand in contending for the English throne.

The barons, with estates in both France and England were divided in their loyalties between the harsh and total power of the English crown and the more free wheeling attitude to power in France where private wars and tax raising were allowed. The situation worsened in the spring of 1101 and Robert invaded England, landing at Portsmouth and marching to meet the defending army of Henry at Alton on Hampshire. The two armies stood facing each other and the two brothers rode forward to talk. The full details of there discussions are unknown, but we are told in the Anglo Saxon Chronicle that the King agreed to give up all the land in Normandy that he held by force against the Duke and that Robert be gifted 3000 marks per year, in return for which he would no longer contest Henry's right to rule and, that in the event of either brother dying without lawful issue, the other would inherit both England and Normandy. Robert stayed on in England as his brother's guest until Christmas and his army was left to fend for themselves 'doing much harm' wherever they went.

This situation could not last and the escape from captivity of devious Ranulf Flambard to Normandy did not improve things, it was said that he was the cause of the scheming and plotting that persuaded Robert to continue his claim for England. Henry still had to contend with rebellious outbreaks from disaffected barons at home and in 1102 marched against Robert of Belleme, Earl of Shrewsbury, besieging the Earl's castles at Arundel and Bridgenorth. Finally defeated, the Earl 'went over the sea' and Henry was once again in control of his contentious kingdom.

During this time, the saintly Anselm held a great Synod of Clerics at Westminster, setting out many new cannons of Christendom and depriving many clerics, French and English of their parishes who had obtained them unjustly under Rufus or had lived in iniquity therein. This was a popular move and was welcomed by layman and godly clerics everywhere.

Henry was at last getting a grip on his estate and had quelled most of the country to his rule. He was not helped however by the droughts and famines of the next few years which together with the heavy taxes made life a burden for all. The Chronicle talks of' blood being seen coming from the earth, the death of cattle, perished crops, great winds and pestilence'.

In 1104 Robert of Belleme and Henry were reconciled and the Earl had his estates returned to him. This greatly displeased Duke Robert as he had given refuge to the Earl when he was driven from England and his presence had helped the Duke persuade many the Anglo Norman barons to side with him in his disputes with Henry.

The following year Henry went to Normandy and gained much territory as well as the allegiance of many of the Norman barons. With typical medieval treachery Robert of Belleme again changed sides and fled to Normandy. Duke Robert visited England in 1106 to try to persuade Henry to give him back the lands taken by force the previous year. This was refused and they parted without reconciliation. Henry knew this situation could only get worse and in July he invaded Normandy. He met Robert's forces at Tinchebrai some 40 miles from Avranches and, during a fierce battle, reported to have lasted less than an hour, defeated Duke Robert, Earl Robert and William of Mortain who was lord of Tinchebrai. The battle took place on September 28th 1106, which was 40 years to the day after the Conqueror had landed in England. Tinchebrai was the first battle in which an English army commanded by a Norman King fought on Norman soil against a Norman army commanded by a pretender to the English throne. Bucking the trend of the time, Henry's army fought on foot against Robert's mounted forces and achieved a decisive victory.

Also captured during the battle was William Clito the son of William of Mortain, who in turn was the son of the Conqueror's half brother Robert and a possible contender for the English crown. Edgar the Atheling was also captured during the battle but, continuing his charmed life, was released by the King to live in obscurity, even being granted a pension of £1 per day (which he subsequently exchanged for a horse) until his death in 1125, It must be presumed that, like his father before him, Henry did not want to let Edgar become a rallying point for a Saxon uprising and his martyrdom might achieve this.

Robert was taken to Cardiff castle where he was to remain a prisoner for the remaining 28 years of his life. Following an escape attempt by him, Henry had his brothers eyes put out. It is strange to think of this man, so well thought of that he was once offered the Kingdom of Jerusalem spending his remaining days in lowly captivity reportedly trying to learn Welsh. Henry was, for a while at least, was supreme in England and

Normandy, but King Phillip pf France died in 1108 and was succeeded by his son Louis Vl.In 1109 Count Fulk of Anjou died and was succeeded by his son Fulk V and in 1111 Count Robert of Flanders died and was succeeded by his son Baldwin Vll, All being hostile to Henry.

Consolidating his victory, Henry destroyed all unlicensed castles, revoked all land grants made since the death of William the Conqueror and subjected the duchy to the same harsh fiscal administration as England.

As for those he considered traitors, Henry displayed his usual cruelty. William of Mortain was blinded and imprisoned for the next 34 years, being released only after Henry's death and being allowed to enter the Cluniac Monastery in Bermondsey for the few years remaining to him. Robert of Belleme was imprisoned for the last 24 years of his life

With his restless energy Henry began the construction and refortification of the English coast and the Welsh and Scottish borders. The major castles at Corfe, Wareham,Portchester and Carisbroke were built in this time.

Henry made conspicuous loyalty a test of royal favour, during his reign he dealt harshly with all who would oppose him, the great conquest families of Grandesmill, Montgomerie and Mortain were all brought down and their leaders killed, crippled or banished. All their estates of course, reverted to the King.

The King spent much time in his new possession of Normandy, reaffirming his rule over the barons. In 1110 the Earl of Maine died. He was a vassal of Henry and on his death the province became the fief of the Count of Anjou who was an ally of the King of France and no friend to Henry. Thus began another period of war and destruction as Henry fought to retain his territories against this new threat. He crushed all his opponents with his customary savagery, even personally hurling a rebel knight called Conan to his death from a tower in Rouen. He continued with his ruthless tax regime and in 1115 instituted the system of Exchequer replacing the older system of pipe rolls which had previously been used to calculate all monies and taxes owing to the King, amounts paid in and sums pardoned. The Exchequer Board was a table covered with a checkered cloth and was used to show the figures being calculated or audited and acted as a kind of two dimensional abacus enabling mathematicians to calculate high numbers in the manner of modern schoolchildren using one Hundredths, Tens and Units. The Royal Exchequer was controlled for many years by the very able Richard Fitzneal who became Henry's treasurer and his adoption of the system was an early example of information technology being used by government. At the board sat the Chancellor, or, during his absence, a deputy known as the Chancellor of the Exchequer ,the Justiciar, Constable, Chamberlain and Marshal and the Sheriff .They jointly audited the annual accounts of the Sheriff's receipts and expenses. These accounts were however, backed up by the older system of tally sticks. Notches giving the amounts rendered were cut in sticks which were then split, one being given to the renderer of the account and one kept by the Exchequer... Unfortunately, these tally sticks, having been stored for some 700 years were burned in 1834 in a bureaucratic clear out; the resulting fire incidentally, also destroyed the old Palace of Westminster.

Returning home, Henry went with his army into Wales to curtail the endless border raids of the local princes. His strength and power were sufficient to persuade the Welsh to make peace with him, but he greatly strengthened the castles of the Marcher barons to ensure security.
In 1120 the Kings of England and France were reconciled, Henry's son William was married to the daughter of the Count of Anjou and peace reigned in Henry's French possessions. The royal party went to Barfleur to take ship to England and a certain Thomas Fitzstephen, captain of the ship 'Blanche Nef' or White Ship, asked if he could have the honour of having the King travel on his ship known as a "snecca" or snakeship, based on the Viking design and very fast. It was Fitstephen's father that had brought Henry's father to Hastings on that fateful day in 1066. The King had already arranged his own sailing plans, but allowed his two legitimate sons William and Richard, plus an illegitimate half brother Ottuel and half sister Matilda to accept the offer. The King's ship sailed on the afternoon tide, but the Blanche Nef, being lighter and faster was to sail later. The princes arranged for much wine to be taken on board before sailing and the three hundred odd passengers and crew became extremely drunk with much carousing and mocking the priests who had come to bless the voyage. The ship struck a rock on the port side shortly

after leaving Barfleur and went down like a stone, leaving just two survivors in the water, a nobleman and a butcher from Rouen called Berold. The butcher was wearing a sheepskin coat which it is thought protected him from the worst of the cold, but the nobleman perished.

When the word reached England nobody dared to tell the King until finally, the youngest son of his sister Adela was coaxed into breaking the news. He is reported as "falling to the ground in his grief and had to be shepherded away to mourn in private. It was said that Henry never smiled again. Ever suspicious and sensitive to being seen as an usurper, Henry had gone to great lengths to ensure the eventual succession of his eldest son. In 1115 he had forced the Norman barons to do homage to William and a year later had his English nobility do the same, vowing to accept William as their true King on the death of Henry. Also, having married William to the daughter of the powerful Count of Anjou, he had established a counterbalance to any scheming that the King of France might attempt in support of William Clito the only surviving grandson of the Conqueror. who, incidentally ,had also married a daughter of the Count of Anjou.

 Still determined to ensure the succession of his line, Henry, being by now widowed, married again, this time to Adeliza of Louvain, but when it became apparent that there would be no children from this marriage, Henry decided to impose his daughter Matilda, a widow since 1125, as his successor and marrying her to Geoffrey the son of the Count of Anjou. This proposal was not received well by his barons. There had never been a Queen Regnant in England and the age was particularly hostile to the notion of a woman wielding political power. Moreover, the alliance with Anjou, a traditional enemy, was not welcomed in Normandy by the Anglo Norman nobility who held lands both sides of the channel. This whole question of wether or not a woman could inherit the Throne continued to be a contentious issue for many years and the issue of the so called Salic laws was raised again in the 15th century when Henry Vth claimed the French Throne. Henry was not however alone in his attempt to declare a woman his successor, both Alphonso of Castille and Baldwin of Jerusalem had designated their daughters as their heirs, Urraca in 1109 and Melisende in 1131.

The English barons were made to swear allegiance to Matilda who married Geoffrey in 1128, the year in which William Clito died. In 1133 Matilda gave birth to Henry (the future Henry 11) and in 1134 to Geoffrey. King Henry now becomes the doting grandfather. It is recorded that Henry presented his son in law with a shield bearing the emblem of 'many lions'. The lion being one of the symbols that William the Conqueror was known to have used as an heraldic device. This lion symbol was originally used by the Viking Rollo when he first settled in Normandy and has been part of Normandy's banner ever since. When Geoffrey's son assumed the throne as Henry 11,he again used the lion as his own standard, this being two golden lions, passant guardant on a red field representing Normandy and Maine, confirming his claim to the French throne through his Norman mother. Later, Richard the Lionheart amended the design to three lions representing England, Normandy and Aquitane ,whose symbol was, and is, also a lion ,this last becoming the recognised symbol of the King of England until Edward 111,claiming France as his right, quartered the English lions with the lilies of France. In the 15th century, the French king reduced the number of Fleur de Lys to three and the English king Henry 1V followed suit. This device becoming the Royal Coat of Arms until 1801 when King George formally surrendered the English claim to the throne of France.

In addition to Henry's continental problems he was frequently at loggerheads with the church. Anselm had refused to do homage for the church estates, believing them to be held from the Pope and Henry had refused to give up the power of appointing senior churchmen. The dispute escalated as far as Rome and the Pope threatened Henry with excommunication. The Archbishop was again exiled until a compromise was reached through his sister the Countess of Blois. Henry relented and the rift was healed, but in practise he still retained his old authority. This dispute did however mark a turning point in the relationship between King and church and it was tacitly accepted thereafter that the royal power was separate from though answerable to the law of God.
The situation in Normandy again became critical when Loius V1 married his daughter to Robert of Normandy's son William Clito. William had divorced the daughter of The Count of Anjou due to papal objections of

blood relationship and Louis, seeing a chance to unite the Norman barons against Henry, began another campaign against Henry's dukedom. Henry spent much of the years 1124/1125 in Normandy putting down various rebellions, the most notable of which involved Waleran, Earl of Worcester who had risen in support of William Clito. The rebels were crushingly defeated at the battle of Bourtheroulde in March 1124 where it is recorded that Henry used archers (some mounted) to achieve his victory. In his aggression and cunning he was able to subdue the rebels and restore order in Normandy, the leaders being treated most cruelly by being blinded although the rebel Earl Luke De la Barre did manage to commit suicide before the punishment could be carried out...

In England the harvests were poor and the cost of food was causing famine and riots, the situation being made worse by the crippling taxes that Henry was raising for his wars in Normandy. To divert attention he found scapegoats in the moneyers who had for years been debasing the coinage through processes known as crimping whereby coins had the edges cut off and melted down, the resulting original coin becoming smaller and smaller. They were commanded to appear in Winchester at Christmas 1125 and were arrested one by one. Each had his right hand and his testicles cut off as a warning to others. The year 1125 ended miserably with great floods, bridges broken up, corn and meadowland ruined, famine and disease and more crop failures than in many years before.

Trouble flared again in 1127 when the Earl of Flanders was traitorously murdered in church by his own men. King Louis ever wishing to provoke unrest appointed William Clito to the Earldom. Hostilities continued on and off throughout the following year until William was wounded in a personal fight and was taken to the monastery of St Omer where he died on 27th July. Thus died the last true claimant to the Conqueror's estate,

There was much unrest in the church during this time, the rise of the Gregorion movement questioning the established church and its worldly ways ,the division of the authority of Rome resulting in there being two Popes, Peter in Rome and Gregory in the west. The riches of the church contrasted cruelly with the poverty of the ordinary man and in 1128 the Archbishop of Canterbury called. at the King's request, a great council of bishops, abbots, archdeacons, monks and cannons who should come to

London at Michaelmas to speak of God's law. At the meeting it was decreed that archdeacons and priests must give up their wives and concubines on pain of their churches, houses and homes being forfeit. This was commanded by the Archbishop and his bishops. Having agreed to this, all were given leave to go, but the Chronicle records that 'They all kept their wives as they did before'

Henry was 65 and still fit enough to balance his time between his two realms... On the 1st August 1135 he left England for the last time. An eclipse the next day was reckoned by men to be a bad omen. In December 1135 he had enjoyed a day's hunting in the forest of Lyon south of Rouen. On returning to the castle he ate a meal of lampreys, an eel like fish with a sucker on its head with which it attaches itself to other fish to draw sustenance. Henry was very fond of this rather unpleasant looking creature, but fell ill immediately after the meal. His physicians, anxious to exonerate themselves from any blame all said that they had advised against the meal. The possibility is that the fish was infected; salmonella could have proved fatal to someone of the King's age. It is recorded that the King developed a fever and finally died very quickly. However, the rapidity of the onset of symptoms argue against such an infection which takes some time to develop. History notes that the meal was followed by immediate illness and a stomach condition such as peptic or duodenal perforation may have been the cause. After such a perforation, peritonitis developments with fever and vomiting and this is what seems to have occurred...

Henry's brain, entrails and eyes were removed and buried in St Denis le Ferment and his body was embalmed for shipment to Reading Abbey. His body had however reached such a state of decomposition that the surgeon assigned to the embalming died of infection, recorded by Henry's enemies as" the last of many whom Henry destroyed". Henry's body was sewn in to a bull's hide for its journey to England, but continued to deteriorate despite the coldness of the weather.

The only one of his many children who was with him on his last journey was the illegitimate Robert of Gloucester who brought the body to the great Cistercian abbey founded by Henry at Reading in 1121 where he was buried.

Reading suffered badly during the Dissolution of the Monasteries and Henry's tomb was ransacked and his bones scattered. A large Celtic cross is all that remains to mark his last resting place.

Stephen and Matilda

Henry had done all he could to ensure that his daughter Matilda would succeed him to the throne and had forced his nobles to swear to this on more than one occasion ,the last being at Oxford when all present, including Stephen of Blois, son of the Conqueror's sister Adela gave his word.. Stephen was a pleasant, affable and likeable man and a favourite of Henry who gave him so much land and property both sides of the channel that he became one of the richest and most powerful of noblemen. He lacked the moral strength and ruthlessness however to be a firm leader which ultimately proved to be the cause of his failure to secure his line through the accession of his son. He was one of the party intended to travel to England in 1120 on the White Ship, but declined due to diarrhea, an attack which probably saved his life.

Matilda was the legitimate daughter of Henry 1st, but was a quarrelsome and difficult woman. Her marriage to the Emperor Henry V of Germany was of huge diplomatic importance to the English King as witnessed by the dowry of 10,000 marks of silver. The marriage gave Henry an ally against the French King and also enhanced status as the father in law of the Emperor. Following her husband's death in 1125 she returned home and it was probably her experience as an Empress which included witnessing royal acta, channeling petitions to the Emperor ,being entrusted with the royal insignia and even becoming titular regent of Italy in 1118,which persuaded her father to put her forward as his successor following the White Ship disaster. Her training had ensured that she had a mind of her own and sufficient self confidence to be her own woman.
Her marriage to Geoffrey of Anjou, who was 10 years her junior, in 1128 was another strategic move by her father always seeking allies in his territorial disputes with the French King and the other nobles ever nibbling at the edges of his lands. Geoffrey's father Fulk went off immediately after the wedding to become the consort of Melisende of Jerusalem leaving Geoffrey as Count and thus, a suitable match for a princess. Fulk would however rule as King of Jerusalem to Melisende's

Queen whereas no such arrangement was envisaged for Geoffrey, the allegiance sworn to Matilda in 1131 being to her alone. It is typical of her that she retained the title of Empress even after her marriage to Geoffrey and her son Henry, born of this marriage was called Henry Fitzempress

The marriage did not have an auspicious start; she had a notoriously sour nature while he was rather shallow. Henry desperately needed a grandson to secure his line but Matilda and Geoffrey lived apart for the first three years of the marriage. It was only the prospect of the succession of Anjou going to a half brother from Palestine (born in 1131) that forced reconciliation. Thus the combination of duty and greed resulted in the birth of Henry (1133) Geoffrey (1134) and William (1136).

Henry, recognizing the weakness in Geoffrey would not let him have any authority or influence in Normandy or England. Matilda spent much of her time in Rouen being taught government administration, but this all came to an end with Henry's death.

Stephen wasted no time in hurrying to England to claim the throne despite his oath to support Matilda. In this he was supported by many nobles, particularly his brother Henry of Blois, Bishop of Winchester and Hugh Bigod, a powerful Earl of East Anglia. They could not countenance being ruled by a woman and also saw some potential personal gains to be had under the rather weak Stephen. Within 3 weeks he had secured the support of London, Henry's officials and the church. It was vital for him to be recognized by the royal administration based in Winchester as it gave Stephen access to the royal treasure. Stephen was duly crowned on 22nd December 1135 by William, Archbishop of Canterbury.

Stephen's swift action had taken his rivals by surprise, Matilda and her husband Geoffrey of Anjou, Henry's illegitimate son Robert of Gloucester and of course, Stephen's elder brother Theobald whom many favoured for the accession. The Only options open to them following the coronation was acceptance or rebellion and civil war

Stephen also ensured his acceptance by the church by enlisting the support of the Pope, in return for which, he opened the way for increased papal influence in English political affairs and granted the church a Charter of Liberties.

All should have been set fair for Stephen, but his precarious position required the ruthless streak of the Conqueror and this trait was sadly lacking in him. His weak attempts to play the nobles off against each other and to seek compromise in an age when only strength was admired soon alienated those who had declared for him. His first test was against Baldwin De Redvers who rose against Stephen in 1136. Stephen attempted to lay siege to to Baldwin in Exeter ,but the disaffection of his Flemish mercenaries and their squabbles with the Norman contingent of his army led to disarray and retreat .Sensing the lack of resolve in Stephen, the nobles started to fight among themselves settling old scores and seizing what they could from each other. Civil war was to scar Stephen's reign and throughout this time it was said that 'Jesus and the Saints slept'

During this time, Geoffrey of Anjou, Matilda's husband had been increasing his influence in Normandy, he was little concerned with England and its troubles but saw an opportunity to further his own ambitions to annex the Duchy. Stephen mounted a campaign against Geoffrey in 1137, but again his army fell into disarray with the Flemish and Norman troops disintegrating into rival factions and fighting each other. In England the barons continued to fight among themselves, frequently changing sides in their support or otherwise of Stephen. A stronger man might have been able to pull all these conflicting factions together, but the situation worsened when Robert Earl of Gloucester, Matilda's half brother, rose against Stephen in 1138 to exploit the dissatisfaction felt by many at Stephen's inability to impose order in the country. It should be remembered that Robert had as good a claim to the throne as any, but had accepted the fait accompli of Stephen's accession up till now. He became alienated however, by the many favours granted by the King to the Beaumont family twins Waleran of Meulan and Robert of Leicester. Many of his neighbours fell in with him and the West Country became the centre of the anti Stephen revolt.

Stephen, with events getting out of hand, and seeing treachery everywhere, ordered the arrest of the powerful Bishop Roger of Salisbury and his relatives, this act losing him the support of the clergy, another wrong move. Heartened at news of the growing uprising, Matilda came to

England, landing at Arundel where her stepmother, now lived. Here Stephen displayed the strange workings of a medieval mind. After threatening to besiege Arundel castle, with incredible chivalry he had Matilda and her forces escorted to her half brother in Bristol. The support Matilda enjoyed was not solely from supporters of her hereditary claim, but more from those who felt cheated from their lands under Henry or were jealous of favours bestowed on others by Stephen and who felt that they may profit better under a change of ruler. Stephen's forces were numerically stronger than those of Matilda and her half brother, but shortage of resources, indecision and lack of resolve to crush his enemies, whose power base was centered around Robert's West Country estates, prolonged the rebellion.

Stephen was beset by enemies all around, Geoffrey in Normandy, Robert of Gloucester in the west and, in July 1138, the Scottish King David invaded England ostensibly to lend support to his niece Matilda's claim to the English throne, but seeing in the turmoil a chance to annex Northumberland. Stephen being preoccupied with the rebellion in the south west, the defence of the north fell to the ageing bedridden Thurstan, Archbishop of York who declared the forthcoming conflict a crusade and promised heavenly reward to the participants and eternal damnation to those who would not fight. As an added inducement, Thurstan provided the banners of four Yorkshire saints which were mounted on poles affixed to a four wheeled wagon. Atop the poles was a silver casket containing the Host, all this designed to give heart and resolve to his forces as well as providing, in the words of a contempory "a sure and conspicuous rallying point by which they might rejoin their comrades in the event of being cut off"Thurstan's methods were successful and a large force consisting of English, Anglo Norman and Welsh moved against the Scottish King.

The two armies met at Northallerton in Yorkshire on 22nd August 1138, Thurstan's forces were drawn up on a slight rise and arrayed in a single division rather than the more usual three. All the knights were on foot having sent the horses to the rear as a sign of their refusal to retreat. In this rank of soldiers were deployed blocks of archers interspersed with the armoured men-at –arms, an arrangement that would figure prominently in many future battles fought by the English both at home and abroad. The

Scots halted six hundred yards away on another small rise, but fell to arguing among themselves as to who should lead the attack. The men from Galloway insisting that it was their traditional right to be first in the Scottish ranks. King David ordered his trumpeters to sound the advance and the men of Galloway" gave vent to to a yell of a horrible sound" and charged the English line beating their swords on their shields. The English archers sheltering behind the front rank took terrible toll of the Galwegians. A contempory writer recorded that "the Scots, bristling all around with arrows and in blind madness rushing forward to smite the foe, but lashing the air with furious strokes".

King David's son Henry, seeing this carnage, led a cavalry charge from the right, screaming his battle cry Albany! Albany! And scattered the defenders of the English left. Had Henry been supported by infantry, he might well have won the day, but in this confusion an English knight held up a severed head, shouting that King David was slain. On hearing this, the Scottish morale was shattered and the Galwegians, unable to endure any more of the arrow storm or the fierceness of the armoured knights, fled the field. Some of David's supporters however, seeing the King's Dragon banner still aloft realized that the David was still alive and rallied to his standard allowing the King to make a fighting withdrawal.

In January 1141, Stephen moved with his forces to attack the pro Matilda Earl of Chester in his castle at Lincoln .On learning of this, the Earl left the castle in the care of his brother William Roumare, while he himself escaped to join Earl Robert in the Welsh Marches. Robert had been busy building up his forces in Wales with the aid of his allies the two Welsh princes Mariadeth and Kaladrius, sons of the powerful Madog who had made common cause with Robert against Stephen and Miles, the hereditary sheriff of Gloucestershire and castellan of Gloucester. Miles had initially supported Stephen, but had turned to Matilda after her landing in England. It is likely that, given the adherence to Matilda of Miles's more powerful neighbour Robert of Gloucester, his change of allegiance may have been more prompted by self preservation. The Welsh had little love for Stephen whose cavalier distribution of the lands of the Marches to his friends, particularly the Mortimers, had driven them into alliance with Robert, a third of whose army were Welsh.

On the 2nd February, Robert's forces crossed the swollen Fossdyke and marched for Lincoln. On hearing of their coming, Stephen called a meeting of his nobles. The older wiser heads counseled that he should retreat to London to raise a more powerful army, but the hot heads argued for an immediate attack on Earl Robert. The hot heads won the day and Stephen's forces gave up the advantage of the high ground around the besieged castle and descended to meet the enemy.

Stephen's forces were led by no less than 6 Earls, Richmond, Norfolk, Southampton who would command the right wing and Surrey, Worcester and York. The latter would command the left wing and the others in the centre with the King. As was usual during the period, speeches were made to the troops before the battle to stiffen resolve and mock the enemy. Earl Ranulf made a short speech and then Robert of Gloucester. Robert called the Duke of Richmond "an infamous man polluted by crime", Worcester was "slothful in deed, last to attack, first to run, tardy in battle and swift in flight" he claimed that Surrey had stolen York's wife and that he was "weaking with wine and unacquainted with warfare", he dismissed Southampton as "a man whose deeds consist of words alone"Stephen, claiming that "he had not an agreeable voice" instructed Baldwin of Clare to address the army. Baldwin accuses Robert of "having the mouth of a lion but the heart of a hare, whatever he begins like a man he ends like a woman". He dismissed the lightly armed Welsh contingent as "objects for our contempt, devoid of skill in the art of war like cattle running upon the hunting spears".

York opened the battle by tearing into the lightly armed Welshmen creating much slaughter, but the better disciplined followers of the pro Matilda Earl of Chester, who it is recorded" stood out in his bright armour", moved in on York's men and routed them. For all his faults, lack of courage was not one of them and there is a contempory account of Stephen's capture which does much to give the flavour of barbarity and bloodshed of medieval warfare.

"No rest, no breathing time was granted them except in the quarter where stood the most valiant King as the foe dreaded the incomparable force of his blows. The Earl of Chester, on perceiving this and envying the King his glory, rushed upon him with the weight of his armed men.

Then was seen the might of the King, equal to a thunderbolt, slaying some with his immense battleaxe and striking others down. Then arose the shouts afresh, all rushing against him and him against all. At length through the number of the blows, the King's battleaxe was broken asunder. Instantly, with his right hand drawing his sword well worthy of a King, he marvelously waged combat until the sword as well was broken asunder.

On seeing this, William Kahammes, a powerful knight rushed upon the King seizing him by the helmet, cried with a loud voice, Hither! , Hither! I have the King!. All flew to the spot and the King was taken. Pulling off the King's helmet, Stephen, foaming at the mouth in his rage finally recognized the inevitable and surrendered to Robert of Gloucester."

Stephen was put in chains and taken first to Gloucester where Matilda could see him in his defeat and then to the dungeons of Bristol castle. Upon his imprisonment, Stephen absolved his vassals of their allegiance, n act which made easier Henry, Bishop of Winchester's defection to Matilda.

Matilda now needed to grasp the reins of power and needed prominent nobles to join her cause. On 2nd March 1141 she arranged a meeting with Henry, Bishop of Winchester and brother to Stephen. If she could persuade him to join her it would add much weight to her cause. The meeting took place outside the gates of Winchester on a cold and wet March day. The rain poured down on the two parties as the Empress promised "that all matters of chief account in England, especially gifts of bishoprics and abbacies should be subject to his control if he received her in Holy Church as Lady and kept his faith to her unbroken" Bishop Henry agreed to accept her as Queen so long as she too kept her promises.

On 3rd she was formally welcomed in Winchester and took up residence in the castle, Henry handed her the keys to the royal treasury and the royal crown. She was acclaimed in Winchester market place as "Our Lady And our Queen", although it is interesting to note that throughout this period she was never openly referred to as Queen, the title 'Dominus' or Lady of the English' being more commonly used. Henry sent for Archbishop Theobald and he duly arrived three days later but was clearly reluctant to abandon Stephen the anointed King.

While Matilda traveled in triumph to Oxford, a church council meeting was convened, William of Malmesbury was present at the meeting and recorded that Henry explained his change of loyalty due to Stephen's failure to keep his promises to the church and the arrest of Bishop Roger of Salisbury. He pompously declared that "though he loved his brother, he loved his Heavenly Father more".

The church did not want the country to be without a ruler and, following more meetings with Henry, were persuaded to support Matalda, who, in the meantime, was having troubles of her own.

Having arrived in London she lost no time in establishing her authority, but her arrogance and high handedness, plus harsh tax demands quickly alienated her from the very people whose support she needed. Her procession through the city turned to a riot when the people rose against her and she was driven from London.

Learning nothing from these experiences and listening to no advice, Matilda very soon lost the support of Bishop Henry, who, turning his coat again returned to Stephen's cause. Henry with a strong force besieged Winchester castle determined to restore the city to the royalist cause. Matilda responded on the 31st of July by arriving with a besieging force of her own and the bishop's men were forced to retreat to the fortified Wolvesly palace, Henry's official residence while Henry escaped to gather reinforcements. A double siege ensued with Matilda's forces besieging the bishop's men in Wolvesly and the royalists besieging the city. Three days later the city was set on fire. It is not known if this was Matilda or Henry's doing, but the fire cost Matilda most of her provisions and she was forced to make a break for it. The royalists and the Londoners then proceeded to sack the town, burning and looting, dragging many away for torture and execution, Stephen's supporters were starting to waver and his Normandy possessions were being overrun by Count Geoffrey. Matilda's fortunes were in no better state however, although she and her supporters had managed to escape from Winchester, her half brother Robert was captured at Stockbridge about 10 miles from the town. This capture enabled Stephen's supporters to negotiate the King's release in exchange for Robert and Stephen thus regained his crown and title on 1st November 1141 after being held captive since 2nd February.

The war dragged on and in October of the following year, Stephen laid siege to Matilda in Oxford castle. The siege lasted 3 months and the situation became desperate enough for Matilda to seek a means of escape and it said that she climbed down a rope from St George's tower and escaped across the frozen river wearing white as a camouflage, finally reaching the safety of Wallingford castle, showing that for all her lack of tact or charm she had some of the Conqueror's spirit in her. She remained the focal point of resistance to Stephen, but her moment had passed. She made a new base of resistance in Devizes being joined by her eldest son Henry in 1142, but was unable to extend her area of influence. Her requests for help from her husband were ignored, he was far more interested in the domination of Normandy which he completed in 1144.

The wars were finally ended when agreement was reached, following the death of Stephens only son Eustace, that Stephen would reign for his lifetime and that Matilda's son would inherit thereafter. Things might have been very different for Stephen had Eustace lived and if Stephen had forced the church to accept the accession of his son .With the death of her half brother Robert in 1147, Matilda gave up, leaving further resistance to her son and returned to Normandy.

The rest of her life was spent furthering the interests of her son and dabbling in the politics of Normandy and its relations with Germany and France .Although unpopular and never achieving he throne, she was the mother of the Plantagenet's who would reign for the next 350 years. Matilda lived to see the first 13 years of her son's reign and is buried in Fontrevault Abbey .It is said that the name Plantagenet derives from the habit of Geoffrey's family, being avid hunters, of planting sprigs of the plant we know as Broom to provide ground cover for game animals. The Latin name of this plant being Genista, therefore, Planta Genista.

We should also remember the role in Stephen's life played by another Matilda (sometimes known as Maude) his wife and tireless supporter in these parlous times. She was the daughter of the Count of Bouloigne, granddaughter of Malcolm of Scotland and a direct descendant of both Ethelred the Unready and Charlemagne She was made of sterner stuff than Stephen. In 1138 Maude supervised the capture of Dover castle, from Matilda's supporters; in 1139 she negotiated a treaty with her uncle David, King of Scotland. She rallied support for Stephen after his capture at Lincoln and was instrumental in persuading Stephen's brother Henry of Winchester to return to Stephen's cause. She also played a large part in manipulating the favours of the Londoners against the Empress Matilda. She is described in the Gesta Stephani as "a woman of subtlety and a man's resolution", who "bore herself with valour like a man", thus showing that it was possible to be both hard and resolute without alienating her supporters through arrogance.

Stephen however, was still to know no peace. The enmities and rivalries of the civil war continued with much death and destruction during a time when, as the chroniclers recorded "the saints slept"

Stephen held only a modest court and little is known of his death. Richard Baker's chronicles state that" he was suddenly seized with the iliac passion and with an old disease of the emroids"Any pain in the Illiac region could be the result of appendicitis which can lead to an abcess ,causing peritonitis and death, it seems that he also had a recurrent attack of Haemorrhoids at this time.

Stephen was buried beside his wife Maud and son Eustace at the monastery he had founded at Faversham in Kent in October 1151

Henry 11

Henry was born in Le Mans in March 1133, the son of Matilda and Geoffrey of Anjou. He was an energetic and powerful man, his red hair and fiery temper revealing his Plantagenet temperament. He is described as having grey blue eyes, bow legs, rough hands and was generally unkempt and grubby. He was careless of his dress and was rarely seen in formal clothes, disdaining the trappings of power as only one born to such high rank can. Despite this, he was supposedly responsible for the introduction of the short continental cloak to England and thus gained the nickname"curtmantle" He was strong willed, restless, always on the move and very fit. On the distaff side, he seems to have suffered from Manic Depression, common in the Plantagenets and was a lecher.

He was educated in England and France and was an excellent scholar, being fluent in both French and Latin and was reputed to have compiled much of his own legislation during his reign.

He became Duke of Normandy in 1150 and Count of Anjou after his father's death in 1151 and, following his marriage to Eleanor of Aquitaine in 1152, became Duke of Aquitaine (named after the Roman "Land of Water") and Count of Poitou. Eleanor, the former wife of Louis V11 had been divorced by the French king due to her being within the fifth degree of kinship, a practice prohibited by the church. She and Henry were to the same degree of kinship and the marriage scandalized Europe.

He also claimed his father's title of Anjou even though this had been promised to his younger brother Geoffrey by family agreement in 1151.

He became King of England and Duke of Normandy in 1154 and thus ruled an empire stretching from Scotland to the Spanish border. He traveled and worked ceaselessly to keep his inheritance together, spending only thirteen of his thirty four year reign in England. He insisted that horses were always kept ready for his use in Abbeys throughout his reign and nobody knew when he might make his sudden appearance. His knowledge of statecraft, intrigue and war were learned during his many English campaigns on behalf of his mother in 1147, 1149 and, 1153. He was determined to reinforce and expand his domains and was very fierce in his defence of what he considered his rights.

He had five legitimate sons, William who died shortly after birth, Henry, Geoffrey, Richard and John.

Often considered one of the most important of English monarchs, at various times being hailed as "the father of Common Law" and "Gravedigger of Fuedalism", a man whose insight laid the foundations of much of our present common law and it was his establishment of permanent professional courts at Westminster and in the counties that changed the relationship between King, Church and society forever. The replacement of the ancient Trial by Battle with Grand Assizes and the creation of Petty Assizes for lesser claims and the appointment of itinerant judges operating in the King's name did much to establish what the common law became.

In fact, Henry had no grand design or strategy for the creation of law and equitable government. He was Lord of his Domain comprising England, Normandy, Anjou, Maine, Brittany and Wales. He held England by right of blood and held Normandy and Anjou by the same right but as a vassal of the French king. Brittany and his main aim was the exploitation of his rights and the collection of revenue as with his other holdings. Many of his laws were framed with this in mind.

His firm reign ,following the tribulations and rebellions of his predecessor Stephen was welcomed by the English magnates and the fierce protection of his inherited rights validated those of his barons The theme of hereditary rights being one which Henry repeatedly used during his reign.

The ferocity with which he pursued his mother's (and therefore his own) cause in the bloody period at the end of Stephen's reign in 1153 became legendary, his scorched earth policy and the destruction of castles signaling his ruthless determination to prevail. It is interesting to note that, during this period he was knighted by King David 1st of Scotland, ever a man who knew which way the political wind was blowing. This was a significant act in view of David's own claim to the English throne through his great great grandfather King Edmond Ironsides which he was effectively renouncing. This act by the Scots king did not prevent Henry from virtually taking over Scotland in 1174 following the defeat and capture of King William "The Lion". The terms imposed by the Treaty of Falaise surrendered Scotland to Henry who granted it back to William as a fief for which homage was due to the English king. English garrisons were installed in Berwick, Roxburgh and Edinburgh and Northumberland was annexed. An independent Scotland no longer existed.

Upon taking the crown, Henry sought to reconcile the many warring factions in the realm and appointed two of Stephen's supporters, Richard de Lucy and Robert of Leicester as Justiciars as well as a protégé of Archbishop Theobald of Canterbury, a certain Thomas, the son of Gilbert Becket, a Norman merchant living in London. Thomas had demonstrated his brilliance in Theobald's service. Thomas, described by his contemporizes as tall, thin, pale complexioned, with a big nose and dark eyes had a likeable personality and a quick mind, he was reported to be of a somewhat nervous disposition and would sometimes stammer. He received a good education and began his career in the service of one Osbert Huitdeniers, (=eight pence, probably his rate of interest) a London banker. The name, Thomas a Becket was not used by him and was first recorded some 400 years later .He titled himself Thomas of London. In 1146 he joined Theobald's household where his career blossomed, eventually being appointed Archdeacon of Canterbury in 1154.
On Theobald's recommendation, Thomas was appointed Henry's Chancellor and quickly became friend and confident of the young King, taking over many of the duties that Henry found irksome, witnessing royal letters and charters, sitting on the Exchequer and sometimes acting as a royal judge. He was instrumental in raising the Great Scutage, (shield money) of 1159 to finance the King's foray to Toulouse. This was the system, first practiced by William Rufus and later by Henry 1st to raise money from the barons in commutation of military service and was based on a percentage of each knight's fief, the rates being from one Mark (13s and 4p) to one Pound. This scutage raised one hundred and Eighty Thousand Pounds for Henry

to enable Henry to employ mercenaries in place of the old feudal levy.

Thomas's influence and friendship with Henry reaped him many rewards of estates from the King who, as a special mark of his esteem freed Thomas from rendering accounts to the Exchequer for the lands he held on behalf of the King. This tax free existence was potentially dangerous for Thomas soon developed a taste for the good life and became notorious for his lavish extravagance. It was said that most of the fifty odd clerks employed by Thomas were assigned to administer his estates and he also maintained some seven hundred knights in his personal household. When sent on an embassy to Paris in 1158,Thomas took with him a retinue of two hundred and fifty servants ,plus eight wagons of furnishings, plate, provisions and twenty four changes of clothes .The locals marveled at his splendour, "how great must be the King to have such a Chancellor". For all this, Thomas was also a man of action even campaigning with Henry's troops. During Henry's ill-fated expedition to subdue Toulouse, Thomas was reputed to have led the attack on three towns and during the Vexin campaigns of 1161, was in command of some six thousand troops. He also beat the French knight Engelram in a joust, claiming the Frenchman's charger as prize. This was no deskbound clerk.

Becket, mentor, close friend and confidant to Henry, shared the King's obsession with the rights of his office and the crown and was driven to excel in their maintenance. All that Thomas held was dependant on his relationship with the King and all was well until the Death of Theobald in 1161 when Henry appointed Thomas as the new Archbishop. The appointment was not popular among the clergy due to Thomas' reputation and lifestyle. Henry felt that the appointment would herald a new cooperation with the church, but also help him regain some royal rights lost under Stephen. He had however seriously underestimated Thomas. Once confirmed in his new role he set about establishing his views on ecclesiastical immunities and jurisdiction much to the annoyance of the King. Part of his stand was doubtless his desire to win acceptance from the clergy who understandably were suspicious of him and his record, but it would have been in keeping with his character for Thomas to pursue his new task with all his vigour .The recurring dispute between King and Church regarding the royal right to clerical appointments, plus the churches' contention that all clerical estates were held from the Pope and therefore were not taxable by the King became the rock upon which their friendship foundered .Henry had expected Thomas to be the portal through which church riches would flow to him, but he had underestimated his Archbishop.

By the autumn of 1163 the two were in open conflict, the King stripped Thomas of all secular honours acquired as Chancellor which, significantly Thomas had failed to renounce on his appointment as Archbishop. Relations deteriorated further in January 1164 when Henry tried to force the bishops to accept the existing customs unconditionally. Surprisingly, Thomas capitulated to these demands, probably reckoning that he could reduce them over time. The King however promptly enshrined these agreements in the Constitutions of Clarendon, a move that enraged Thomas, whose' arrogance was by now alienating many of his colleagues. He was summoned to Northampton in October 1164 to answer charges of peculation and unlawfully withholding property.

However, on his arrival, was further charged with treason. In typical style Thomas defended himself and defied his critics, he denied the jurisdiction of the royal courts and declared the issue was one of clerical independence .He appealed to Rome and then fled in disguise to exile in France where he was to remain for the next 6 years.

Thomas, well versed in politics and intrigue, spent this time fomenting discord in England and gathering support for his position among the French clergy. The increasingly heated and extravagant propaganda campaign alienated many of his former supporters who felt that it achieved nothing but weakened the whole church. It was during this exile that Thomas began to adopt more extreme symbols of religious piety by wearing a hair shirt and indulging in violent flagellation.

Frequent attempts of reconciliation notably organized by Louis 1V of France and the Pope founded due to the obstinacy of both parties. Henry and Thomas met at Montmiral and Montmatre during 1169, but failed to affect an end to their dispute. Henry was however anxious to have his son, also called Henry, crowned to ensure his succession on his father's death and, in the absence of Thomas ,had the ceremony performed by the Archbishop of York in contravention of what many saw as the cherished right of Canterbury. Ironically, this blow to Thomas' position led to a reconciliation with Henry at Feteval in 1170. This agreement returned Thomas' lands and allowed his return to England but left the wider issues unresolved.

Returning to England, Thomas traveled ostentatiously through southern England and with a total lack of any sense of reconciliation refused to lift the excommunication of the bishops involved in the coronation of young Henry. The King, in Normandy for Christmas, was angered by this and possibly fearful of the rising popularity of Thomas, flew into one of his rages declaring" What miserable drones and traitors have I nourished in my house who let their lord be treated with such shameful contempt by a low born clerk". Later recorded as "who will rid me of this turbulent priest"

On hearing this outburst, four of his knights, Hugh de Moreville, William de Tracy, Reginald FitzUrse and Richard le Breton embarked for England. It is probable that their motive was to arrest Thomas, but events slid out of control once they reached Canterbury, arriving on 29th December 1170.There are a number of contempory accounts of the murder of Thomas, perhaps the most detailed is by the monk Edward Grim, who was present at the time and received wounds to his arm while trying to protect Thomas. He records that, after some strong words with the four knights outside the cathedral, the monks took Thomas inside for shelter. The knights followed together with a sub deacon of the cathedral, one Hugh, described as The Evil clerk. The monks tried to bar their entrance by closing the great doors, but Thomas would have none of this saying" It is not proper that God's house be made a fortress". The knights entered with weapons drawn shouting "Where is Becket traitor to the King and kingdom" Thomas replied,"Here I am, not a traitor of the King but a priest". The knights replied "Then absolve and restore to communion those you have excommunicated". Thomas replied "No penance has been made so I will not absolve them". Grim then records that Thomas was struck on the head by the first knight, Reginald FitzUrse and this blow almost severing the arm of the writer. This was swiftly followed by another strike to the head by a second knight, but Thomas remained on his feet .partly supported by Grim. The third knight then struck detaching the crown of Thomas' skull and breaking his sword as it struck the stone pillar. At this blow, Thomas at last fell, the fourth knight pushing the monks back from the slaughter so that the others might finish their work. The cleric Hugh, who had entered with the knights then put his foot on Thomas' neck and kicked so that blood and brains spattered the floor exclaiming" We can leave this place, he will not rise again"

It is clear that Thomas had resigned himself to death and had made no move to escape or defend himself from the attack, perhaps knowing that this would make the crime seem even more heinous

To the world. Thomas would seem to have achieved more in death than he had in life .He had been one of the least successful archbishops ,he had effectively performed his duties for only two and a half years and during that time had managed to alienate many of his supporters, including Pope Alexandria 111.

Henry at once realized that the murder had alienated all Christendom and that Thomas had now become a saint and a martyr, a victim of a terrible and sacreligious outrage in his own cathedral. A huge gesture of penitence would have to be made .Surprisingly; Henry seemed in no hurry to complete this. He did, after all, have many other problems. The rift with the church was deep, but the business of church and state went on. It was not until the Compromise of Avranches in 1172 that Henry was absolved for his part in the murder of Thomas and in1174 that Henry appointed a new Archbishop, one Richard of Dover. In the same year he decided to carry out his penance. Henry walked to Canterbury wearing only a shirt. Arriving at the cathedral he knelt at the porch and then, with bleeding feet, he walked to the murder spot and kissed the stone floor where Thomas had fallen. A ceremony of penitence and absolution was then held, following which, Henry was beaten, receiving three strokes from each of the eighty monks and five strokes from each of the bishops and abbots present. Unwashed and bloody, he spent the next night in the cathedral crypt, fasting and praying.

Throughout this troubled time a further problem had been quietly festering in the west. As long ago as 1155, the Pope had, in the papal bull Laudabiliter, asked Henry to intervene in Ireland to clean up a corrupt and lax Christianity. With other more pressing problems in his own domains Henry had deferred involvement this obscure island in the west .The situation took a turn for the worse however ,when in 1166,Diarmait,King of Leinster was ousted from his Dublin fastness and forced to flee by an alliance led by the High King of Ireland Ruaidrai Ua Conchobair. Diarmait appealed to Henry for help in regaining his kingdom, but was refused. Henry did however give permission for Diarmait to recruit help from the Marcher barons on the Welsh border... These savage barons were ready for some diversion, the various attempts to subdue the princes of Gwynedd had resulted in the loss of castles, land and peasants The stalemate, plus a chance of perhaps easier plunder was seized upon by men such as Robert fitzStephen and Richard fitzGilbert de Clare, Earl of Pembroke, (known to his friends and enemies alike as Strongbow). The Anglo Norman mercenaries duly reinstated Diarmait in his kingdom and were rewarded with land.Diarmait going so far as to marry his daughter to Strongbow. He further promised that, should his sons not survive, Strongbow would inherit the kingdom (it should be noted that, at that time, one son had been blinded, another had been taken hostage and the third was illegitimate). However, in 1171 Diarmait died and Strongbow became King of Leinster. Henry at last began to take notice. The last thing he needed was another upstart Norman with delusions of grandeur on his doorstep. He already had enough of these within his realm. Gathering his forces Henry sailed for Ireland and quickly subdued Strongbow who turned Leinster over to Henry and was surprisingly made Lord of Leinster in return.

Henry then toured Ireland and in Dublin was offered the fealty of all the Irish kings apart from Connacht and O,Neill in the north. The Anglo Normans swiftly consolidated their hold by building motte and bailey castles, setting up market towns and large scale colonization. Although the Irish kings may have settled for Norman rule the general population was not so enthusiastic and the barons had to deal with a number of rebellions until relative peace was established. Strongbow died in 1176 ,but another Anglo Norman invasion by John de Courcy in 1180 who ,following his capture of the region then known asUlaid changed the name to Ulster and built his base at Carrickfergus , adding south west Ireland to his domain a few years later. In the early part of the 13th century, a major rebellion broke out and many barons were killed, their homes being burned and the lands wasted. The rebellion dragged on for many years, but by 1260 most of the land was owned by Anglo Norman barons and the rebels defeated.

If these events were not trouble enough, Henry's sons were losing patience with their father's desire to keep all power to himself. The young Henry was heir apparent to the English throne,Poitou and Aquitaine were to be settled on Richard, Geoffrey was to have Brittany and John was made Lord of Ireland. They all wanted some part to play in these domains and in 1173 Henry, Geoffrey and Richard formed an alliance with their formidable mother Eleanor, Louis V11 of France ,the Scottish King William and the Count of Flanders ,plus assorted disaffected barons in England and Normandy and launched a series of revolts to depose the king. King Henry could however rely on the loyalty of certain key barons led by his justiciar John de Lucy. These allies, coupled with Henry's drive and determination resulted in his defeat of the rebels.

Henry wasted no time in reinforcing his victory. Although lenient to his sons he set about the tightening of royal rights through his own courts superceding baronial ones. The itinerant justice was overhauled and given greater authority (Assize of Northampton 1176); Forest Laws were resumed in full severity. Rebel castles such as Hugh Bigod's in East Anglia were destroyed.

Henry's restless energy kept him constantly on the move, in 1172 he traveled from Ireland to Normandy in a month, this prompting the French King Louis V11 to remark "the King of England seems to fly rather than travel by horse or ship". This constant movement enabled Henry to keep his finger on the pulse of his domains enabling him to impose his personality and will on events. Where he was absent, his interests were protected by agents and judges acting in his name, but answerable to himself. A contempory noted that Henry" hunted through the kingdom inquiring into everyone's doing and especially judges who he had made judge of others"

From 1174 there began a period of extended peace in England even though his sons champed at the bit of Henry's continued authority. This erupted in 1183 when the young Henry launched a major rebellion against his father, this rebellion died out following the young prince's death through dysentery... In 1185 Henry's youngest son John attempted to enforce his lordship over Ireland a venture ending in fiasco.

As has already been noted, Henry was a womanizer and had many mistresses, including Prince Henry's betrothed, Alice the daughter of the French king Louis. Following the death of Prince Henry she was then betrothed to Prince Richard. The love of his life however was Rosamund Clifford "the Fair Rosamund" who bore him two sons and for whom he built the castle at Woodstock. His wife Eleanor, ever on the side of her sons against Henry, was imprisoned at Winchester for the last sixteen years of his reign.

In 1186 Henry was asked by the Patriarch of Jerusalem to lead a crusade and, although he had been toying with the idea for some years, Henry declined. On October 3rd 1187 Saladin captured Jerusalem and Pope Gregory V111 called for a 3rd crusade to return the city to Christian rule. Henry took the cross in 1188, but never made the journey.

Henry was to face further tests of his energy and will. In 1186.his son Geoffrey Duke of Brittanny died after being stamped on by a horse after a fall at a tournament near Paris. Henry's two remaining sons, Richard and John were still no closer to being given any real power and Richard, jealous of the favourite John, feared that Henry would now give all the French inheritance to his brother and in 1188 openly rebelled. aided by the French King Philip and, although no pitched battle took place, finally forced Henry to concede the advantage, It seems that Henry simply gave up, dismissed his army and retired to Chinon. His age, health and the treachery of his sons finally robbed him of the will to continue.

There were many contradictions in Henry's character, his attention to detail in lawmaking, his classic rages when foiled, his attitude to his sons and his refusal to defer any power to them, his power struggles with the church must be set against his achievements. His annexation of Northumberland to settle the border with Scotland, his accommodation with the Welsh, his Anglo Norman colonization of much of Ireland and his establishment of the courts giving legal redress to all are among the changes for which he will be remembered. In Europe his unflagging energy in keeping his vassals under control including his son Richard in Anjou and Aquitaine, and

Geoffrey in Brittanny kept his borders safe from French expansionism.

There is no precise record as to the actual cause of Henry's death, he is reported to have contracted "a lingering fever" which, together with acute depression led to the development of pulmonary complications and fever .Henry's last words were reported as "shame, shame on a dying King". He died on July 6th 1189 attended only by his illegitimate son Geoffrey and was buried at Fontenvrault in Anjou.

Richard 1

Richard was born in Oxford on 8th September 1157 the third son of Henry 11 and, as such, never expected to succeed to the English throne. History has rather glamourised his reign endowing it with an air of romance and chivalry as epitomized by his statue outside the Houses of Parliament.

A better description may be that of an absentee warlord forever seeking to consolidate and expand his rule through the force of arms and spending only six months of his ten year reign in England. His undoubted military prowess earned him the title of Lion Heart throughout Europe while in the East, mothers would threaten their children with his Arabic name Melec Ric "King Ric".

What is known is that he was a handsome figure,6'5" tall with the fair hair and blue eyes of the Plantagenets. He spent his early years in England before moving to Aquitaine. He was a bright scholar and became a talented linguist. It is recorded that he could make jokes in Latin and recite poetry in French and Provencal. A man of some intelligence and insight, he realized that there was more to successful warfare than just being skilled at Arms. He combined these qualities with a gift for strategy and tactics that enabled him to consolidate his rule, first in Aquitaine where he was not initially popular with the barons, then, as king in launching the Third Crusade. As with all the Plantagenets, he combined the contradictory qualities of being romantic and poetic with aggression and cruelty.

Despite his marriage he was probably, homosexual, this preference being well documented. Richard of Howden, one of Henry's clerks records with reference to the rather close relationship between Richard and Phillip of France that "Phillip so honoured him that every day they ate at the same table, shared the same dish and at night, the bed did not separate them, such was their friendship that King Henry grew much alarmed". There are however, other references to Richard's appetite for young girls, described by one contempory as" voracious, even on his death bed".

In 1167, at the tender age of 10 Richard inherited the lands of his mother Eleanor, the county of Poitou and the Duchy of Aquitaine for which he did homage to the king of France in 1169. He was formally installed as Duke in 1172 and immediately set about imposing his authority on the unruly barons who, during his minority, had had things very much their own way. King Henry was however, still unwilling to give real power to his sons. The young Prince Henry had been crowned as King in waiting to ensure the succession, Richard had Aquitaine, Geoffrey had Brittany and John was made Lord of Ireland. One can imagine the frustration of these high stomached princes at being constantly overruled by their seemingly tireless father. This was particularly true of Prince Henry "The Young King", while Richard and Geoffrey were allowed to exercise some powers in their respective duchies; Henry was not given similar powers in England. This may have been due to his rather feckless and shallow nature.

Much is recorded of the young Henry's bored pursuit of leisure rather than duty and preferring to spend his time in tournaments and the fashions of chivalry. The king had appointed William Marshall as Tutor at Arms to the young prince, but even that honest and loyal knight sometimes lost patience with him. Matters came to a head in 1173 when the king arranged a marriage between Prince John and Alais, the daughter and heir of the Count of Maurienne which would extend English control to southern France. The king also granted John the castles of Chinon, Loudon and Miribeau in the heart of Anjou without consulting his other sons. Prince Henry was furious, the castles were strategically important to Anjou which had been given to him in 1169. The princes Henry and, Richard formed an alliance with their mother Eleanor, Louis V11 of France, the Scottish King William, the Counts of Flanders, Boulogne and of Blois , plus the Earls of Leicester, Chester and Norfolk to depose the king. Henry could however count on the loyalty of the key barons and the rebellion was easily crushed.

There was reconciliation between Henry and his sons and Richard, Richard being the last to submit to his father. He finally backed off from fighting his father face to face and gave a new oath of subservience to Henry in 1174. Richard then resumed his campaigns in Aquitaine and the region of Gascony to put down disaffected nobles, assisted by his elder brother Henry. It is interesting to note that, despite Richard's reputation as a brave and noble knight, he was considered very cruel in his French domains and there were many reports of rape and murder committed by him and his followers. The young King however, still frustrated by his lack of power, invaded Poitou himself on a shaky pretext and Richard's opponents flocked to him. The King tried to negotiate a peace between his sons, fearing that fighting between them could destabilize his kingdom, but was unsuccessful. Geoffrey of Brittany then joined forces with his eldest brother and set themselves against Richard and their father. Henry brought the French part of his army to assist Richard and things might have become much worse but for the death of Prince Henry from dysentery in 1183. William Marshall was with him to the last and, on his deathbed, Henry gave him his cloak and made William swear that he would take it to the holy land and place it on the sepulcher in Jerusalem/ William carried out his promise, spending two years in the holy land and, returning to England to serve in high office for both Richard and John.

With the deaths of Henry and Geoffrey, King Henry named Richard as heir and attempted to settle Aquitaine on his youngest son John. This did not suit Richard who regarded Aquitaine as his own and having fought so hard to settle it he was not about to give it up. He allied with the French king Phillip against his father, but as we have seen in an earlier chapter, Henry eventually simply gave up and retreated to Chinon to die. Richard was declared king following the death of his father at Chinon in July 1189 and was duly crowned at Westminster. The celebrations and feasting were recorded as lavish and exotic. Jews had been expressly forbidden to attend the ceremony, but many had gathered to watch the spectacle and to attempt to offer gifts to Richard who ordered them to be thrown out, which resulted in a riot and massacre, followed by major religious and political persecution. The word spread that Richard wanted all Jews destroyed and the populace, fuelled by envy, gladly complied attacking Jewish houses, killing the people and looting. The word spread to other cities and many Jews were killed. In York the Jewish community tried to seek refuge in the castle from the mobs, but, realizing that they could not hold it, murdered their wives and children, throwing the bodies over the wall to the mob below, before torching their own houses and dying inside them. The local citizens lost no time in rushing to the castle where all the loan records were kept and burned them all. The Jews being the major lenders of money to Richard and his father were the only religion allowed to make money by the interest charges made on loans, usury being considered a sin to Christians, became a target when Richard began to use Italian sources bankers for loans and had no further need for the Jews' services.

Richard was determined to join the crusade. The first crusade of 1096-1099 attracted little support among the English nobility, but the second crusade of 1146-1149 provided them with a respectable excuse to leave the country with its power struggles and infighting and look good in the eyes of the church. In July1187 the holy land had been captured by Saladin the Egyptian Arab and Jerusalem had fallen by October after the battle of Hattin. All of Christendom was calling out for a restoration of a Christian kingdom and Richard was the man to do it.

Richard was taking a great risk by joining the crusade without leaving a male heir and with his scheming brother John ever ready to foment trouble. Richard had attempted to sweeten John by granting him the lordship of 7 English counties, but this merely enlarged his power base.

Richard did however, have a number of loyal and able administrators who would protect his interests in his absence. He appointed his chancellor William Longchamp as his representative in England, who although very efficient was very cold and high handed and not popular with the barons. A coalition of the barons and the restless John set out to discredit him and things came to such a head that Richard was forced to send his special envoy Walter of Coutances to mediate between them. John continued to foment troubles for Longchamp and a chance came when Lonchamps men attempted to stop the King's half brother Geoffrey from entering the country. They dragged him violently from sanctuary to custody and Geoffrey played up the incident by drawing parallels with Becket. John orchestrated baronial outrage and Longchamp was forced to stand down. He then attempted to flee the country disguised as a woman "a sex he always hated" but his flight ended in a humiliating farce when, waiting on Dover beach, he was picked up by a fisherman whose attempt at rape was only halted after he lifted Longchamp's skirts. Hubert Walter, Archbishop of Canterbury was finally appointed Justiciar and remained in the post until Richard's return.

This period of Richard's life reveals his drive and attention to detail, plus his skills as an administrator and commander. He realized that he would need huge amounts of money to mount a proper crusade, even offering King William of Scotland freedom from his oath of fealty for 10,000 marks and, as his clerk, Roger of Howden writes "that the new king put up for sale all that he had. offices, lordships

Earldoms, castles, forest rights, castles and town charters" King Richard once remarked" that he would sell the whole of London if he could find a buyer".

His efforts raised and paid for over 100 ships with around 8000 men, his land army which was scheduled to meet the fleet at the ports of Marseilles and Massina, was over 9000 strong. It was here that he proclaimed his nephew Arthur of Brittany as his heir, perhaps to head off any attempt by John to seize the throne in the event of Richard's death.

His preparations and logistics for the crusade were a revelation for the time. From the hiring of ships to the ordering of horse shoes, cheese, bacon, arrows, armour etc, his dynamism drove everything. While the French and German leaders relied on their contingents to be self supporting, Richard was determined that his forces were to be paid and supported by himself. It is unfortunate that, while organizing such a venture with all its detail, he did not unlike the other senior crusaders; arrange safe passage for his return home.

The Combined forces of Richard and Phillip of France reached Sicily in September 1190 where King William 11 of Sicily had recently died. He had named his aunt Constance (later to become Queen Constance of Sicily) as his heir. Constance was married to the Emperor Henry V1.

King William's Cousin Tancred had other ideas however and seized control of the island and was duly crowned king in 1190 as Tancred 1st. He might have avoided any input by Richard except for the fact that he then imprisoned King William's widow Joan, who also happened to be Richard's sister. Further, he had refused to pay to her a large sum of money bequeathed to her by William. Richard demanded that her rights be restored to her and that she should be released. Meanwhile, the two armies were causing much unrest among the population and in October the people of Messina revolted. Richard attacked Messina and captured it on 4th October 1190 and after looting and burning much of the town he made a base there. Sporadic fighting continued until Tancred agreed to a treaty in March 1191. The main terms of the treaty being,

That Joan be released and given her inheritance

Richard and Phillip to recognize Tancred as King of Sicily

Tancred to marry one of his daughters to Arthur of Brittany when he came of age ,he being 4 years old at the time (it will be remembered that Richard had named Arthur as his heir previously)

This arrangement was not well received in the Holy Roman Empire and made it possible later for John to gain support from the Pope for his bid for the crown.

Traveling onwards Richard arrived at Limassol in Cyprus on 6th May 1191 and immediately set out to attack. the city. The ruler of Cyprus was one Isaac Comnenus who arrived too late to intervene and Richard captured the city. Isaac continued to resist, but was decisively defeated at the battle of Tremetusia and finally surrendered at Kantaras. Richard subdued the island brutally, looting and burning and massacred all who opposed him.

Richard's mother Eleanor in the meantime, had not been idle. She was determined tat Richard should have an advantageous marriage and had arranged for Berengaria, the daughter of the king of Navarre to accompany her to Cyprus to meet up with Richard, who had originally been betrothed to Alice the sister of the French king Phillip. Richard's father Henry had however, seduced Alice some years before and, while he never admitted as much, it was sufficiently well known at the time for Richard to withdraw from the arrangement. This affair was one of the causes of the friction between Richard and his father, and, following his marriage to Berengaria, was the beginning of the rift between Phillip of France and Richard which culminated in the French king returning home and commences plotting with Prince John against Richard.

Richard and his forces arrived at Acre in July 1191, the city fell a month later after a siege of over 2 years. During this period ,in addition to falling out with king Phillip , Richard quarreled with his other ally, Leopold of Austria over the relative height of their respective banners placed over their tents, Leopold demanding that his should be raised higher than Richard's. Richard considered himself the senior partner in the coalition and refused. Phillip and Leopold left for home leaving Richard to continue the struggle.

The issue of banners, badges livery etc was of great importance, all serving as rallying points in battle as well as advertising the wealth and power of their owners. It is ironic that the leaders should fall out over the height of a banner when they had already come to agreement on the much wider issue of uniforms. It was recognized that a multinational army would have problems communicating and the leaders had arranged for each nationality to wear the cross in a different colour. France would have a Red Cross, England white and Austria green. Thus, any soldier could find someone who could speak his language.

Richard twice attempted to assault Jerusalem, but each time had to withdraw due to the vulnerability of his supply lines and his realization that even if he captured Jerusalem he could not hold it. It says much for Richard's leadership that he could get his followers to accept this fact after the years of fighting for this goal. The fighting ended in stalemate and a 3 year truce agreed between Richard and Saladin. Richard undertook to return territory to Saladin and to leave Palestine. Saladin was to give Richard the remains of the True Cross, payment of 10000 marks and Christian access to Jerusalem. The littoral of Palestine was restored to a Christian kingdom and knights were allowed to fulfill their vows and pray at the holy sepulcher. When Saladin reneged on payment, Richard had some 3000 Arab prisoners killed before sailing from Acre in 1192.

Richard then had the misfortune to be shipwrecked and landed in the territory of Leopold whom he had offended so he now attempted to continue his journey disguised as a pilgrim. Traveling with only two companions he arrived at Erperg near Vienna. Sending one of his attendants into the village to barter for provisions with his royal gloves. These gloves were recognized by an Austrian knight and the servant was forced to reveal where Richard was hidden and he was captured. Leopold was however, forced to hand Richard over to his suzerain Emperor Henry Vl who bore no love for Richard due to the affair in Sicily. A mock trial was held and Richard was accused of having imprisoned the king of Cyprus and of having insulted the Emperor. Richard defended himself and characteristically demanded trial by combat. He carried the day and was released to house arrest. The Emperor demanded a ransom for Richard's release of 100,000 marks, a vast sum requiring a tax of 25% of income from all of Richard's estates. It says much for the efficiency of Richard's administrators and the esteem in which Richard was held that over 70,000 marks was paid within the first 6 months. Such a sum could not be coerced from an unwilling populace.

During Richard's absence, his mother Eleanor had ensured that John could not make too much mischief in England, but this was not the case in France. Phillip, with the tacit acquiescence of John had been laying claim to much of Richard's Norman lands. Both knew that Richard would not take their treachery lightly and upon hearing of Richard's release, Phillip sent a note to John,"look to yourself, the devil is loose".

There was much rejoicing in England on Richard's release, but he wasted no time planning his return to France to regain the lands usurped by Phillip. Within 6 months of his return he was off again having first raised yet more money from his subjects for the campaign by various means including a new land tax, the carucage and extracting protection money from wealthy individuals, towns and the vulnerable Jewish community. By 1199 almost all the lands lost to Phillip had been regained. In April 1199 he was besieging the castle of Chalus-Chabrol near Limoges. This was nothing special for Richard; he was merely policing a minor rebellion in what was a strategically important part of his realm. Just before the assault he rode around the castle walls wearing no body armour and protected only by a shield when a defender, one Bertrand de Gourdon, who had been waiting this chance, fired a crossbow at him hitting the king in the right shoulder. When later captured, de Gourdon said that he was revenging his father and two brothers slain by Richard's forces.

Richard's wound was not considered serious, but following a botched attempt to remove the bolt it became infected and probably gangrenous. There are a number of versions of the event that all agree to Richard having been shot with an arrow or javelin, but some conflicting accounts of whether it was his left or right shoulder that was struck.

Gervase of Canterbury wrote, "The king was fatally wounded in the left shoulder. He was fatally wounded in the right shoulder by an arrow in such a way that, the bolt being driven down from the shoulder reached the area of the lung or liver, nor could it be checked by any skill of the physician"

Roger de Hoveded writes, "Bertrand de Gourdon wounded the king in the arm with an incurable thrust. Then the king entrusted himself to the hands of Marchadeus, a physician, who after trying to pry out the javelin, removed only the wood, and the head remained in the flesh. It was only when the bungling rascal cut freely round the king's arm that he succeeded in removing the head, but the king died on April 6th, eleven days after he had been wounded".

Matthew Paris records roughly the same, but states that he was shot by a Peter Basil on 25th March and died 12 days later. Richard is recorded to have forgiven the bowman, but another account states that Richard's General Marchadeus had the man flayed alive. Yet another version casts Marchadeus as the physician and he himself was executed for his bungling.

Richard left an empire stronger than that which was left to him. We know more of his exploits and legend than we do of his personality. He was clearly a warrior, oblivious and sometimes reckless regarding his own safety and yet capable of organizing, planning and leading his forces with great skill. He was capable of both kindness and great cruelty. He remained fond of his wet nurse Hodierna and rewarded her with estates recalled in the parish of Knoyle Hodierne, and yet after the siege of Acre, he ordered 3000 Muslim prisoners executed. His failure to leave a natural heir however led to the coronation of John and subsequently the loss of most of the possessions that he had fought so hard to retain.

Richard was buried at Fontenvrault at the feet of his father. His heart was buried in Rouen cathedral in a very beautiful tomb that can be seen to this day. In 1838 a small statue was discovered in Rouen containing a small lead box within which was a silver casket, wherein lay, apparently the Lion Heart of Richard, reduced to the semblance of a dry reddish leaf"

Arthur

Arthur was born in Nantes Brittany on 29th March 118, the son of King Henry's fourth son Geoffrey and Constance of Brittany. In 1190, on his way to the holy land, King Richard had named Arthur as his heir, a move which no doubt first turned Richard's younger brother John's mind to rebellion. It is thought that Richard's declaration was little more than symbolic in that he was about to be married to Berengaria and could have expected heirs of his own.

The unexpected death of Richard in 1199 changed all of these expectations, English law was unclear as to the rightful heir should be, should it be the last surviving son of King Henry or offspring of the old king's deceased elder son Geoffrey. In the event, the French inheritances of Anjou, Maine and Touraine all declared in favour of Arthur, while in England the Archbishop of Canterbury, Hubert Walter supported Arthur in his succession to England and Normandy. John did however have powerful allies to assist in his claim and by a mixture of force and diplomacy isolated Arthur from his Angevin support and the young prince was forced to make peace and accept John as his overlord.

Phillip of France watched all this from a distance and when, in 1202 he confiscated all John's French dominions, Arthur seized the moment and did homage to Phillip for all his French lands except Normandy which Phillip had determined to keep for himself as a useful buffer between his kingdom and the turbulent English. As might be imagined, this did not suit John and hostilities broke out with John launching another campaign to retake what he believed was his. During this campaign, while besieging the castle of Mirabeau, held by his grandmother Eleanor of Aquitane, Arthur was captured and on the 31st of July was imprisoned in Falaise castle, but taken to Rouen shortly afterwards, where he disappeared from sight. It was rumoured that he had been murdered by John, thus beginning the reputation for evil that still surrounds him.

A contempory account of Arthur's end was written by Ralph, Abbot of Coggeshall which discusses the concern of John's supporters over the continuing violence in Brittany by Arthur's followers and how it could only be ended by the death or incapacitation of the young prince. His account begins at Falaise where John sent two servants to blind Arthur.

"Some of the king's counselors thought there would never be quiet as long as the prince lived in a sound state and suggested that John should deprive the noble youth of his eyes and render him incapable of governing. Some wretches were sent to his prison to carry out the deed but were so moved by the youth's pleas and prayers that they stayed their bloody hands. Hubert de Burgh, the castle warden, took it upon himself to suspend all cruelties until the king be further consulted. This merciful appeal only resulted in the prince being transferred to Rouen. On the 3rd of September, Arthur was startled from his sleep and invited to descend the stairs to the foot of the tower which was washed by the Seine. At the portal he found a boat and in it, his uncle the king attended by his squire Peter de Mulac.

Making a last vain appeal, the youth threw himself upon his knees and begged for his life, but John gave the sign and Arthur was murdered. Some say that Mulac shrank from the deed and that John, seizing his nephew by the hair, stabbed him with his own hand and then threw the body into the river. Others that Mulac did the deed and this is possible as he was later rewarded with the heiress of the Barony of Mulgref for his part"

In another account from the Annals of Margram Abbey in Glamorgan, John is said to have killed Arthur in a drunken fury, a story which may have been started by the Abbey's patron William of Brioze, who although being a one time supporter of John and had coincidentally, been the captor of Arthur at Mirabeau , later fell out with the king and he and his family were treated most cruelly.

Arthur could be described as either a very naïve young man, easily influenced by the devious Phillip ,or as a catalyst in Anglo French relations which hurried the inevitable separation of the English king and his French dominions. John's view was that Arthur was a liar and a cheat and deserved his fate, this view being shared by many at the time. There are references in both the Barnwell Chronicle and the Life of William Marshal to the pride and high handedness of Arthur and perhaps he was not just the innocent young man thrust into the spotlight by the power games of other kings and princes.

King John

John was born on Christmas Eve 1167, the fourth son of Henry 11 and Eleanor of Aquitaine. Due to growing interfamily feuding, John's parents drifted apart and he divided his early years between his brother Henry and the house of his father's Justiciar Ranulf Glanvil .John learned the arts of chivalry and knighthood from Henry while Ranulf schooled him in the business of government.

History treats John poorly, mainly because of his suspected murder of his nephew Arthur, but also due to the romance that has grown to surround the romanticized legend of Robin Hood and his battles to protect England from the evil John in the absence of the king. John's reign was, however, momentous in that it saw the birth of civil rights in the signing of the Magna Carta(this having little effect during his reign) and the coronation of a French prince at St Paul's as the King of England. John was however, a shrewd tactician as seen by his gaining of the throne, defeating his rival Arthur, gathering support for a coalition against France and exploiting the financial potential of his kingdom. His misfortune was to follow a charismatic king, seen at the time as the very embodiment of chivalry (although in truth Richard had had very little regard for England and its troubles) and to be secretive and scheming.

In contrast to his Plantagenet forebears, John was small and dark although he did possess the family trait of titanic rage on occasions. It is recorded that, following his signing of the Magna Carta, he withdrew to Windsor where his chroniclers say "his behavior was that of a frantic madman, for, besides swearing, he gnashed his teeth, rolled his eyes and gnawed sticks and straws", fairly typical Plantagenet behavior. As the fourth child of Henry whose vast empire had already been allotted to his older sons, John was not born with an automatic inheritance of his own, thus earning him the nickname" Lackland". He was, however Henry's favourite son and had sided with his father in the rebellions of his elder brothers in 1173-1174. It was his father's wish that John be given Aquitaine when his elder brother Richard became king, but Richard reneged on this arrangement and family feuding began again.

John married the heiress Isabella of Gloucester on 29th August 1189 Richard endowed John with vast estates in England. The honour of Lancaster and the counties of Nottingham, Derby, Dorset, Somerset, Devon and Cornwall and, in Normandy, the county of Mortain. This was seen as an attempt to appease John for his lack of inheritance and to ensure his loyalty. There seemed no doubt at this time that John was Richard's heir. His marriage was childless and was annulled in 1200 on the grounds of consanguinity, a common device of the time. John then married Isabella of Angouleme in August 1200, a move that made him many enemies in France as she had been betrothed to the powerful High de Lusignan. With Isabella he had two sons and three daughters, his eldest son Henry becoming king on John's death, Richard, Earl of Cornwall, Joan, later married the Alexander 11 of Scotland, Isabella, later married to the Emperor Frederick 11, and Eleanor, later married to Simon de Montfort of whom we shall hear more later. He also had five illegitimate children including Joan who married Llewyn of Wales, from which the later Tudor dynasty was descended. Like his Angevin predecessors, John was a lecher and a bad loser and pursued many women, it is said that he once sent a poisoned egg to a woman who had spurned him. He was predatory and seduced many of his noble's sisters, daughters and wives
.

In 1185 John, who had been given the title of Lord of Ireland back in 1177, visited Ireland in an attempt to establish his position there. The expedition became a disaster due to John and his retinue frittering away the monies given by his father in feasts and carousing while mocking the locals as hairy and stupid and showing disdainful patronage to the Anglo Norman settlers sent there by his father.

When Richard left for the third crusade, (selling to the Scots the counties of Westmorland, Cumberland and Northumberland to help finance his travels) he left regency in England led by William of Longchamp his chancellor. This did not suit John who felt that he should rule in the king's absence. John set up his own rival court complete with his own Justiciar, Chancellor etc. John being resentful of not being regent, led the opposition to Longchamp and forced his removal in 1191. Matters were made worse when Richard announced at Messina that Arthur was to be his heir, prompting John to declare himself temporary ruler and heir to Richard. He further conspired with Phillip of France to dismember Richard's continental empire, this betrayal, especially of a crusader, further alienated baronial opinion.

During this time, as a thank you for aiding Phillip in his theft of Richard's French estates, John had been given the lands of Evraux and, following Richard's release in 1194 and rather remarkably being forgiven by the king for his treachery, John returned to Evraux and massacred his French garrison, probably as a gesture to show Richard his renewed loyalty, a move which did not endear him to the French king.

Richard, during this time, had not been idle. In a series of campaigns, plus some aggressive diplomacy he had regained most of the lands grabbed by Phillip and by 1199 was tidying up small localized frictions when he was fatally hit by an arrow.

On hearing of Richard's death, John, ever true to the family traits of opportunism and. rapacity, seized the royal treasure and sent the Archbishop of Canterbury to England to call a great council at Northampton. Not all the English and French barons or clergy were in favour of John's accession, many believing that Arthur was the rightful heir. After a short and successful military campaign John had largely settled his problems. He had gained the agreement of the English barons and clergy, plus the submission of Arthur and his mother Constance and crucially, his acceptance by Phillip and at the Treaty of Le Goulet in May 1200 Phillip recognizes John as the rightful heir to all his French lands in return for homage and a relief (tax) of 20,000 marks. John's divorce and subsequent remarriage to Isabella of Angouleme reopened the rift between the two kings and was further soured by Arthur's death reportedly at the hand of John in 1203.The French king Phillip had earlier knighted Arthur, declaring him the true successor to Richard. Arthur in turn did full homage to Phillip for all the French territories previously held by Richard. It was during this second outbreak that Arthur was captured by John and his lieutenant William of Briouze at the battle of Mirebeau where they had marched eighty miles in two days to outmaneuver Arthur who was besieging the castle there owned by his aunt(and John's mother) Eleanor of Aquitaine.

Arthur's death, reputedly at John's hand has been recounted in the previous chapter and did much to further alienate John from his subjects. Phillip continued with his takeover of John's French possessions and by the end of 1205 was in control of Normandy, Anjou, Brittany, Maine and Touraine, leaving just Aquitaine and a part of Poitou. To further add to John's problems, his Chancellor and Archbishop of Canterbury Hubert Walter, died and the Pope and some of the English clergy chose Stephen Langdon as his successor. Langdon had been a fellow student with Pope Innocent 111 in their younger days in Paris. John however, wanted his own candidate John de Gray, while some Canterbury monks wanted their own man Reginald. The Pope was asked to mediate and not surprisingly chose Langdon. John refused to accept the ruling and Langdon was effectively exiled in France while the Pope excommunicated John and placed England under an Interdict, an extremely serious event in an age where the only solace of all men was God. Under such conditions church services, marriages, burials, church tithes, etc were suspended. The church became poor, no doubt causing much of the bad press that John received in clerical records over the next few hundred years. John was facing trouble on many fronts, the loss of his French possessions ,the raising of ever more taxes to pay for his attempts to regain them, the Interdict and yet more incursions in the north by the Scots who were still disputing the ownership of the border counties. It will be remembered that Richard had sold these to Malcolm, but John refused to accept this and rested his case on the homage that Henry 11 had exacted from the Scots fifty years earlier.

For all his faults, John was no pushover, he possessed all the cunning and aggression of his Angevin ancestry as had been seen in his campaign against Arthur, he had managed to retain control of Poitou by his clever campaign of 1206. In 1209,using only the threat of force, had imposed a harsh treaty on his troublesome neighbor William the Lion of Scotland and his naval preparations had resulted in the first major English victory at sea at the battle of Damme in 1213 .He reestablished his authority on his Anglo Irish subjects during a brief expedition in 1210 and in 1211, finally subdued Lleywelyn of Wales ,prompting the Barnwell chronicler to note that "now no one in Scotland, Ireland or Wales did not bow his head to him". He was also an able administrator, he suspended the Westminster judicial bench and had the justices follow him around the country, he established the distinction between the civil or Common Pleas and the criminal Kings Bench divisions instigated the creation of a national Customs system based on standard weights and measures and created a royally funded navy. He developed household bureaucracy and judicial records were instituted. His restless and suspicious nature had him forever on the move, particularly in the north where previous kings had hardly bothered to visit and the presence of an inquisitive and avaricious king on the doorstep must have come as a rude shock to some.

John's suspicious and treacherous nature led him to many poor decisions and through his greed alienated many former friends and potential allies. , his nickname "softsword" stuck because of his willingness to abandon a cause before decisive action. He was ever the architect of his own downfall. Instead of compensating Hugh de Lusignan for the loss of his intended wife Isabella of Angouleme, John seized the Lusignans' duchy of La Manche, forcing him to appeal to his and John's overlord Phillip, thus setting in train the confiscation of John's continental estates. His dealings with the English nobles were no less harsh. At every turn he sought ways of extracting monies from his barons, a favourite method being to force them to become royal debtors by accusing them of some misdemeanor and then demanding money in return for "The King's Grace" (protection money). It is recorded that William de Briouze, a former favourite, was ruined and exiled in this way and his wife and son starved to death in prison. In these ways he pulled down the over powerful and installed his own supporters in key positions.

In addition to the national property taxes of 1203 and 1207, he exacted ever more expensive levies on his richer subjects including, on top of the scutage, a tax in lieu of military service calculated on the number of knights owed, each baron had to pay a fine foe personal exemption. The barons had had enough, it was one thing to execute thirty Welsh hostages as he did in 1212, or let captives from Mirabeau starve to death in Corfe castle, but the persecution of the English barons without trial was different and by 1213, were refusing to pay scutage at all..

The leader of the growing baronial unrest was Lord Robert Fitzwater, his own record was however, far from clean, he had surrendered Vaudreuil in France to Phillip in very suspicious circumstances, a major factor in the loss of Normandy. This first rebellion was suppressed with relative ease by John and Fitzwater fled to France and his chief ally Eustace de Vesci took refuge with the Scottish king William.

John went again to France in an attempt to win back his inheritance and was making good progress to that end when further unrest in England forced him to return, leaving his campaigns in the hands of his nephew Otto the German emperor, in the event, a disastrous move.

Seeing these clouds gathering, John submitted to the power of Rome and Had the Interdict and his own excommunication lifted, a move that made the Pope a powerful ally in subsequent events. This settlement acknowledged the Pope's authority, but committed Innocent 111 and his successors to support their newly repentant vassal. Thus John regained the authority to appoint The English clergy with all the monies and influence this brought.

On the death of the Scottish king William in 1214; his son Alexander 11 took up his father's claim to the three disputed northern counties, despite being John's son in law and also having his sisters held in England as hostages. Alexander raided northern England prompting John to march north and torched the towns of Berwick, Roxburgh, Coldingham and Haddington. Alexander resurrected the Auld Alliance with the French and invaded northern England again, secretly enlisting the aid of the unhappy northern barons including Robert Fitzwater and de Vesci who recruited a hard core of about 2000 barons who where equally frustrated by John's constant demands for money and his interference in what they saw as their own affairs. The barons tried to ascribe their uprising to the will of the common folk, but in reality it was to rid themselves of John. The ordinary people of England had been treated fairly by John who had reserved his rapacity for what he saw as his over mighty barons. This supposed will of the common folk breaking out into rebellion fueled the later tales of Robin Hood fighting the supposed oppressor. Robin of Loxley, if he existed, was probably a minor player fighting to regain his inconspicuous family seat in Staffordshire. History does however record the existence of one Robert Hod, aka Robert of Wetherby, outlawed by the king's justices who was captured and executed in Barnsdale by Eustace, Sheriff of Lowdham, who later became Sheriff of Nottingham.

The barons uprising did not go well, John, by his clever placement of loyal supporters had some support throughout the land and managed to outmaneuver his opponents, but the net was closing. With more nobles turning to the rebels, John finally agreed to a meeting, but made promise after promise without settling a date and forcing the rebels to traipse after him around southern England for a month. John was probably playing for time to calculate how much support he had and could he capitalize on it. The rebels had marched from Northampton to Bedford to Stamford, to Brackley and to Oxford and many were becoming irresolute with supplies running low. The barons delivered to John their "Articles of the Barons" to John on the 27th April and on 5th May they arrived in Wallingford and formally renounced their allegiance to the king. Fitzwalter was elected leader and took upon himself the title Marshal of the Army of God, probably to counter the religious and moral high ground that John had assumed by taking the cross as a crusader at Easter. The two sides finally met at Runnymede on the 10th June .John first offered some compromises that in themselves amounted to very little and were really just a rehash of the Charter of Liberties first agreed by Henry 1st. The barons however pressed for more, mainly concerning taxation, payments of "relief" and hereditary rights. The major additional concessions were the release of hostages, of which John had many and the virtual handover of authority to the 25 surety barons, effectively a senior council to oversee and ratify John's rule It is of interest to note that, of these 25 barons, 22 of them were related by marriage, illustrating how small was the ruling elite in England since the conqueror. The discussions lasted around five days, but this was probably to show how important and momentous the occasion was. Stephen Langdon had really argued and agreed the details some five days earlier.

This is where John's foresight in bringing England back to Papal authority paid off. The Pope annulled and abrogated the charter and described it as a conspiracy against his vassal King John of England and ordered Stephen Langdon to excommunicate all the signatory barons to the charter. On September 24th he excommunicated all the barons again because Stephen Langdon had refused to comply .The barons attempted to implement the charter and fighting again broke out. When John had accepted the Pope's over lordship of England he had effectively became a vassal of Rome, thus making his barons sub tenants and as such, legally landless. John, careful as ever, began to withdraw all his jewels and royal regalia from the monasteries and then retreated from London and made a few half hearted gestures to comply with the charter by releasing a few hostages and making some adjustments to his administrative functions .One of the provisions of the charter was that, any concocted grievance raised by the barons, if not corrected by John within 40 days could lead to his dethronement, would any man dare this?. It would seem that John had little intention of complying with the charter and was playing for time in the hope that he could increase support for his cause, but he was misreading the minds of his barons. Even the loyal ones realized that John's excessive demands should be curtailed even if they stopped short of actually supporting the rebels. This was recognized very quickly following his death by William Marshall, John's half brother ,Lord Protector and Regent of England during the minority of Henry 111,when the charter was reissued in 1216 and again in 1217 with some amendments making it more acceptable to both sides. And it was not until 1225 that a third reissue, again amended, became the definitive law of the land. The rebel barons had made their headquarters in London, but still lacked real power. The charter had, in reality, negotiated an instrument which legalized high treason and were apprehensive about John's loyal tenants in chief who were the real power in the land. John still held control in the rest of England, Ireland and Wales through his own placemen, Further, he had a ring of castles stretching from Norwich, through Wisbech,Cambridge Nottingham,Oxford,Wallingford,Corfe,Winchester,Dover and his base at Windsor. The stalemate could have continued indefinitely, but a new element was added when the French Dauphin invaded England with a force of 600 ships, almost as many as the Conqueror's 696. The timing of the invasion and the logistics required must have been secretly planned for many months beforehand and confirms John's suspicions of the plotting between the French, the Scots and the barons.

The French force landed at Stanhope on May 21st 1216 despite the wrath of the Pope. John had stationed his navy in the mouth of the Thames, but a storm enabled the Dauphin's forces to avoid a sea battle. The Dauphin himself disembarked at Sandwich and marched towards London, John offering only token resistance before tactically retreating to Winchester. On June 14th, the French laid siege to both Winchester and Dover castles, but John, being a smarter tactician than his predecessor Harold had left. Ten days earlier and moved on to Windsor. Winchester was taken, but Dover held out until October 14th.

The Dauphin sent emissaries to the North and West claiming all of John's territories as his own. He was welcomed by the barons and their wealthier allies in London and was declared king of England by them in a very grand coronation on June 2nd. England now had two kings, a fact that rates little mention in history, Encyclopedia Britannica calling it "an intervention". London and most of the Home Counties were now occupied territory by a French army of around 35,000 men. The Dauphin received fealty from emissaries sent by Alexander of Scotland and Llewelyn of Wales promising support, probably to ensure the return of their hostages including the Scots King's daughters.

The Pope again showed his support for John by excommunicating the King of France, the Dauphin and all their accomplices by name at a great conclave in Rome on May 28th. Heartened by the Pope's support, John began a series of assaults against the French with much success. But on October 9th he passed through the town of Lynn where he was feasted by the burgers and nobility. He fell ill shortly afterwards with what was thought to be dysentery, but continued on his march, raising troops and support against the invading French. It was on this southward march on the 12th October that he decided to cross the Wash at an arm known as the "Cross Keys", an area which is passable at low tide but is always a dangerous crossing. It is not known why he chose this route, but it has been suggested that certain guides had been bribed by the French to falsely guide the king. John and his army had almost reached the opposite shore when they became trapped by the tide. John and the bulk of his troops got across, but the baggage train was trapped and lost. Mathew Paris records in his Chronicle that"carriages, horses, treasures and man all swallowed up by the whirlpool by the impetuous ascent of the tide".

John's sorry band moved on to the Abbey of Swinshed where he was said to have eaten immoderately of some peaches or pears and to have drunk large amounts of new cider. He spent the night in much pain and was unable to mount his horse the next morning. He was carried on a horse litter to the castle of Sleaford and spent another painful night before being moved the next day to the castle at Newark on Trent. It is likely that John had suffered a perforation of a duodenal ulcer. Such a perforation would cause acute pain and collapse followed by peritonitis causing death within days. We know that John took some time to die since he was able to name his son Henry as his successor and begged his knights to be true to the new king. Ironically, during his last days, messengers arrived from some of his barons who becoming disenchanted with their French rulers, wished to rejoin John, but it was all too late. On the 18th October 1216 John died Matthew Paris records that "He fell into such despondency on account of his possessions having been swallowed up by the waves that being seized by a sharp fever, he began to be seriously ill. But he aggravated this by disgusting gluttony, for that night, by indulging too freely in peaches and copious draughts of cider, he greatly increased his fever".

It is possible that the French had a hand in the king's death, John had been fairly successful in his skirmishes with the invaders and support was gathering for him among some of the barons. The Dauphin knew he had to finish the stalemate before things became worse and it is likely that the French were involved in the attempt to drown John and his followers in the Wash. For John to die from stomach pains so soon after this event makes it likely that poison could have been administered, its taste being masked by the cider, history does not record a food taster being present at the meal.

John was buried in Worcester Cathedral; his tomb was opened during some restoration work in 1797 and revealed that John was probably a little concerned regarding his passage to heaven as his decayed body was shrouded in a monk's cowl, worn to protect him on his passage through purgatory. His sword and scabbard were also found beside him.

Henry 111

Henry was born on in Winchester 1st October 1207, the first of five legitimate children born to King John and Isabella of Angouleme. He was a little over nine years old when his father died and William Marshall, the Earl of Salisbury and half brother to the old king was appointed Lord Protector and Regent of England for the period of the prince's minority. Henry was a rather poor specimen physically compared to some of his Plantagenet ancestors. He was medium height, thickset and with a narrow forehead and suffered from a drooping eyelid, a genetic disorder also present in his son Edward. He was a gentle man, loving the arts and did much to aid the rebuilding of Westminster Cathedral and other great cathedrals such as Wells, Peterborough, Lincoln and Salisbury.

He succeeded his father at a time of great turmoil. the country was divided by the rebellion against John and a French army occupied most of southern England, while the son of the French king Phillip had been crowned king of England at St Paul's by the rebel barons. His mother Isabella immediately had Henry proclaimed king and, as a precaution against the French invaders, sent her younger son Richard to safety in Ireland. William Marshall immediately set about strengthening the forces under his command by hiring mercenaries from friendly Anglo/Norman barons. His first aim was to rid England of the Dauphin and his French forces. It must be remembered that Marshall and most of the ruling classes of England were from Norman stock and even in the short time since the Conquest, would consider themselves English or Anglo Norman rather than French.

Henry struggled to assert his position in these early years as his various guardians jockeyed for power and was sixteen before he was allowed to sign documents with his personal seal and only then

By appealing to Pope Honorius 111.His life is one long saga of being in thrall to others, firstly his guardians, then his in laws, then the rebels and finally his son. He failed to stamp his authority on the kingdom and, in the end, took comfort in religion and piety. He was a gentle man, born in an age when respect was earned through strength and violence.

The Dauphin and the Surety barons had based themselves in London and had sworn fealty to France. William Marshall began his campaign by seizing the castle of Montserol from the rebel Saire de Quincey. When the rebel leader Fitzwater heard of this he raised an army of 600 knights and 20,000 men and together with the Dauphin and his military commander the Count of Perche, marched on Montserol where they found that Marshall had abandoned the castle and had retreated to Nottingham.

The rebels moved on to Lincoln castle as Marshall gathered his forces including his son, another William, who ironically was one of the surety barons, whose signature appears on Magna Carta, but who had since relented, plus a growing number of barons previously supporting Fitzwater, but now for the young king, laid siege to Lincoln. The French army and the rebel barons were forced back into the castle by the superior numbers of Marshall's troops and some 300 knights were taken prisoner, including most of the charter knights. The battle was a particularly bloody one, chroniclers tell of "much blood running in the streets". The remnants of the French army retreated towards London and were attacked and badly mauled all the way with even the common people rising against them. William Marshal reached London retook London without resistance and the Dauphin and the remnants of his forces were allowed to leave England after signing a pact relinquishing all claims to the English throne, this, significantly, being signed at Runnymede in 1217 almost a year after Magna Carta. *too many spaces??*

The young king had been crowned by the Papal Legate at Gloucester on 28th October 1216.The royal crown having been lost in the Wash by his father, Henry was crowned using his mother's gold circlet or Torque. The coronation was to confirm Henry as the rightful ruler and it would be another six years until he assumed his majority and was crowned anew on 17th May 1220 and only then by gaining the support of the Pope to declare his minority at an end.

During his minority, the country was administered by the Justiciar Hubert de Burgh and later by Peter de Roches ,Bishop of Winchester. Some of the old rebels still caused trouble, but de Burgh gradually restored order. The Magna Carta was reissued, with some amendments. The Crown was now expected to rule through consultation and within the limits of law and custom although it was not resolved how this would work. The clause placing the king under the scrutiny of 25 barons had been dropped in 1216 and there was no agreed mechanism to interpret law and custom, During the minority, William, Marshal, Hubert de Burgh and others careful balanced the differing factions and had consulted widely on all major issues to make policies acceptable. The problem was that the charter did not lay down specific rules as to what the king could or could not due and while this was not a problem in his minority, Henry, having gained his majority, wished to exercise his royal prerogatives in what he saw as the traditional areas of kingly rule such as, patronage, foreign policy, justice and the appointment of officials. The king did not wish to act as a tyrant, but being a religious man, believed in his divine right from God to rule, but the barons, having had a taste of what they considered democracy, were reluctant to let it go. Many of the barons were angered by Henry's appointments to administrative office of trained bureaucrats (mainly from Poitou) whom Henry consulted on government matters instead of the barons and a revolt in 1233 forced Henry to dismiss these officials. He was ever suspicious of the Baronage and Mathew Paris records him exclaiming, during a stormy meeting," You English want to hurl me from my throne as you did my father".

Although he was not a natural warrior, Henry was determined to retrieve his French inheritances of Normandy and Anjou, lost, he believed through the scheming of his English barons and the French king and also to regain control of Ireland, Scotland and Wales His attempts at invasion, first of Brittany in 1230 and then of Poitou in 1242, both ending in failure although he did make peace with Alexander 11 of Scotland at the Treaty of York in 1237 when the definitive border between the two countries was set as a line from Solway Firth to the River Tweed.

In January 1236 Henry married Eleanor, daughter of the Count of Provence. She was thirteen years old and hitherto, had led a sheltered life. With the French invasion debacle still fresh in their minds, the English were not happy with this despised foreign Queen and on one occasion, while traveling down the Thames on her royal barge, had to take shelter in the palace of the Bishop of London, to escape from a jeering London mob.

Henry and Eleanor had nine children of whom four survived to adulthood. Edward,Margaret, Beatrice and Edmond. Henry seems to have been a loyal and chaste husband, but did come under the influence of many of Eleanor's relatives including Peter of Savoy, who was to become his principle advisor and who was given the Savoy Palace as a reward. This reliance on foreigners was made worse when his mother, who had, before marrying John, been engaged to the French nobleman Hugh de Lusignan, returned to France and met again her old betrothed. He was now betrothed to Isabella and John's daughter Joan, who, being only ten years old was not yet ready for the marriage. In typical medieval fashion the engagement was cancelled and de Lusignan married Isabella instead. Together they had five sons and three daughters and it was these half brothers of the English king that were later invited to Henry's court and were shown much favour, a move which further alienated the barons. They were also responsible for urging Henry into the disastrous campaign in Poitou to expel the French king.

In 1238, Henry secretly married his sister Eleanor to the powerful Simon de Montfort, Earl of Leicester, a move designed to strengthen the King's authority. Simon de Montfort had come to England in 1231 to attempt to reclaim some English lands formerly owned by his father. He became a friend and advisor to Henry who returned de Montfort's estates also bestowed on him the Earldom of Leicester, for which Simon was reported to have paid one hundred pounds, plus an undertaking to supply the king with six armed knights. Simon became increasingly concerned at Henry's refusal to consult the barons in matters of state and sided with the barons, a move which ended with a council being convened in 1244 where he was elected by the barons to demand that the king consult them in all financial matters. The king rejected the demand and attempted to bribe some of the barons with gifts. The Earl was sent to Gascony to attempt to restore English authority in 1248 and had some success before being recalled in 1252 to answer charges of maladministration move that totally alienated de Montfort.

Henry's close relationship with the papacy was also becoming a cause of much resentment and matters became worse when, in 1254, the Pope offered the kingdom of Sicily to Henry's son Edmond in return for Henry financing the conquest of the island from the Hohenstaufen dynasty whom the Pope wished to be ousted from southern Italy and Edmond did achieve some success in his venture until his father could no longer support the costs and the kingdom was given to the French king's son who made rather a better job of it.. The English barons were much disturbed by Henry's subservience to the papacy which had already resulted in an influx of foreign clergy into England and an increase in papal exactions. The barons however were outraged that they had not been consulted over the Sicilian affair and refused to grant the necessary funds. The Pope threatened Henry with excommunication and thus forced the king to come to terms with his barons, now lead by the resentful de Montfort.

Henry, at odds with the powerful barons, was forced at last to come to terms with them and in 1258, signed the Provisions of Oxford, which required Henry to govern with in consultation with a council of fifteen barons, who would meet three times a year with twelve other barons in a parliament. The parliament we know today was decades away, but the Provisions of Oxford set an important precedent. Earl Simon made these meeting further representative by later inviting attendance from two Burgesses from each borough and from this can we see the beginnings of a real Parliament.

These were supplemented a year later with the Provisions of Westminster, strengthening the power of the barons over the king. The rebel barons headed by Simon had won the support of most of the major towns and cities including London. Simon was well thought of by the general population, but began to fall out with the barons over what they thought was his arrogant and superior manner. The ruling classes were dividing into these two very distinctive camps, culminating in Henry raising an army against the rebels. Sporadic fighting broke out and, following papal intervention, the French king was asked in January 1264 to mediate between the two sides. This resulting treaty known as the Mise of Amiens was little more than a declaration completely in the Henry's favour. A broken leg had prevented Simon from attending the meeting, doubtless he would have been more forceful in the debate. Needless to say, fighting recommenced.

Traditional loyalty to the king and a respect for legality had already induced some barons to return to the royalist camp. Simon de Montfort could rely on the support of six Earls and fifty nine barons, while the king had around fifty barons and another six Earls on his side leaving around fifty barons uncommitted... Henry could count on the support of his brother Richard of Cornwall who, throughout Henry's reign, had attempted to be a bridge between the king and the nobles. This was not entirely altruistic as the luxury loving Richard received large sums regularly from his brother to keep him "onside". Richard was an extravagant man, a lover of fine things and yearned for his a crown of his own. He eventually became king of the Romans by buying the votes of German Electors and lobbied for the Pope to declare him Emperor.

By the spring of 1264 both leaders were ready for war and on 5th April the king's son Edward struck the first blow by attacking Northampton and capturing de Montfort's son, a number of knights, and some Oxford scholars who joined the fight with slings, stones and crossbows. The rebels replied by besieging Rochester where much blood was shed. The king sent a small detachment of cavalry to London to reconnoiter the city walls, but the London rebels, fearing attack sent word to de Montfort who began to withdraw towards London. Henry's forces reached Rochester and easily overcame the remnants of the besiegers and cruelly maimed those taken prisoner.

King Henry continued westward and were much harried by Welsh archers loyal to de Montfort on the way. They stopped at Lewes, knowing that de Montfort's army was pursuing them. The rebel leader stopped at Fletching about eight miles from Lewes and sent three bishops to Henry with peace terms, which, unsurprisingly, were rejected. On the evening of 13th May, de Montford knighted Gilbert Rufus, Earl of Gloucester (known as Gilbert the Red) plus some other young nobles. Early on the 14th, his forces advanced towards Lewes and climbed the steep track of the Coombe valley and the high ground of Offham Hill. It is said that they encountered a solitary sentry placed there by Henry, who, on being rudely awakened, begged for his life. It is not known if he was successful.

Earl Simon arranged his forces of around 5000, including 600 knights in three divisions with a fourth in reserve. The royalists had not advanced more than 300 yards when de Montfort ordered his cavalry to charge. Henry had around 9000 men including 1500 mailed knights and knowing it would be fatal to receive a cavalry charge while standing still, ordered his own cavalry forward and the two sides met .Henry's son Edward led the royalist charge and cut through the rebels to reach the infantry behind. The infantry broke and ran, many being drowned in the Ouse and others cut down as they ran. Edward continued his pursuit and attacked the rebel baggage train believing that de Montfort was hiding there. The rebels in the meantime had pushed on to the royalist infantry and a vicious no quarter battle ensued. Henry had two horses killed beneath him amidst the slaughter and fought valiantly, but was forced to retreat to St Pancras priory. When Edward and his cavalry finally returned from their pursuit they found only the remnants of Henry's army, he tried to rally his troops to attack the rebels who were now trying to batter down the gates of Lewes Castle. To his right he could see some of the enemy shooting flaming arrows "spryngelles of fyre"at the wooden gates of the Priory. Before he could rally his men, de Montfort sallied from the town with a band of cavalry, Edward tried to renew the fight but his other commanders had no stomach for it. The prince, with his personal retainers fought their way into the priory and joined his father.

The priory was not built to withstand a siege and the king sued for peace .On 15th May Henry signed an agreement with Earl Simon known as The Mise of Lewes. The Abbot of St Pancras estimated the dead at 2700, a figure generally accepted. In 1810, three burial pits were in the area were uncovered, revealing 1500 skeletons. It seems that very few of the leaders were slain, it was worth far more in ransom to take noble prisoners alive, plus the efficiency and quality of plate armour aided the survival of those who could afford it. Earl Simon's victory can be attributed to his radical use of dividing his army into defined divisions and the creation of a reserve force. Further, he made good use of the ground and launched his cavalry early and, like all good medieval leaders, placed himself in the forefront.

The superior royalist forces suffered from divided command, Edward's relationship with his father was not harmonious and the king's insistence on command did not sit well with the prince or the headstrong Poitevin and Scottish allies and they may have all decided to "go their own way" in the battle. Edward's charge, while initially successful, left the royalists without proper cover and by the time of his return it was too late to save the day.

In the period after the battle, many bitter quarrels broke out among Earl Simon's followers over the question of ransoms. Again the Earl's high handedness in allocating monies to his cronies rather than to those who actually made the capture caused dissent and a further drift back to the royalists.

Earl Simon was now the de facto ruler of England, with the king isolated and Prince Edward imprisoned at Hereford, he now discovered how difficult it would be to rule such a divided nation. He was forced to take more dictatorial measures to keep his factions loyal, but rebellion in Wales and the steady drift of barons back to the royalist cause were progressively weakening his base. Matters became much worse when Prince Edward escaped from captivity in Hereford by the simple expedient of challenging his captors to a horse race which he won and simply kept going, reportedly shouting a valedictory "Have now a good day" as he sped off.

Earl Simon and his four, equally high handed sons continued to alienate their supporters and he was dealt a further blow when his main henchman Gilbert de Clare (Gilbert the Red) changed sides and met up with Edward at Ludlow where they agreed to restore the king. The gentry of Shropshire and Cheshire flocked to the new army. With Earl Simon at Hereford, Edward was determined to stop him joining forces with his son's army at Kenilworth. He marched along the east bank of the Severn burning bridges and dredging fords to prevent Earl Simon crossing. On 10th June, the Earl met with Prince Llewellyn of Wales who promised him 5000 spearmen in return for lands and castles in the Welsh Marches. His forces attempted to cross the Wye at Monmouth, but he was stopped by his former ally John Giffard. He then moved on to Southport to ship his army across the Bristol Chanel,but Edward, having foreseen this move, had sent three war galleys to destroy the merchant ships destined to carry Montfort's men.

Edward, after a night march, arrived at Kenilworth and surprised the rebel army at dawn, falling on the enemy and "killing them in their nightshirts". Simon's son managed to escape but his forces were severely depleted, a deciding factor in the coming battle.

Earl Simon, unaware of his son's defeat, crossed the Severn at Kempsey, just south of Worcester and arrived at Evesham a small town in the loop of the River Avon on 3rd August. Edward, showing his qualities as a leader and recognizing that Earl Simon was now trapped, stationed a part of his force at the bridge at Bengeworth to cut off any escape route. The royalist army marched on to the high ground at Green Hill. Earl Simon sighted the first of the royalists at the bridge and, because they carried many of the banners captured at Kenilworth before them, mistook them for his son's forces. It is said that it fell to his keen sighted barber to discover that they where in fact, Edward's "We are all dead men" he shouted down to the Earl" it is not your son who comes, but the king's son with Gloucester and Mortimer". Earl Simon replied" let us then commend our souls to God for our bodies are theirs"

Simon formed his force into a single column led by a steel tip of 100 knights, followed by his Welsh archers and the rest of his troops. In all he had about 350 knights and 5000 foot soldiers. The Prince had assembled their main force in two long divisions on top of Green Hill facing Evesham, his force comprising 1000 knights and about 7000 infantry. At about 10 o clock in the morning trumpets blared and with banners flying Earl Simon hurled his forces at the enemy, aiming at its centre and hoping to break through at the weak point where the royal divisions joined. The shock forced the royalists to give ground, but rallied and the line held. It now started to rain heavily adding to the confusion. Finding itself underemployed, the two wings of royalist cavalry charged the flanks of the rebels. This broke the infantry who began to run to the Avon in an attempt to escape.

The battle raged for several hours, no quarter being asked or given, but Edward's superior numbers forced the rebels back towards the centre where Earl Simon, his sons and household knights fought beneath his White Lion standard. He was last seen alive in the melee, wielding his sword with both hands. Simon had brought the captive King Henry to the battle dressed in the Earl's colours and was only able to save himself in this final slaughter by shouting" I am your King Henry of Winchester, do not kill me".

The rebels finally scattered, some heading for Offenham Bridge were cut down in the fields nearby in a place now known as Dead Mans Ayot The Prince ordered his soldiers to bury the dead and it was found that some of the fighting had been so fierce and the bodies so mangled that they were unable to strip them for burial. Edward wept at the funeral of his boyhood friend Henry de Montfort, but showed no mercy to the Earl Simon. A rider was sent with the Earl's severed head on a lance point, plus his hands and testicles to Roger Mortimers wife at Wigmore Castle. The Lanercost chronicles list the baronial losses at 180 knights, 220 squire and 5000 infantry, but the last figure hides the number who slipped away as the battle wore on. Edward was reported to have lost only 2 knights and 2000 infantry." Such was the murder at Evesham for battle it was not".

Thus Prince Edward had broken the rebel army, at 26 years of age he had taken over the reins of power and readied himself for a lifetime of soldiering in Wales, Scotland and France and laid the foundations of an army that would conquer at Crecy,Poitiers and Agincourt.

The rebel remnants, known as "The Disinherited" returned to their castles to hold them against retaliation while in Ireland De Montfort's son Simon the younger carried on his father's struggle.Baronial resistance did gradually crumble and in 1267 Edward captured Kenilworth Castle after a two year siege and yet more rebels returned to his camp when he incorporated much of the Provisions of Oxford in the Statute of Westminster at his first Parliament in 1275.

The King played little part in these proceedings and, growing older and more vague, spent more and more time in his devotions. He was taken ill at Bury St Edmunds, probably due to a mild stroke and after some rest, felt better enough to call a council in the town. Before it could be convened, he again was ill and decided to return to London, He died on 16th November 1272 at Westminster, probably from a second stroke and was buried in the Abbey he had built, over the site of Edward the Confessor's original grave.

Edward 1

Edward was born at Westminster on 27th June 1239, the first born son of Henry 111 and his wife Eleanor of Provence.He was to live for 68 years, and reign for 35 years. It is unfortunate that so much of the goodwill and admiration earned by him in his early years was to be dissipated in his decline.

Edward is described as a tall but thin man, earning him the nickname "Longshanks". He was healthy, fit and energetic with the drooping eyelid of his father. Like his Angevin ancestors he could also be subject to titanic rages. He became a great warrior, learning his trade during the revolts of the barons as well as his years spent on crusade. His desire to unite the kingdom resulted in forays into Wales, Ireland and Scotland, where he became known as "The Hammer of the Scots" as well as seeking to consolidate and expand his domains in France.

He received a disciplined and thorough education, reading and writing in French and Latin in addition to the arts, science and music. In 1254 he was sent to Spain for an arranged marriage to the 9 year old Eleanor of Castille and, at this time, his father endowed the prince with the Duchy of Gascony , plus some estates in Ireland, Wales and the Channel Islands. Edward was to have sixteen children by Eleanor and a further three by his second wife Margaret. Edward spent the next year in Gascony studying its administration and governance. He spent much of his early life learning the very harsh lessons of his father's failure as a ruler, which resulted in civil war and his fight to defend the king against the barons. The ill judged campaign to install Edward's younger brother Edmond on the throne of Sicily ended in failure and also aroused the barons to anger at the financial demands that Henry made to pay for the venture. Bankrupt and threatened with excommunication,
 Henry was forced to submit to a reiteration of the main terms of the Magna Carta in the Provisions of Oxford, under which, his debts would be paid, but he had to agree to various reforms including sharing power with a Great Council consisting of 24 of his most powerful barons. Henry repudiated these terms in 1261 and sought assistance from the French king, a move which caused Prince Edward temporarily to side

with the barons. When civil war broke out however, Edward was firmly on his father's side. Following the king's defeat at the battle of Lewes, Edward was held hostage to ensure his father's adherence to the peace terms, he escaped in 1265 and on 4th August defeated the barons, led by his brother in law Simon de Montfort at the very bloody battle of Evesham. Edward supported his father in social reforms aimed to reconcile the disinherited and by 1267 the country was largely pacified.

In 1270, the new Parliament agreed an unprecedented levy on all citizens of one twentieth of all goods and possessions to finance Edward on a crusade to the Holy Land. He planned to join the French king Louis 1X in returning these lands to Christian rule, but Louis was taken ill and died in Tunis and his armies were bought off and returned to France. Edward was determined to continue," By the blood of God though all my fellow soldiers and countrymen desert me, I will enter Acre, I will keep my word and my oath to the death"

Edward arrived in Acre in May 1271 with a force of 1000 knights and though he did relieve the city, his small force was not sufficient to realize his ambitions and he finally made a truce with the Saracens, but not before an attempt was made by them to assassinate him He was attacked with a knife, but was able to disable his opponent with a stool and received only a cut to his arm. It was feared that the knife was poisoned and there is a tale of Eleanor sucking the poison from the wound. Edward was clearly worried for he made a hasty will, but prompt attention to the wound ensured his recovery... Hearing of his father's death, Edward headed for home but not, it seems, in any great rush. He visited the Pope on his journey and also accepted a challenge to take part in a great tournament at Chalons, where it seems another attempt was made to kill him, but he managed, with his company of a thousand knights to to defeat twice that number ,he himself defeating the Count of Chalons in single combat. There are a number of instances reported at various times of this seemingly charmed life, narrowly escaping being struck by lightning in Paris where his two attendants were killed, narrowly escaping death when a javelin thrown from the walls of Stirling Castle as he rode the perimeter landed between his feet, and on another occasion, also walking away unharmed when a stone fired from a mangonel brought his horse down beneath him.

Edward arrived back in England in August 1274, he had been proclaimed king on the death of his father without opposition reflecting the regard for his prowess and renown as a warrior, called in his time "the best lance in the world". He was crowned in 1274 at Westminster Abbey. With the barons now quiet, Edward was determined to enforce England's claim to primacy in the British Isles and set out to return Wales to his rule, Wales at this time consisted of a number of princedoms, broadly divided into the south, where the Welsh princes had an uneasy alliance with the English Marcher Lords, who had been given the lands in Norman times to protect the English against Welsh raids. The northern Welsh were based at Gwynedd and ruled by Llywelyin ap Gruffid, the Prince of Gwynedd, who, in 1247, had agreed to hold the North Wales in fee to the king, but, seizing his advantage during the English civil war to consolidate his territory and his rule, which, under the Peace of Montgomery, confirmed his position as Prince of Wales. Llywelyn thereafter maintained that "the rights of the Principality were entirely separate from the rights of England" and refused to do homage or attend Edward's coronation.

Finally, running out of patience, Edward declared Llywelyn "a rebel and disturber of the peace" and in a short campaign, aided by Llywelyn's brother David, defeated him. The rebellion broke out again in 1282 when Llywelyn , now joined with his brother, again attempted to reclaim his lands. All this ended in December 1282 with the death of Llywelyn in a chance skirmish at Builth where Llywelyn was forced to fight with a knight named Adam Frankton who killed him and sent his head to be displayed on London Bridge. David was captured and executed for treason and has the dubious distinction of being the first recorded example of hanging, drawing and quartering. He was hanged for the murder of knights in Harwarden Castle, disemboweled for committing the crime on Palm Sunday and quartered for rebelling against his lord.

Under the Statute of Wales, in 1284, Wales was divided into the English framework of Shires and control was assured by the building of many castles. In the same year a son was born to Edward and Eleanor. This son, also called Edward was to be named Prince of Wales in 1301.There is a tale that Edward presented his son to the Welsh as Prince of Wales" who could speak no English" this is unlikely however as he already had an elder son,Alfonso alive at this time. Prince Edward was only named to the title following the death of Alfonso

Edward now turned his attention to Scotland, its throne had become vacant following the death of Alexander 111 and the only direct descendant was a child Margaret known as the Maid of Norway., her claim being that her mother, Margaret of Scotland, daughter of Alexander had married the King of Norway. The Scottish nobles recognized her as the rightful heir and she became Queen under regency. Edward arranged a marriage between Margaret and his son Edward at the Treaty of Birgham in 1290, but she was unfortunately drowned in a storm on her journey from Norway. To add to Edward's troubles his beloved wife died in the same year and he had her body brought from Lincoln to Westminster, erecting a cross in her memory at every resting place on the journey. There were over a dozen claimants for the Scottish throne and Edward was asked by the Scottish claimants to call a meeting at Norham in Northumberland to decide the issue. The two strongest claimants were John Balliol and Robert Bruce; both descendants of David, Earl of Huntingdon, brother of the Scottish king William the Lion. Edward favoured Balliol who had agreed to do homage to the English king and he was duly crowned King of Scotland at Scone. Balliol was never seen as a strong king in Scotland and was given the nickname "Toom Tabard"=empty coat and was considered spineless and in Edward's thrall. Edward's plan was to install Balliol. goad him into rebellion and take the country over. In the event, he succeeded only in turning Scotland into an enemy and forcing the Scots into an alliance with France.

With the north temporarily under control, Edward then faced another rebellion in Wales. His Statute of Rhuddlan had created the counties of Anglesey, Caernarfon, Merionith, Flint, Carmarthen and Cardigan, dividing Wales up into the English system. This was backed up by further castle building garrisoned by English troops and English immigration to new towns in the shadow of these fortresses and all was to be ruled by English Justices.

The Welsh rose, attacking and destroying the English presence, pulling down and burning the great castle and town of Caernarfon, but in a swift campaign, Edward ruthlessly crushed the rebellion. His grip on Wales was now so tight that it would take another one hundred years before the Welsh made any serious attempt at rebellion.

The French chose this time to invade Gascony, but Edward was unable to rush to its aid as Balliol, in typical medieval style, formed an alliance (later known as The Auld Alliance) with France and rose in rebellion against the English king. He had been summoned by Edward and ordered to provide troops and funds to assist the planned invasion of France, but on his return to Scotland he convened a war council and resolved to send emissaries to France to warn the French. He also proposed that his son, Edward Balliol should be betrothed to Jeane de Valois, the French king's niece and that, if the English king invaded France, the Scots would invade England together with troops supplied by the French. He also arranged a treaty with King Eric 11 of Norway, who agreed to supply one hundred ships for four months each year for as long as hostilities between England and France continued, in return for a payment of 50,000 groats .Edward learned of Balliol's treachery in 1295 and responded by strengthening the northern defences and appointing the Bishop of Durham, Antony Bek and the Earl of Surrey, John de Warenne (Balliol's father in law) as custodians of the border. He also appointed the Lord of Annandale, Robert Bruce (father of the future Scottish king) as governor of Carlisle Castle. The Scottish campaigns saw the raising of one of the largest armies ever assembled by an English king. It is reported that Edward had a force of some 15000 men, including troops from Gascony and some Welsh Archers. These forces were a formidable combination of mailed cavalry, infantry and archers and it was these longbow skills that laid the foundations of future English victories at Crecy, Poitiers and Agincourt.

To finance his wars against all these adversaries it was necessary to raise money through taxes and Edward would summon a Parliament (from the word parley=to talk) twice a year for this purpose. In 1295 he summoned what was to be known as the Model Parliament, consisting of Barons, clergy, knights and townspeople to obtain money specifically for his war against Phillip of France. This became the pattern for future parliaments and Edward, as astute a statesman as he was warrior used this forum to establish the rights of the Crown, often at the expense of feudal privileges, to raise income for his many wars, to consolidate a countrywide administration of justice and to formalize the legal system.

He began a thorough survey of the local government, not only defining royal rights and possessions but also uncovering administrative abuse such as extortion by royal officers and bailiffs and the rigging of elections.

His Model Parliament also enacted legislation on wool, England's most important export, the king claiming a customs levy on all such exports that earned him £10000 per year. He also, through the Statute of Mortmain, imposed a licence fee on all gifts of land to the church (normally a device to avoid death duties).

In 1296 Edward advanced against Balliol and sacked the city of Berwick the townspeople of Berwick, showing their contempt, climbed on the roofs and mooned at the English, shouting insults at the king. Edward retaliated by destroying the town and slaughtering the inhabitants including women and children. The English army continued up the coast towards Dunbar, but on April 27th, was met by a large Scottish force who immediately attacked the English from their higher ground position. The English, led by John de Warenne were well prepared and withstood the charge. They then counter attacked and the Scots turned and fled a not unusual move in medieval warfare. A massacre ensued and some senior hostages taken. Earlier that year, Balliol had formally renounced his homage to the English king, speaking of "Grievous and intolerable injuries, as your own whim dictated….we renounce the fealty and homage we have done to you", but by now he was a beaten man.

Edward continued his foray and overcame all further Scottish resistance by taking the castles of Roxburgh, Edinburgh and Stirling. Scots leaders were taken hostage and on July 7th Balliol was forced to renounce his kingdom and dressed in only a shirt and underwear he handed over a white wand, signifying the surrender of Scotland to the Bishop of Durham and on 10th July repeated the ceremony before the English king and was banished to exile in Normandy.

Edward, determined to further humiliate the Scots, removed the Stone of Scone, the traditional stone on which Scots kings were crowned and brought it to London where it was to remain for the next seven hundred years. He set up an administrative system based in the newly rebuilt city of Berwick and ensured control of all southern Scottish castles would be in English hands. All landowners in Scotland were forced to sign their names to an oath confirming that they recognized Edward as their king. This list, known as the Ragmans Roll still exists and contains some 2000 names including Robert Bruce, who asked that Edward name him as rightful successor to Balliol. Edward is said to have replied" Do you think I have nothing to do but win kingdoms for you?"

Edward was now facing his next crisis ,the costs of the wars in Gascony, Flanders, Wales and Scotland were costing more than four times his income and the clergy were refusing to pay their taxes and when he tried to force them, the Archbishop of Canterbury threatened him with excommunication. The barons also were reluctant to continue financing the wars and presented Edward with a formal statement of their grievances. The Earls of Hereford and Norfolk refused to serve in Gascony and the king was becoming increasingly isolated. Edward was ultimately forced to reconfirm the charters (including Magna Carta) to obtain the monies he needed.

While he was thus engaged, another rebellion flared in Scotland, led by William Wallace, Earl of Elderslie ,a supporter of Balliol and, at 6'7" tall, a giant of his time. He first comes to prominence in a brawl with English soldiers in the market place in Lanark where an English sheriff was killed .Edward sent an army of some 300 men at arms, plus several thousand infantrymen, led by John de Warenne, Earl of Surrey to crush the rebels. On the 11th September 1297, Wallace's forces of about 5000 men had based themselves in a loop of the River Forth near Stirling and the only direct approach to them was over Stirling Bridge and along a causeway flanked by fields. John de Warenne immediately decided to attack, but Sir Richard Lundie,a Scottish Earl in de Warenne's army, urged caution ,noting that the bridge could be crossed only two abreast and suggesting a ford two miles downstream as a better place to cross. John de Warenne dismissed the suggestion and with the arrogance of his class declared that he wished only to get to grips with the enemy and would take the direct route. The army began to cross and, waiting until the vanguard had arrived, Wallace advanced on the English. As they fell on the flanks of the vanguard, the remainder of the English army surged forward in support, rushing across the bridge, which collapsed under the weight, isolating the troops on the other side from the main force. The vanguard was now trapped with little room for manouvre and no hope of reinforcement and were swamped by the rush of Scottish spearmen. A few of the lightly armed infantry managed to escape by swimming the river, but the bulk of the vanguard were slaughtered where they stood. The remaining English forces slunk away to the safety of Berwick castle. Wallace was rewarded with a knighthood and the title "Guardian of Scotland"

The success of Edward's negotiations with the French king made Wallace realize that he had little prospect of reviving the Auld Alliance and with his ally Moray ravaged the border country ,burning ,killing and stealing corn and sheep.

Edward moved north making his headquarters in York and gathering his armies together, archers from Gascony and Wales, Slingers from Ireland, spearmen and mailed knights. He then marched north accompanied by a great host led by no less than eight Earls, including Warwick, Arundel, Lancaster and Pembroke. In June 1298,he reviewed his forces at Roxburgh where it is reported that he had 12500 infantry,3000 mailed cavalry"armoured from head to crupper" and a new addition to warfare,4000 hobelars ,lightly armed fast cavalry. He also had his 500 Gascon bodyguards. Moving his forces northward, the Scots retreated, burning and destroying all as they went. Edward's troops were short of food, due to bad weather delaying the arrival of ships sent to provision the force, Old rivalries together with hunger caused many outbreaks of fighting between the various factions and Edward reluctantly returned to Edinburgh to reprovision...

When he again set out northwards, the army was still short of food and Edward, still, no doubt wishing to punish the Welsh for their various rebellions,favoured the English in the distribution of what little food was available and fighting again broke out between the English and the Welsh Edward was forced to use his knights to restore order, but not before many Welshmen were killed. When some of the Welsh threatened to join Wallace, Edward replied" let them do so", thus showing a contempt that was undeserved.

Wallace in the meanwhile had not been idle. He had raised an army of some 10000 men, mostly peasants, but with some cavalry under John Comyn and moving across country, burning and destroying crops to deny Edward of them .Wallace set out his battle lines at Falkirk. He intended to make a surprise attack at night before the English were aware of how close he was, but he was betrayed by two traitors who warned Edward of the plan. It says much for Edward's fitness that he carried on despite having suffered three cracked ribs some days earlier when his horse stepped on him while he slept.

Wallace moved to a position with marshland at his front and secured his flanks by erecting palisades driven into the ground.

He set out his troops in circular formation with their 12 foot pikes facing outwards, these units being known as schiltrons from the Old English meaning "Shield Troop". The schiltron ,partly, based on the Greek Phalanx and the Roman Testudo, differed in that they remained static in their positions with shortbowmen between these blocks and further protecting the pikeman by erecting sharpened stakes in their front with ropes stretched between them to hamper cavalry.

The English advanced in three columns, led by the Earl Marshal, followed by the Bishop of Durham and Edward himself with the rearguard Wallace is reputed to have told his troops "I have brocht ye hear to the ring, hop (dance) if ye can". The English cavalry without waiting for support, charged and soon became bogged down in the marsh where they were much damaged by the Scottish bowmen, those that reached the pikes found their horses impaled and were soon struck down. Some of the cavalry managed to swerve to the sides and soon rode down the Scottish archers spaced between the schiltrons. When Edward arrived, he called the cavalry back and assembled his secret weapon, the Welsh longbowmen. At this moment, Red John Comyn drew back all his forces and quit the field, leaving Wallace with no cavalry to harry the English archers. It is not known why Comyn deserted when he did, some say he had been bribed by Edward, but it is more likely that, seeing how the fight was going and ever jealous of the popularity of Wallace, he took the opportunity to escape and leave the Scots leader to his fate It is alternatively possible that Comyn, realizing that the battle was already lost, withdrew the cavalry to be saved for another day rather than waste them in a lost battle. The Scots certainly had cavalry available at the later battle of Bannockburn .Films such as Braveheart show the Irish section of Edward's army shaking hands with the Scots defenders, but it more likely that it was the Welsh longbowmen who refused to fight and there is some evidence to show that it was in fact the Irish bowmen and slingers that finally broke the schiltrons down sufficiently to enable Edward's cavalry to finish the job.

Wallace was now in serious trouble and did the only thing he could do, he rallied his men and leading from the front with his great two handed Bastard Sword, he stood his ground. Edward's forces began to fire point blank at the schiltrons, aiming directly at their targets unlike the tactics of later years when arrows would have been fired high to arc down on the enemy. The schiltrons suffered and began to break under the terrible rain of death, Edward set his cavalry lose on the collapsing schiltrons. It was said that "they fell like blossoms in an orchard when the fruit has ripened".

It is said that Wallace lost between 6500 and 8000 men at Falkirk, which, if true, would be a terrible loss in one engagement. This figure would however include those who drifted away during the fighting, a common occurrence in battles of the time. Wallace and the remainder of his forces escaped ,pursued by the English who caught up with them while crossing the River Carron.It was here at Brian Ford that an English nobleman, Sir Brian le Jay was killed by Wallace in single combat. The horse ridden by Wallace that had carried him throughout the battle and retreat was now covered in wounds and arrow shafts and collapsed and died in the water.

Following his defeat, Wallace was stripped of the title, Guardian of Scotland and is believed to have traveled to France to attempt to gain support for his cause. Edward meanwhile, set up a government of sorts under Bishop Lamberton of St Andrews, Robert Bruce and Red John Comyn, the same Comyn who had fled Falkirk. Rebellion and border raiding continued however and in 1300, following Robert Bruce's next defection and Edward's marriage to Margaret, he again came to Scotland with his army, laying waste to large areas, but could not bring the Scots to battle .In 1301, Edward was in a fury to receive a letter from the Pope informing him that Rome recognized Scotland as a Papal fief. He again attacked Scotland, this time with two separate armies, but the Scots still refused battle, harrying, raiding, destroying and melting away. Edward's solution was to be the same as the Welsh problem, to build chains of castles and divide the Scottish Marches into shires.

With dwindling support for the devastating wars, Robert Bruce surrendered and did homage to Edward, hoping no doubt for Edward's support for Bruce's claim to the Scottish throne over those of Balliol and Comyn.Scotland was still far from peaceful and in 1303 Edward is again in Scotland and suffers defeat at a minor battle at Roslyn which infuriates him and he resolves to settle the problem once and for all. He moves further northwards, crossing the Forth using prefabricated floating bridges, he captures Stirling, Perth and, by September, had reached the Moray Firth. The Scots finally sue for surrender leaving Wallace's supporters isolated. Edward exacts oaths of allegiance from the Bishops and nobles of Scotland and in March 1304 at St Andrews, he establishes Robert Bruce and Bishop Wishart as Guardians of Scotland, together with the English nobleman John Mowbray and 18 months later, frames his Ordinances for Scotland, proposing a government of 20 Englishmen and 10 elected Scots, based on the presumption that Scotland was now "justly" an English province.

This continued misjudgment of Scottish aspirations soon resulted in further outbreaks of violence, but by May 1305, only Stirling castle still held out against the English. The walls fell at last to the two famous siege engines War-Wolf and All-The-World. The English were still unable to track down Wallace but in August of 1305, he was betrayed by his supposed friend Sir John Mentief. Wallace was believed to be hiding in a tavern and Mentief's signal to the searchers was to be the turning over of a bannock (oat cake).Wallace was captured and taken to London and paraded like an animal through the streets, he was charged with illegal assumption of Guardianship, invasion of England, burning of English monasteries and a bogus accusation of murder of nuns. Dragged on a hurdle from Westminster to Tower and thence to Smithfield, he was hanged, cut down while still alive and disemboweled with blunt knives ,his intestines torn out and burned before him, emasculated and finally (and mercifully) beheaded, his head being displayed on a pike on London

Bridge. His torso was then cut in four parts that where then sent to be displayed in Newcastle, Berwick, Perth and Aberdeen. Thus was the end of Braveheart.

In 1306 at Greyfriars Kirk in Dumfries, Robert Bruce argued with, and killed John Comyn, again reneging on his oaths and declared himself King of Scotland, and was duly excommunicated by the Pope. Edward again sent an army under the command of Pembroke northwards to punish the Scots and capture Bruce. The English reached Perth and took the city and on 18th June the Scottish army had reached the city walls, but for some medieval reason, agreed to a proposal from Pembroke to postpone the battle until the following day. The Scots camped a few miles away at Methven and during the night the English made a surprise raid on the camp, killing many and scattering the rest. Bruce escaped with some of his followers pursued by John Mcdougal, son of the Lord of Argyle and sworn enemy of Bruce. He made his escape to the Western Isles, returning in the New Year to continue his fight for independence. Edward, now an old and tired man, led his army northwards once again, but was taken ill at Burgh on Sands .He asked that his body be boiled down and his bones carried into Scotland at the head of a victorious army. He also asked that his heart be taken to the Holy Land by 100 knights; neither the journey, boiling nor victory took place.

Thomas Walsingham wrote" The King began to be troubled with dysentery and gave up hope of living longer. This disease increased on the Saturday. Bidding farewell to to the present life, he ended his days in well doing and his years in England".

Edward died, probably of cancer of the rectum on the 6th July 1307. His tomb in Westminster, made of black marble, is inscribed "Edward the First, Hammer of the Scots"

Edward 11

Edward was born at Caernafon on 25th April 1284, the fourth son of Edward 1st. He grew to be a tall attractive prince, in good health with a strong build and fair hair. The romantic story of the young Edward being presented to the Welsh as their future native prince is unfounded as Edward was only made Prince of Wales in 1301. He was only a few months old when. by his brother Alfonso's death, he became heir to the throne and received the standard military education of his class and although thought able by his teachers, never showed the ruthlessness and aggression required of a medieval ruler as exemplified by his father.

He took part in several of the Scots campaigns led by his father, but despite his father's efforts, developed the habits of frivolity and extravagance which where to dog his reign. It was said that" Had he practiced himself in the use of Arms, he would have excelled King Richard the Lionheart". He further outraged his father and many of the barons by his close, some believe homosexual, relationship with Piers Gaveston the son of a Gascon knight in the service of Edward 1st,showering gifts and favours on a man who will be shown to have had a much stronger will than Edward's. The king quarreled often with his son over the relationship, the last occasion shortly before he died when the prince asked his father to give the rich province of Ponthieu to Gaveston. King Edward flew into a rage calling Edward a" baseborn whoreson, do you want to give away land now? You who have never had any?" The prince was kicked to the floor and a handful of hair pulled from his head by the king's rage.

The king, aware of the influence that this favourite held over the prince, had Gaveston exiled, hoping that Edward would return to more manly pursuits and skill at Arms. The prince however, showed no interest, preferring to practice the lowly arts of hedging, thatching and consorting with the working class, much to the disgust of his father. It is said that he had no interests other than amusement and diversion. Edward was a man of little confidence and therefore relied heavily on the advice of his favourites to the exclusion and anger of the barons. As he grew older he became ever more shallow, capricious and distracted, only on a few rare occasions did he display any real interest in government or in consulting his barons.

Upon his accession, Edward wasted no time in recalling Gaveston back to court and when, in January 1308,he went to France to marry Isabella the daughter of Phillip the Fair, he left Gaveston in charge as Regent, an act seen as another insult by the nobility. Isabella was 12 years old, later to become known as "the most beautiful princess in France". When the couple returned to England Edward wasted no time in rushing back to the companionship of favourite.Gaveston.in the meantime, had done nothing to improve his popularity, his haughty and arrogant manner, plus his flaunting of the finest and most expensive clothing and jewellery, including the wearing of much of the royal crown jewels "loaned" to him by Edward, only increased his unpopularity.

 Edward created further rifts with the nobility by bestowing the Earldom of Cornwall on Gaveston and giving him the hand of his niece in marriage. Gaveston had an acid tongue and created nicknames for many of the senior gentry, calling the Earl of Warwick "the black dog of Ardenne" and the Earl of Pembroke "Joseph the Jew". To make matters worse, Gaveston was an expert in the lists and in various tournaments had defeated Pembroke, Warenne, Hereford and Lancaster. He became more and more unpopular with the barons who managed to have him exiled twice, but each time, Edward found ways to have him reinstated. He was finally banished with the threat of death should he return, but, once again Edward brought him back under his protection. This was too much for the barons to stand and they finally confronted the pair at York. Gaveston was placed in Scarborough Castle "for his own safety", but the castle was not strong enough to withstand a siege by the Earl of Pembroke determined to bring Gaveston to account. Gaveston surrendered on the promise that he would be given quarter and was sent immediately south to the Earl of Warwick. He was tried, condemned, stabbed to death and beheaded. Edward was beside himself with grief when he learned of Gaveston's death and had the body brought to Windsor for burial with all pomp. The humiliation of the king was completed by the barons electing a committee of 21 Lord Ordainers to govern the country who, in 1311, drew up a series of ordinancies by which the country should be governed, but these merely reinforced the old ideas of baronial control that King John was faced with at Runnymede and did nothing for the clergy or the working class. With the death of Gaveston, the barons hoped that Edward properly take up the duties of king and husband. Isabella gave birth in 1313 to Edward, the first of their four children and it was felt that, at last, the king was showing signs of properly ruling his inheritance. He did, on occasions make some effort to consult and to listen to the affairs of state but soon relapsed into frivolity and shallow pleasures.

During this time, Robert the Bruce of Scotland had not been idle and was gradually retaking the castles captured and garrisoned by Edward's father and by 1313 only Stirling castle remained in English hands. The Scots besiegers were led by Edward, the brother of Robert Bruce. Edward Bruce arrived at a compromise with the English governor Sir Phillip Mowbray and agreed to a year's truce on condition that if the castle was not relieved by 24th June 1314, it would surrender. Robert Bruce was furious with this arrangement, he realized that the English king would not let strategic Stirling drift into Scottish hands and that he would have to face an invasion and a pitched battle. Edward assembled an army, which included over 1000 heavily armed knights and more than 20,000 infantry and archers and marched north, ordering these forces to muster at Berwick on 10th June. On 12th June, the king continued northwards together with the Earls of Pembroke, Hereford and Gloucester, it is recorded that, behind his army trundled 110 supply wagons and 106 four horse carts. The English arrived in Edinburgh on 21st June and replenished their supplies with provisions unloaded from the fleet and moved on to Falkirk by 22nd June. Meanwhile, the Scottish army of around 500 cavalry and possibly as many as 10,000 infantry camped at Torwood and then moved on to a wooded plateau fronted by the marshy Bannockburn just two miles from Stirling and prepared for a defensive battle.

This English army was not the cohesive disciplined force of Edward 1st. The young king lacked the ruthless control of his father and there was much squabbling over precedence between the Earls. Edward was then contacted by Mowbray the keeper of Stirling castle, who asked for a force to be sent to relieve him. Edward's plan was to split his forces and send Hereford and Gloucester straight up the Stirling Road and drive straight at the Scottish force while another force of 500 knights led by Sir Robert Clifford and Sir Henry Beaumont where sent up a bridle path, hidden from the Scots that led to Stirling. Unfortunately they were spotted and Bruce sent Randolph, Earl of Moray and his spearmen to intercept them. Hereford and Gloucester meanwhile, moved off still at loggerheads, made worse by the sight of the foppish Henry de Bohun, a nephew of Hereford's, prancing in all his finery 50 yards in front of the army. This young knight saw another horseman some way ahead who, upon closer inspection, rode "a grey palfrey, little and joly"and wore a gold circlet on his helm. This rider was Bruce himself checking on his troops hidden in the woods and seeing de Bohun bearing down on him, lance at the ready and not wishing to retreat from a challenge in full view of his troops, Bruce waited his moment and as de Bohun charged close, swerved his smaller more nimble horse and swung at his opponent with his battleaxe," cleaving de Bohun to the brisket".

The second English force under Clifford and Beaumont had ridden to the east, crossing the Bannock Burn lower down to reach the bridle path and outflanking the Scots. They then sighted the Scottish infantry under the Earl of Moray advancing on them from the woods. An argument broke out between Clifford and Beaumont as to whether they should delay attacking the Scots until more of them were in the open .The Yorkshire knight Sir Thomas Gray disagreed strongly and urged that the attack be made before the Scots could form up behind their pikes in the schiltron formation. Beaumont angrily accused Gray of cowardice and without another word, Gray charged the Scottish line which by now had formed their squares and perished on the enemy spears, together with his friend Sir William Deyncort who had bravely tried to rescue him. The English, secure in their military superiority, charged the Scots who formed into the defensive schiltron hedgehog with their 15 foot spears pointing outwards. The schiltrons held and the English knights died on the points of their spears, seeing the confusion, the Scots did the unthinkable and charged the cavalry and sent the remainder retreating back to the main force, leaving more than 100 dead on the field. Edward decided that a frontal assault was too risky and moved his forces across the Burn to camp for the night, breaking up the nearby Bannockburn village and using doors and thatch to cover the "evil deep wet marsh". Meanwhile Bruce had turned his forces to face the new English position, dividing the troops into four divisions under Douglas, Moray, Edward Bruce and Bruce himself. Bruce knighted some of the squires in his force and the Abbot of Inchaffray gave the soldiers absolution as they muttered the Pater Noster. Edward, on seeing the Scots kneeling, joked that they were begging for mercy, but was reminded that, though they prayed, it was not to him. Bruce then gave the order to advance.

The English had also completed their formations, the front consisting of nine cavalry squadrons of about 250 men each, with the infantry massed behind. A further squadron, usually known as the vanguard was stationed on the English right. Gloucester and Hereford continued to argue, this time about who should command the vanguard and the king, silencing them accused Gloucester of cowardice .Gloucester rode back to gather his troops and without waiting to don his surcoat, flew at the Scottish lines and died on the spear points of the schiltrons.

 The four Scots divisions moved closer together as they neared the English line and this was the signal for the English cavalry to hurl themselves at the oncoming Scots. The chronicler of Lanercost records" The two hosts came together and the great steeds of the knights dashed into the Scottish pikes as into a thick wood, there arose a great noise from rending lances and dying horses, and they stood locked together". Behind this clash the English infantry stood idle, some archers made an effort to shoot on a low trajectory over the heads of their own cavalry, but, as one chronicler reported" they hit some few Scots in the breast, but struck many more Englishman in the back". Other archers rushed to the side and began to shoot into the Scottish flank so well that Bruce feared that they could turn the battle. He ordered his cavalry to scatter the archers who, without spearman to protect them, retreated.

The Scots pressed their attack, sensing victory, but the battle hardened English gave blow for blow until they sighted more troops appear on the ridge behind Bruce, fearing that these were reinforcements the English suddenly lost their nerve. These reinforcements were in fact the sutlers and grooms from Bruce's baggage train who had come closer to observe the battle. Edwards's personal guard fought their way through the melee to guide the king to safety at Stirling castle. As in all battles of the time, once an army broke it was at the mercy of the enemy and the Scots pursued their foes mercilessly until darkness and weariness ended the slaughter. It was said that so great was the spilling of blood that pools of it stood all around, bodies lay half submerged in the mud around the burn and bridges formed of dead bodies stretched across the stream. The total English casualties are unknown but records show that 22 barons and 68 knights surrendered to the Scots and although many Scottish spearmen were killed, only two Scottish knights were recorded as casualties.

King Edward and his party reached Stirling castle, but Mowbray, with the chivalry of the time, refused him entry stating that as the Scots had kept to their word regarding the siege, Edward's defeat meant that the castle had not been relieved and Mowbray must therefore keep his word also. The king, dispirited, moved on to Dunbar and eventually took ship for England. The remainder of his army also headed for Stirling and again Mowbray refused admission to all but a few favoured knights, the remainder camped outside the walls and were again attacked by the victorious Scots with many English being slaughtered.

Bruce was now undisputed leader in Scotland and had won the crown by right of conquest. He wasted no time in starting a pitiless devastation of the north of England, wreaking his vengeance for all the sufferings of his people at the hands of the English.

Edward's defeat made him more dependant on his barons than ever, but the barons jockeying for power and influence, were divided. Edward's uncle,Thomas,Earl of Lancaster, a great power in the land but with little ability, led a faction nominally loyal to the king, but was suspected of making a secret understanding with Bruce. Described in his own time as "immoral, quarrelsome and vindictive" and with a repulsive nature" Hereford was a great landowner, much favoured by Edward 1st and had become jealous at his perceived reduced influence under the new king. A counterforce arose under the leadership of Aymer Valence, the Earl of Pembroke, who, in his determination to frustrate Lancaster backed the royal camp. With these two camps in open disagreement, Edward was to regain some little portion of his authority,

 Lancaster became increasingly distanced from the king, ruling his lands like an independent state and in the words of McKisack,"the supreme example of an over mighty subject". The weakness of Edward can be seen by the treaty contracted between him and Lancaster at Leake in 1318, resulting among other things in the banishment of a number of Lancaster's enemies and paving the way for the rise of the Despenser family.

Hugh Despenser was a justicier, related by marriage to the powerful Earl of Warwick, but had been excluded from court by Lancaster who feared the Despenser's influence. By 1316 Despenser was back in court but now his son Hugh had captured the attention of the king and by 1318 this younger Hugh had become Chancellor and had all the power and control that Gaveston had earlier enjoyed. His relationship with the king raised again the question of the king's homosexuality, but not to his face, It was said of the Despensers that" No baron or knight could approach the king without their consent and then a bribe was usually necessary, they answered petitions as they wished, removed household officials without consulting the baronage and any who displeased them or whose lands they coveted they threw into prison" The king would take advice from no other but them" (Maddicott) This situation infuriated the long suffering Queen Isabella and she was not going to be humiliated again by her husband's lovers. The opportunity arose when Edward, long overdue to travel to the French royal court to pay homage for his French lands, but fearing for his safety passed title of his French estates to his son . Edward sent Isabella to France in an attempt to persuade her brother the French king to reconciliation with Edward over their differences. Having reached the French court, Isabella stayed. The young Prince of Wales, now 13 was sent to do homage for his French lands and, like his mother, stayed there despite urgent orders from Edward for their return. Later during her stay, Isabella was to meet Roger Mortimer the Earl of March who escaped into exile after being sentenced to death for aiding the Despenser's enemies in their Welsh sequestrations and in Lancaster's rebellion and the two became lovers, one can imagine the scandal of a royal queen in an openly adulterous relationship in the French and English courts. Unfairly dubbed "The She Wolf of France" due to her tyrannical rule with Mortimer between 1326 and 1330,she had, for most of her life been a faithful wife and mother, even though she had taken second place in precedence to Gaveston and Despenser. Daughter of a king and brother of three successive kings, she showed her strength during her eldest son's minority and in her unremitting hatred of the Despensers. Their rapacity and corruption finally proved too much and culminated in Hereford bringing an army to St Albans to demand the banishment of the Despensers. The king's hatred of Lancaster festered, had Lancaster not been responsible for the death of Gaveston? And now had forced the banishment of Despenser.

In 1322 Lancaster raised a rebellion, but did not receive huge support, he lacked the charisma or personality to achieve his aims and had raised only some 3000 troops when he met with the king's forces at Burton on Trent. Greatly outnumbered, he retreated northwards. Meanwhile, the kings Warden of Carlisle Sir Andrew de Harcla had summoned "under heavy penalty, knights, esquires and other men of the border region" and with a force of some 4000 men, marched south to block Lancaster's retreat at Boroughbridge. When Lancaster reached Boroughbridge on March 16th 1322, he found the royal force deployed by the River Ure, with some knights and pikemen stationed on a bridge and more pikemen arrayed in schiltron guarding the ford from attack by cavalry. Lancaster ordered an attack on the bridge to be led by his son in law, Roger de Clifford and the Earl of Hereford, a man much admired for his physical strength and the two carved their way on to the bridge as a rain of arrows where showered on them. Things were going well until" a worthless creature" in the manner adopted many years before at Harold's battle at Stamford Bridge," lurking under the bridge, and fiercely with spear smote the brave knight in the fundament so that his bowels came out there". Sir Roger de Clifford was then badly wounded by the arrow storm and the remaining knights could make no headway. The remainder of Lancaster's forces were faring no better at the ford, unable to cross in force due to the royal archers. Lancaster sent a message to de Harcla requesting an armistice till morning, when he would either give battle or surrender. De Harcla was in no mood for soft words, and bellowed across the water "Yield Traitor, Yield". Lancaster knew that the charge of treason hung over him and now knew that he could expect no quarter, he replied"Nay,traitors we are none, and we will never yield while our lives last". Darkness was now falling and the overnight truce was accepted.

With hundreds already dead, Lancaster's men knew that they stood little chance of victory, many crept away under cover of darkness and by dawn, Lancaster could see that he did not have sufficient forces to continue. Many discarded their armour and fine clothes, donning rags to look like peasants and tried to escape, but it was said that "not one single well known man among them escaped". Lancaster was found in a nearby chapel, on his knees praying, he was grabbed, stripped of his armour and dressed in the clothes of his squire and taken to prison at York

Throughout this period the Scots had not been idle, becoming ever bolder and moving further south with their raiding. So destructive were these raids that in 1318, Pope John XX11 excommunicated Bruce and placed an Interdict on Scotland. In 1320 the Scottish barons and prelates drafted the Declaration of Arbroath to Pope John whose recognition they needed to declare an independent Scotland. The Declaration stated that" For so long as one hundred men remain alive we will never, in any way, be bound beneath the yoke of English domination, for it is not for glory, riches or honours that we fight, but for freedom alone" The Declaration fell on deaf ears however and it was not until the Treaty of Northampton in 1328 that the Pope lifted the Interdict. Some captured spies revealed to Edward a plan for the Scots to attack York and abduct Queen Isabella. By the time the king learned of this plot, the Scots were already at Myton, only 13 miles from York forcing the local Mayor and Bishops to raise what forces they could to from hastily co-opted "laymen, clerks and men of religion" oppose the Scots. This rag tag army moved untidily, arriving at Myton on 20th September 1319.The Scots were delighted at the sight of such a shambles of a force sent against them and were mainly concerned that the English would scatter before they could be brought to battle. To hide their strength, the Scots fired a number of haystacks to obscure the English view of their opponents. Puzzled and unnerved by these events, the English moved through the smoke only to come face to face with the Scots, who, uttering bloodthirsty shouts charged... This was too much for the poorly armed and untrained English who began to flee, but had failed to secure their line of retreat over the River Swale. Scottish hobelars galloped to cut of the only escape route over a bridge and many of the English (reckoned at 1000) drowned trying to swim the river. The slaughter continued till dark with a reputed death toll of a further 3000 with minimal losses to the Scots. This disaster was a further blow to

Edward's standing and resulted in raising the siege of Berwick and eventually agreeing to a two year truce.

Edward paid lip service to the truce but allowed privateers to attack Flemish vessels trading with Scotland. The privateers would steal the cargo and kill any Scots found on board and matters worsened when privateers captured the Pelarym carrying a cargo worth £2000, all the Scots on board, including women, children and pilgrims were massacred. Bruce demanded justice and when his demands were ignored, he reopened negotiations with France, reforging the Auld Alliance and promising mutual support against the English at a meeting at Corbeil on 26th April 1326

From 1322 the realm was effectively ruled by the Despensers with Edward being a mere cipher and the period being described as a corrupt reign of terror. Isabella, aware of the unrest among the baronage in England proclaimed that the Prince of Wales should usurp his father's throne and on September 26th 1326 landed with a small force in Essex and was enthusiastically received with many flocking to her banner including some of the king's brothers. Edward, now realizing how bad he had let things become, fled with the Despenser's to Bristol Castle, but the elder Despenser was captured and later executed. Edward and the younger Despenser attempted to escape to Lundy Island, but the weather forced them to South Wales where they were betrayed. Edward was imprisoned in Kenilworth Castle and Despencer was taken to Hereford where he was hanged, drawn and quartered as a traitor and his private parts cut off.

At the Parliament held on 7th January 1327, the Prince of Wales was proclaimed and a long list of charges was brought against Edward. A deputation sent to Kenilworth secured a formal abdication by the king, but "under protest". The new king was crowned at Westminster on 29th January and it was now obvious that the old king's fate was sealed.

Parliament set up Regency, but Isabella circumvented it, using her son's undoubted affection for his mother to give legitimacy to her power. Parliament became a mere rubber stamp and her ever more rapacious rule together with Mortimer had merely replaced the tyranny of the Despensers with her own. Hurried treaties with the Scots and the French only served to postpone problems while Isabella and her lover enriched themselves.

With England looking inward, Bruce launched a new campaign of raids and in 1327 sent three battalions south, defeating the English at Stanhope and Weardale, while another force was sent to invade Ulster. Bruce declared he would annex Northumberland and share it out among his followers and Isabella, being unable to raise a force to respond, agreed to a truce on Bruce's terms. The resulting Treaty of Northumberland virtually renounced all English claims to Scotland by Isabella, who, in the name of the young Edward 111."Renounced all pretensions to sovereignty and betrothed her daughter Joanna to Bruce's son David. The Scots paying a settlement of £20,000 for the treaty, but on paper at least, gained all that they had fought for. The Treaty stated that the borders set by Alexander 111 "shall forever to the eminent Prince Lord Robert, by the grace of God illustrious king of Scots our ally and dearest friend and to his heirs and successors divided all things from the realm of England, entire, free and quit"

Meanwhile, King Edward was in the custody of the Earl of Leicester and was fairly treated, but Mortimer had him removed and put in the charge of two cronies Sir Thomas Gournay and Sir Robert Maltravers and became subject to many insults and humiliations including having his beard shaved off. He was finally lodged in Berkeley Castle near Gloucester under the charge of Gournay and Sir William Ogle. On the night of 20th February, screams were heard coming from the castle as Edward was murdered. It is said that he had a heavy door laid on him to hold him down and a horn pushed into his rectum through which a red hot iron was passed to burn his bowels. Capgrave's Chronicle states "Edward was slain with a hot spit put into his body which could not be spied when he was dead for they put a horn in his tewhel and the spit through the horn that there should be no burning appear outside".

Thus ended the reign of Edward 2nd which began with so much promise and sunk to civil strife and near anarchy through his weakness. The conquests made by his father all but vanished, the stability achieved in his father's reign wrecked by the ambition and rapacity of Gaveston, Despenser and finally, his wife and her lover

Edward 111

Edward was born at Windsor Castle on the 13th November 1312. His reign was to be marked with great victories such as Halidon Hill, Crecy and Poitiers, plus humiliating defeats at Stanhope and Weardale, the surrendering of his Scottish claims at the Treaty of Northampton, The Black Death and the start of the Hundred Years War.

Edward was a typical medieval king, generous to his friends and pitiless to his enemies, he inherited all the warlike qualities of his grandfather and was filled with noble ideas of grandeur and was inspired by the legends of King Arthur and the Knights of the Round Table. He set out to recreate the courtly life of Camelot and it was at a Round Table tournament in Windsor in 1334 that he swore to establish a new order of Arthurian knights and did so four years later, at a ball to celebrate the capture of Calais, the garter of one of the Court ladies fell to the floor. Edward picked it up and tied it round his own leg and famously remarked "honi soit que mal y pense" (evil be to him who evil thinks) which became the motto of the Garter Knights, England's noblest order of chivalry. The Order of the Garter.

Edward grew into a fine, strong and healthy man, large framed, 6ft tall and fair haired, delighting in jousting and feats of arms. It is said that, in 1330, in company with twelve knights, he took on all comers at a three day tournament. He was a popular king, the English being ever pleased with victories, although few liked the taxes levied to pay for his wars,

At the age of 3 his father bestowed on him the Earldom of Chester and at 7 was made the first Duke of Cornwall. At 13 he was taken to France by his mother Isabella who refused to continue to play second fiddle to the Despensers at her husband's court. When she returned in 1326 with her lover Roger Mortimer, she used the young prince as a rallying point for all who wished to see an end to the feeble King Edward and his court favourites. Isabella and her lover ruled England in the name of the young King to be and through their greed and rapacity soon became as unpopular with the barons as had her predecessors

In 1328 Edward married Philippa of Hainault with whom he was to have 8 sons and 5 daughters, 9 surviving to adulthood.Philippa proved a loving and loyal wife to Edward and was well loved by the people. She is known for her compassion, twice interceding to divert the king's anger, first at a tournament at Cheapside when, following the collapse of some staging erected as seating for the queen's party, Edward ordered that the carpenters involved should be hanged. It is said that Philippa refused to rise from the ground until Edward promised to forgive them.Later, following the battle of Crecy, Edward attacked and captured the port of Calais and decided to take revenge on the town by executing 12 of its burghers. Philippa persuaded Edward to release them to her care and subsequently freed them. Their first child Edward, later known as the Black Prince was born in 1330. Contrary to popular belief, his nickname did not stem from the colour of his armour but from his remorseless aggression in battle, giving and expecting no quarter and was probably bestowed on him by the French.

His other sons, through their various marriages and alliances were to sow the bloody seeds of the Wars of the Roses one hundred years later. In October 1330 the King's Court came to Nottingham for the Parliament being there held. Edward and his wife and son were lodged in the town while Isabella and Roger Mortimer remained in the castle being guarded by 180 knights and some Welsh mercenaries. On the night of the 18th October Edward showed his mettle and, led by the castle's constable William de Eland, plus 24 companions entered the castle by a secret door, climbed the stairs to the upper bailey and entered the hall where Isabella was sitting in council. One can imagine the surprise when the young Edward, thought by all to be in his mother's thrall. Burst in and arrested Mortimer and Isabella. Within a month Mortimer, who had given himself the title the Earl of March, was executed and Isabella imprisoned at Castle Rising for the rest of her life, although being allowed to retain a pension of £3000 per year, courtesy of her son.

Thus began the reign of Edward, the years of rebellion, the squabbling and civil strife, plus the weakness of his father had resulted in the loss of his French and Scottish inheritance. The young king was however, made of sterner stuff than his father and was determined to regain the estates and power of his predecessors. He must however, tread warily, it was imperative that he retained the goodwill of his vassals and weld them together in an enterprise that promised profit and France would provide such an opportunity. To make safe the crown of England he had decided to beggar France but knew that with the Scots at his back he must neutralize them and renounce the hated Treaty of Northampton that had given so much back to the Scots before moving against Phillip VI... He also knew that if he was seen to break the treaty, the French would not only come to Scotland's aid, but would certainly confiscate Aquitaine. Edward began a dialogue with Phillip suggesting marriages between the two royal houses and in this cordial atmosphere, the French king invited Edward to go on crusade. Edward was enthusiastic, but asked if he could delay the journey for three years while he led an expedition to Ireland. This delay was just a cover, the Northampton Treaty had promised the return of Scots and Irish lands taken by Bruce to various disinherited English gentry, but Bruce had failed to fulfill this part of the treaty before his death. Edward secretly prompted Balliol to rebellion against the child king David 11 and while publicly denouncing Balliol and refusing permission for the rebel to cross royal lands, supplied Balliol with ships to launch an invasion resulting in Balliol's seizure of the Scots throne from the four year old David on 24th September 1332.

Balliol duly acknowledged Edward as overlord and surrendered Berwick to English control. This was too much for the Scottish nobles who had fought so hard to drive out the English; they promptly rose and drove Balliol from the kingdom "in his bedclothes, bareback and with only one foot booted". But in doing so, the Scots had crossed the border and broken the treaty. Edward could now appear as the injured party; he engineered his parliament to demand that he divert his Irish expedition money to defend the realm from the barbaric Scots and Edward declared war on the rebellion and supported Balliol again. At Dupplin Moor Balliol met a Scottish force led by the Regent Donald Earl of Mar. The Scottish leader positioned his main force covering the bridge that separated the two forces, but during the hours of darkness Balliol sent men across a ford and attacked the enemy camp causing much slaughter. At daylight, Donald formed his troops in one central column flanked by two lesser formations in support and marched on Balliols position. Balliol retreated to higher ground and positioned his forces in one main battle with dismounted knights and men at arms in the centre and skirmish lines of archers borrowed from the English extending to the flanks. The Scottish column crashed into the enemy centre and by sheer weight of numbers, forced it back, gradually the English men at arms, taking advantage of the slope, forced the Scots back and the archers, quickly moving in from the sides began to fire directly into the flanks of the attackers, the rain of arrows forcing the Scots in to an ever decreasing area. The flanking columns moving forward in support where met with hails of arrows forcing them to retreat and leave the main body of attackers at the mercy of the English who now moved forward to finish off the Scottish main body. The press became so thick that many fell from heatstroke and exhaustion and the living had scarcely room to lift their weapons. Within a short time the mound of Scottish dead was several feet high. The survivors tried to turn and retreat down the hill which quickly became a burial heap in which the twitching bodies were said to be piled" fifteen feet high "with troops desperately trying to climb over and escape, but the English poured volley after volley of arrows into them. The Scots lost all their leaders, eighteen lesser nobles and some seventy men at arms, plus some thousands of infantry in the battle. By contrast, Balliol recorded thirty three knights and men at arms slain, plus some two hundred infantry This victory enabled Edward to occupy Scotland again and install Balliol as his vassal king while also sequestering much of southern Scotland into English ownership. As stated earlier, the puppet king was not in power long before the Scots chased him from their lands. In 1333 Edward was again in Scotland with an army of some 10,000 men laying siege to the strategic town of Berwick. The citizens finally appealing for a truce under the terms that, should the the new guardian of the infant King David, Sir Archibald Douglas, not relieve the siege by 19th July, the town would surrender. On the morning of the 19th, Douglas, leading an army of 1,200 men at arms and 13,500 spearmen arrived at the foot of Halidon Hill where the English forces were arrayed. Before them lay an area of boggy marsh which proved impassable for their horses. The Scots advanced in schiltrons through the marsh and began to ascend the hill having learned nothing from the lesson of Dupplin Moor and the butchery inflicted on them by English archers

King Edward's army was drawn up in three divisions to receive them with the king in the centre, the Earl of Norfolk on the left and Balliol on the right with archers angled between. The English troops were greatly disheartened at the sight of so large an enemy force and Edward was obliged to ride among the troops to encourage them and promise them much reward for victory. The Scots rushed on, but, as at Dupplin, the English archers released their arrow storm into the packed infantry wounding and killing hundreds before they could even reach the English line. Lanercost records that hundreds "were so grievously wounded in the face and blinded by the host of English archery that they were helpless and began to turn away their faces from the arrow flights". Douglas and many of the Scots leaders were slain and with their deaths died Scottish resistance. The Scots King David was invited to seek protection in France and Edward was now free to turn his attention to France.

During the early 14th century France was the richest country in Christendom but with many latent problems beginning to stir. The French king Philip 1V had died in 1314 leaving the Capet line seemingly secure with three sons and a grandson. All of these offspring however, died in quick succession, with the last, Charles IV leaving a pregnant queen. Philip of Valois, a nephew of Philip IV, was appointed regent and it was agreed that, if the queen produced a daughter, Philip would become king. The queen duly produced a daughter and Philip became King Philip VI. The succession was legalized by the adoption of the new Salic law which stated that no woman could rule France and that no claim could be made to the crown through a female relative. This law also excluded several other princes who could have claimed the crown, one of them being King Edward 111 of England, whose mother was a daughter of Philip IV.

A dispute over the succession of Robert of Artois to the County of Artois left the French king supporting a rival claimant and feeling
Cheated and betrayed, Robert transferred his allegiance to King Edward. A similar situation arose shortly after in Brittany when Philip ruled that his nephew Charles of Blois should get the Dukedom against the rival claim of Jean de Montfort, who also turned to Edward for support.

The situation was worsened by the ongoing Anglo French dispute over the Duchy of Aquitaine the vast area of south west France from La

Rochele to the Spanish border and are sometimes referred to as Gascony or Guyenne although, in reality, they are provinces of the Duchy that was held as an English possession from Philip and for which Edward owed homage to the French king. The nobles of Aquitaine were adept at playing the English and French against each other to further their own interests. If an English ruling was unacceptable they could appeal to Philip and vice versa.This, plus the unclear borders of the Duchy gave rise to many disputes and French kings in the past had frequently reclaimed Aquitaine as punishment in disputes with England. Philip continued to give aid to the Scots and with the promise of this help, the Scots Lords Randolph and Steward Drove the English back to Berwick and ravaged much of northern England. Pope Benedict XII arranged a six month truce in 1335 and had ruled that no new Crusade could begin until there was peace in Europe, but not before Edward had raided Lothian in what became known as Burnt Candlemass due to the large number of towns and villages burned.

With the hopes of a Crusade gone, Philip had no need to be soft on Edward and when Edward again marched on Scotland In 1336, Philip confiscated the Duchy for the Third time precipitating outright war between the two countries, a time generally viewed as the start of the hundred year's war. Philip attacked northern England with a fleet of twenty seven galleys and also moved his fleet from Marseilles to Normandy as an invasion threat to England. In September 1336 in the Parliament of Nottingham, the meeting denounced Philip's aid to Scotland and voted Edward money to begin military preparations, send war material to Aquitaine and to collect a fleet in the English Channel. By 1338 Genoese sailors under French command were regularly attacking the south coast and in April a great comet was seen in the sky over England and was reckoned a bad omen. On January 25th 1340, Edward formally made claim to the French throne, probably as a way of raising the stakes and to be used as a bargaining counter to extract French concessions later. Following his invasion of France however, he had obviously hardened his resolve and Amended the Royal Coat of Arms from the three golden lions of England that had been the royal symbol since the reign of Richard 1st, and quartered them with the twelve fleur de lis of the French. This new standard was to last for sixty six years until, in the reign of Henry IV when it was amended to the three fleur de lis of the de Valois . On the 22nd June 1340, Edward sailed from Orwell with a fleet of 200 ships and was joined on the Flanders coast outside the town of Sluys by his Admiral Sir Robert Morley with 50 others. These ships, known as cogs, would have weighed around two hundred tons and would differ from cargo ships by the erecting of "castles" at the front and rear "aftercastle and forecastle" from which archers would fire on the enemy. Some of these vessels were transports as the king had brought with him the household of the queen who was at that time in Bruges.The French fleet was anchored in the inlet between West Flanders and Zeeland, at that time a wide roadstead but now silted up the river Eede and amounted to some 190 vessels commanded by the French Admiral Hugh Quiret and assisted by Nicholas Bhuchet. Part of the fleet were Genoese galleys with a crew of mercenaries under the command of Barbavera who was little more than a pirate.

At the approach of the English fleet,Barbavera advised Quiret to put to sea, but Quiret refused to leave the anchorage and arranged his forces into three or four lines with the ships tied to one another, a common defensive tactic of the time.Edward, in a letter to his son, described the English fleet on the morning of 24th June maneuvering to windward and forming two lines, the first attacking the front and the second turning the opponent's flanks. The battle quickly became a confusion of boarding and hand to hand conflicts. A French version of events claims that Edward was wounded during the battle in personal combat with Bhuchet,but the only certainty was the almost total destruction of the French fleet, during which,Quiret was slain together with a reported 30,000 Frenchmen although little credence should be given to medieval estimates.

Following the battle Bhuchet was hanged on orders of the king and Barbavera escaped with most of his squadron intact plus two captured English vessels. The battle left Edward in control of the English Channel and prevented any invasion threat from France; Edward could now concentrate on stirring unrest with Philip by supporting John de Montfort in his claim for the Duchy of Brittany over Philip's choice Charles of Blois in what became known as the Breton War of Succession. This together with various campaigns in Gascony dragged on for some years without any real gains for either. Early in 1346 Edward began preparations for all out war, his officer's recruited men, requisitioned ships and purchased arms and supplies. One of Edward's orders states" for the sake of our expedition of war in France, we have immediate need of a great quantity of bows and arrows, we now firmly order and command you that you shall immediately cause to be brought and provided for us out of the issues of your jurisdiction, 200 bows and 400 sheaves of arrows" Similar instructions were sent throughout the country and huge stocks of weapons were gathered at the Tower of London.

In July 1346 Edward mounted a major invasion, landing at Saint Vaast on the Cotentin Peninsula with a force between 10,000 and 15,000 men, first destroying the French ships in the harbour and then burning the town. Edward landed around midday and Froissart records that he tripped with his first step on the beach. This was regarded by some as a bad omen, but Edward was reported to have remarked "I look upon it as a sign that the land desires to have me". His force marched through Normandy towards Flanders, pillaging as he went in a manner that became known as "chevauchee", merely destroying rather than attempting to occupy captured land.

Between 13th and 17th July he continued landing men and supplies, his forces attacked Barfleur and pillaged and burned the town and the warships in the harbour. It was said that there was so much loot that the soldiers could hardly carry it all and an area 35 kilometers around the landing area was devastated. Edward advanced northwards in three divisions while some of his fleet sailed along the coast destroying or capturing any French warship they found. It was Edward's intention to link up with another invasion force led by Sir Hugh Hastings that he had dispatched to Flanders to link up with a force being collected by Count Henry of Flanders. Arriving at the city of Caen the English forces attacked and after fierce fighting, defeated the French and proceeded to rape, massacre and loot. Over 2,500 citizens died, many being buried in a mass grave at the church of St Jean. The English rested for the next five days, systematically burning and destroying the surrounding area. Edward sent orders to England for additional 1,500 archers ,more weapons and equipment and 100 more ships to bring reinforcements, instructing them to land at Le Crotoy on the northern side of the

Somne,in territory the English had yet to conquer, giving some insight to Edward's confidence.

Philip was in the meanwhile gathering forces, but had to spread them thinly to cover all potential areas of the English advance. Edward left a small force at Caen and moved on to the Seine, threatening Paris. The French sent two cardinals to discuss terms, even proposing a marriage between the houses of Valois and Plantagenet, but Edward would have none of it, he even issued a challenge to battle south of Paris forcing Philip to move his army to the southern wall in preparation. Edwards challenge was merely a ruse to gain time. He had to cross the Seine, but all the bridges were destroyed. Edward's forces moved to Poissy and started to rebuild. When Philip learned of this attempt at a crossing he sent a force to intercept, but by then the English had managed to span a single beam across and sufficient troops were now over the river and drove them off.

On the 16th August English marauders road south to confuse the French, but Edward's main force crossed the river and headed north towards the Somne, being harassed all the way by local militias, brushing them off easily except at the village of Poix where the English turned back and burned the town. Edward's forces needed to cross the Somne before Philip and began to abandon some of the baggage wagons for the sake of speed, but as foraging became more difficult in the abandoned countryside, the English were forced to scour far afield and slowed the army down. The French force overtook Edward, arriving at the Somne on 20th August. The people of Picardy heartened by the arrival of French forces began to attack isolated groups of English troops. On the 22nd Edward's tired army reached Airaines, whose garrison had been withdrawn to guard the bridge at Pont-Remy.

The main French army had now reached Amiens and Philip ordered the destruction or Garrisoning of the Somne bridges. Edward sent scouts to look at the Somme bridges, but found that all were too strongly defended. The English seemed trapped, but Edward was on familiar territory,Ponthieu had been his own county before Philip had confiscated it at the outbreak of war and some of his commanders knew the area. Edward had been gone from Airaines only two hours before The French arrived and the trap was closing. Edward had some hard choices, he could make a stand and fight, he could retreat to Saint Valery and take ship home or he could try to cross the Somne. Some of his men through local connections knew of the ford at Blanchetaque (whitestones) on the Somne estuary, so called because the traffic using it stirred up the chalk bed of the river and left white trails on the banks.

The English had little choice but to head for the ford and arrived at nearby Saigneville on 24th. Before dawn they began their crossing and within a few hours had the bulk of their forces across, a remarkable feat for the time. The French had also set out at dawn, a party of some 500 men at arms and 3,000 foot soldiers being sent to oppose any English attempt at crossing. The French crossbowmen attacked the English vanguard and some men at arms charged into the water to close with them, but the English under the command of Hugh Despenser, Reginald Cobham and the Earl of Northampton drove them off. By the time the English rearguard came ashore the battle was over. Edward's position was precarious, he received information that his Flemish allies with whom he had hoped to unite had suffered some setbacks at Bethune and Lillers and that the Flemish forces had began to argue among themselves and had lifted their siege on Merville. Edward clearly could not rely on any aid from them and sent Hugh Despenser to capture the coastal towns of Novelles, Le Crotoy and Rue, which they did, but there was no sign of the English ships bringing urgently needed supplies.

He decided he had no option but to stand and fight and sent Warwick,Cobham,Suffolk and Sir Geoffrey Harcourt ahead with the main force to occupy the high ground on a hill outside the village of Crecy while the rest of his force followed. Philip's scouts reported that the English had made a stand and called a council to decide on the next move. Some advocated moving ahead of the English to cut them off, others suggested waiting for reinforcements who were still moving to join the main group, but many demanded an immediate attack. Was not the French army the most experienced and ablest in Christendom? Philip's forces were strung out over a wide area on the road from Abbeyville and Philip placed his infantry ahead of the cavalry as a precaution against ambush as they marched through the forestland. This decision meant that his Genoese crossbowmen were separated from their pavisse shields in the baggage train, an error that would have serious consequences later. Philip called a halt, the Genoese who had been leading were tired and the men at arms following were greatly disorganized, the bulk of the army and baggage was further back while hordes of locals filled the lanes hoping for a chance to strike a blow or to collect loot. Once Philip decided to fight the disarray became worse, every unit jostling to be first through pride and everyone wishing to surpass his neighbour.The French unfurled the sacred Oriflamme banner indicating no quarter and the Genoese were ordered to advance.

Edward had placed his divisions in the same three lines as when they marched. His son, Edward the Black Prince, now 16 was placed with his division on the right of the battle line with archers in a block in front and to one side together with some artillery. The left was held by Northampton and Arundel also with a wing of archers in front, while Edward commanded the rearguard. Potholes were dug in front of all positions to slow down cavalry. The baggage train was to the rear at the edge of Crecy Grange wood surrounded by field fortifications of carts and wagons with just one opening for the speedy replenishment of arrows. Food was cooked in the baggage area and troops were sent back by units to eat and relieve themselves leaving their bows or helmets as a marker for their place in the line.

The Genoese were not keen to advance; they were tired and did not have the protection of their pavisses which were normally used for shelter while rewinding their crossbows. Furthermore they did not have adequate reserves of ammunition and with the lowering sun in their eyes were at a disadvantage, but their complaints to the Count of Alencon were ignored.Nevertheless, the 6,000 Genoese crossbowmen and spearmen began their advance on the Black Prince's line. To the sound of drums and trumpets, the force, under the leadership of Carlo Grimaldi moved forward in three stages, each pause being signaled by a great shout to dishearten the enemy and also to enable them to adjust ranks. A sudden and violent rainstorm erupted, quickly turning the lower ground into slippery mud. The rain also soaked the strings of their crossbows making them lose power. A combatant Jean de Venette records that the English longbowmen took the strings from their bows and kept them dry beneath their helmets. This cannot be done with a crossbow and explains how the English easily outranged their opponents. The Genoese opened fire after their third shout at about 150 meters range, they did so uphill with the sun in their eyes, a major disadvantage for men who aimed direct at targets rather than dropping arrows on them. They were then hit by the English arrow storm from the Black Prince's division and from the bombards on the wings. Outshot and outranged and without the protection of their pavisses the Genoese faltered and began to fall back into the path of the following Count of Alencon's cavalry who were trying to ride past the archers to get to the Black Prince's position. It is said that the men at arms attacked the Genoese for cowardice or treachery, riding over them to get at the English bowmen who continued to rain storms of arrows into the confusion. Furthermore, the cavalry had to attack uphill over muddy fields and through the broken remnants of the crossbowmen. French plate armour was good enough to protect from most types of English arrowheads, but visors, joints and chain mail were vulnerable. Furthermore, the horses were only protected by padded caparison easily penetrated and the arrows caused fearful damage, throwing their riders and trampling them in the mud. The frightened horses reared, fled or panicked and lay down refusing to move. The French knight Jean le Bell describes how" The English arrows were directed with such skill at the horsemen that their mounts refused to advance. Stung to madness some reared hideously, some turned their quarters to the enemy; others simply fell to the ground". The English, seizing the initiative, advanced into this melee and slaughtered the struggling horsemen. The straggling French forces, arriving on the field, rushed impetuously forward, eager for a share of the glory.

Among Philip's commanders was the near blind John of Luxembourg, King of Bohemia and Poland and knowing that his son Charles, king of the Romans was with Alencon, ordered his companions to to tie their bridles to his before leading them in a charge against the Black Prince, saying" place me so far forward that I am able to strike a blow". The charge broke through the archers and the fighting became so fierce that at one time the Prince was forced to his knees before being rescued by his standard bearer Sir Richard FitzSimon. The English line held and pushed the French back. King John and his companions were all killed. The Earl of Northampton, seeing the French charge, ordered his nearest unit under the Earl of Arundel to help the prince and a message was also sent to

King Edward for help. The King was reported to have replied" is my son dead, fallen, or wounded so that he cannot help himself? Then let him earn his spurs, for it is my wish that the glory of the day be his"

Despite the death of Alencon and Luxembourg,the French made a further 13 cavalry charges, mostly against the Black Prince's division and some against Northampton's but were met with the same arrow cloud, breaking the charges and enabling the English to hack down the survivors. As dusk fell, the charges became fewer and less intense. Edward ordered the English to advance. The horses were brought forward and forming in conrois formation, charged. The remnants of the French fled, leaving Philip and some 50 of his followers, plus his Orleans militia to fight on. The royal banner and the sacred Oriflamme were captured and the standard bearer killed. Philip himself had two horses killed under him and was wounded in the face by an arrow before being dragged off the field by the Count of Hainault. The king and a few survivors fled to Labroye castle. Some fighting continued until after dark when the English infantry moved forward to kill the wounded and loot the bodies. Edward ordered the burning of a windmill that stood behind his position, plus French baggage wagons to illuminate the battlefield during the first tense hours of the night as French troops were still arriving, separated from their leaders, wandering around and shouting their passwords as they tried to find their units. Many were found and killed as the English still refused to take prisoners. Many estimates have been made of the French losses at Crecy, but the most realistic gives combined losses of men of aristocratic rank as 1,542. Of the men at arms, spearmen and other infantry, estimates range from 8,000 to 12,000 who were unceremoniously tipped into grave pits.

The old king of Bohemia was carried from the field, his body washed, wrapped in linen and returned to Luxembourg with honour.It is said that Edward the Black Prince of Wales adopted John's motto "ich dien" (I Serve) and John's badge of three feathers as his personal arms, this being quite separate from the Prince's own Royal Arms with the three vertical white stripes indicating his status as heir apparent.

The English army continued slowly northwards, staying close to the coast in the hope of receiving supplies by sea. They followed the usual pattern of looting and foraging, destroying an area over 30km wide. On

September 1st they rested at Neufchatel and next day stopped at Wimille to review the situation after hearing that the English force at Caen had been destroyed. Edward realized that he would not be able to retain Normandy, a heavy blow to the Norman knights that had supported him against the French king. Edward decided to besiege Calais rather than Boulogne because it would be a better base and was closer to his Flemish allies, moving north he destroyed the port of Wissant and on 4th September reached the marshes surrounding Calais. On the same day, the English fleet attacked Boulogne but were driven off, they did however make contact with Edward who sent letters home demanding fresh troops and supplies for the siege of Calais.The supply fleet arrived a few days later under the command of Sir John Montgomery and the English settled down for the siege.

The Scots meanwhile, had not been idle. Despite the truce they were eager to aid their French allies and the young King David assembled a force of some 15,000 troops and crossed the border into northern England. The streetwise Edward, anticipating such a move, had appointed Sir Henry Percy, Sir Ralph Neville and the Archbishop of York to defend against just such a move and with an army of 700 cavalry and 10,000 archers and hobilars, set out to confront the Scots. On 17th October Sir William Douglas and a band of 500 hobilars were plundering the town of Merrington. There was a heavy mist over the town masking the approach of the English army and Douglas was suddenly confronted by a large force of men at arms and heard" the trampling of horses and the shock of armoured men". In the ensuing skirmish Douglas lost over half his force, sending the remainder streaming back to the safety of the main force. The English deployed on a narrow ridge at Nevilles Cross near Durham. The ground was not ideal for cavalry so the knights and men at arms were stationed in the rear with the archers and infantry drawn up in three divisions to the fore.

The Scots king was confident enough to remark "ready my breakfast, I will return to it when I have slain the English on the point of the sword". Such confidence was not universal, the Earl of Patrick who had been put in charge of the vanguard, on seeing the English line, asked that he instead take command of the rearguard, leaving the Earl of Moray to lead the Scots first attack which soon ran into difficulties being funneled into an increasingly narrow front by a ravine on their right. This vanguard became entangled with the central division led by King David and lost momentum. The English lost no time in loosing off their usual arrow storm into the mass. Seeing this, the Scottish left surged forward and engaged the English line, but was stopped by a charge from the English cavalry. More cavalry charged into the disorganized Scottish right, forcing them back and exposing the Scots centre to the full might of the English. By dusk the Scots were routed, many escaping into the darkness leaving King David and his liegemen surrounded. The King fought to the last, knocking out two front teeth of John of Copeland, an English knight who finally took the king's surrender.

King David was taken with other Scots nobles to London and imprisoned in the Tower. The Scottish lords Mentieth and Fife were charged with treason as they had previously sworn allegiance to Edward. It seemed at last that Scottish rebellion was over. Not only was their King and senior lords in captivity, but even the most sacred of Scottish artifacts were in English hands. The Stone of Scone had been in English hands since the reign of Edward 1st and now the Black Rood, a casket said to contain fragments of the True Cross, taken from its place in Edinburgh by David to bring him luck, had been captured and was put on display in Durham Cathedral.

Edward meanwhile continued the siege of Calais. As food became scarcer, the defenders expelled 2,000 old men, women and children. These "bouches inutiles or useless mouths" were given food by Edward and sent on their way, but three months later, when the garrison was reduced to eating rats, they expelled 500 more, Edward refused them food or safe passage and they were left to die between the two forces.

Following the defeat at Crecy, the French king's son John, Duke of Normandy, who had been fighting a small English force in Gascony under the command of Henry of Derby, Earl of Lancaster, moved his main army north to aid his father. Henry seized the moment and renewed his efforts to recover the whole of Aquitaine for the English. In seven weeks he had retaken the Duchy, cleared the County of Poitou and captured Poitiers

Calais surrendered on 4th August 1347. Edward was furious that the town had defied him for so long and ordered the deaths of twelve leading burghers. It is said that his wife Philippa intervened and begged Edward to change his mind. It is more likely however that Edward's officers pointed out that, if the Burghers were killed, the French would no doubt do the same to the English at any subsequent siege. Edward expelled all citizens of rank and brought over English tradesmen and their families to the town. He also moved the Wool Staple to Calais to aid its prosperity, making it the only entry point for English wool to be sold in Europe. Calais was to remain in English hands until 1553.

In October 1348 the Black Death arrived in England. This plague, originating in the vast deserts of Mongolia and carried by fleas living on rats, followed the medieval trade routes bringing death on a large scale as it swept through Europe. It is thought that the first outbreak was in Weymouth, other sources give it as Bristol. Soon it had spread throughout the country decimating towns and villages. It is estimated that the plague killed between a quarter and a third of the English population and claimed in excess of 25 million victims throughout Europe. Its name was first thought to describe the blackened and putrefying flesh of its victims, but the septicemia type of the contagion that turns flesh dark purple was not common in the 14th century. It is more likely that the name derived from the Latin "atra pestis . Atra is translated as terrible/dreadful but can also mean black. With the loss of so many of the common folk, there were too few left to adequately work the lords lands and the working man soon realized that his scarcity could command a better standard of living. The king and his nobles were not having any of this and in 1351 passed the Statute of Labourers designed to freeze wages and restrict movement. This had little effect and in the same year Edward turned to the church for more funds by publishing the Statute of Provisions and the Statute of Praemunire, both designed to exact more revenue from the clerics, thus setting in chain a series of events that would result in a near civil war some 20 years later when the clerics under John of Gaunt and Alice Perrers the king's mistress opposed the court party under Edward, the Black Prince.

The effects of the Black Death brought major campaigning to an end in France apart from sporadic conflicts mainly in Brittany.It was during this lull that a party of 30 French knights challenged a similar number of

Englishmen to a chivalric tournament that became known as the Battle of the Thirty. The French won and the captured English were ransomed. This incident in itself, typifies the attitude of the knightly classes of both countries to warring as a way of life. In Florence the Bardi and Peruzzi banks who owned England's entire state treasure went bankrupt. In France, Philip VI died and was succeeded by his son John II "John the Good". The France that he inherited was weakened by disease, famine and the English chevauchee raids. Unlike the English, the French nobility had their own power bases in which they ruled without interference from the king and John would need their cooperation for any new taxation to pay for war. In 1352 he gave his daughter in marriage to King Charles "the Bad" of Navarre, a move which would cause serious problems in the future as Charles believed that he should be King of France. With fewer men available for war, John set out to improve the fighting abilities of his forces by appointing prelates to command and train them. He also commanded that every crossbowman be issued with a belt, spanning strap and hook and to train in loading and firing. The English meanwhile, being content with the proved effectiveness of the longbow, made little attempt to change.

When major military operations resumed in 1355 the English continued the policy of destructive chevauchee in Normandy, Brittany and the French occupied parts of Aquitaine. A treaty had been signed in Valonges marking reconciliation between Charles of Navarre and the French king, this being seen as a threat to English interests. King Edward ordered his son to launch a great chevauchee in the lands of Jean de Armagnac whose lands bordered the Spanish kingdom and a key ally of John. The Black Prince marched from Bordeaux to the Mediteranian and it is reckoned that over 500 towns and villages were destroyed in the campaign. Coming so soon after the ravages of the Black Death, this was a disaster for France. Things got worse when, in 1356, John again quarreled with Charles of Navarre and had him arrested for treason. Charles, in addition to his Navarre kingdom was also a senior member of the French nobility and held vast estates in France which were now confiscated. The English, ever ready to exploit French dissent formed an alliance with Charles' brother Philip of Navarre, thus opening strategic possibilities in south western France as well as in the north where Philip held large estates.

The early months of 1356 were busy for both sides of the Channel. In anticipation of an English attack the French began to coordinate their southern defences, while in Normandy, the Duke of Lancaster begins a series of raids. The Black Prince assembles his forces at Le Reole and begins his chevauchee towards Bergerac with the Duke of Lancaster moving south to meet him. It was not the prince's intention to force a major battle with the French; he wanted to show that the French king could not protect his own lands and persuade its nobles that a better future lay with the English. King John in turn was determined to shadow the English and bring them to battle at a place of his choosing. On the 16th September the English prince learned that John had overtaken him and was now in front, cutting off his route to meet with Lancaster. Prince Edward decided to retreat southwards but kept his forces away from the main routes and instead marched through woodlands and minor tracks, causing the French scouts to lose touch with them.

This cat and mouse movement continued until a force of about 60 men at arms led by the Gascons Sir Eustace de Aubricourt and Sir John de Ghistelles were sent scouting and blundered into the French army moving through a thickly wooded area. A force of French knights, recorded only as "a great number" gave chase to the scouts who raced back to the safety of the main force. Froissart records that "they rode so hard in pursuit they got so far forward that they came upon the Prince's army where it had halted in the heather and bracken waiting news of their scouts. There was great astonishment when they saw them thus pursued". As a result, most of the French were killed or captured and there where some English losses. The English moved on and set camp in the wood of Breuel la Abbaye. The Anglo Gascon forces were so low on provisions and so close to the French that it dare not consider outrunning the French and now considered battle inevitable .Early on the morning of Sunday 18th September, the Black Prince's army broke camp and marched toward the Poitiers to Bordeaux road, skirting the woods at Nouaille. The Prince, fearing an ambush, stationed archers along his left flank. It is known that he dismounted and spoke to the archers and men at arms, calling on the memory of the great victory at Crecy and the

147

might of England. He also promised them great rewards of booty after the battle. The Prince disposed his forces on the top of a slope with the Nouaille wood behind him, the Earls of Oxford and Warwick on the left where the ground sloped down to the Miosson stream and Earls Salisbury and Suffolk commanding the right with the Prince's division in the centre. A reserve of 400 archers and some men at arms where stationed behind the right flank. The main bodies of archers where deployed at right angles to both flanks with ditches and potholes dug in front of their positions to slow down cavalry. The Prince had chosen his spot wisely, with woods behind him, thick hawthorn hedge and scrub, plus vines and brambles in front making footing difficult for any attacker. During these preparations the Cardinal of Perigord rode from Poitiers to attempt some form of peace treaty between the two armies. The Prince clearly did not want to fight and offered at one point to give up his captured towns and castles and free his hostages without ransom; he also demanded however that he be given the King's daughter in marriage and the County of Enghien as dowry. The French countered with a proposal that the Prince and 100 knights surrender and the remaining troops would be allowed to go home.

During these discussions, the French Marshal Clermont came face to face with the English Lord Chandos and Froissart describes that they both wore the same heraldic device, a Virgin azure with a sunbeam sinister on their surcoat. Clermont raged at Chandos claiming the Englishman had stolen the design, but Chandos was equally aggressive in denial, saying "you will find me on the field tomorrow ready to defend and prove by force of arms what I have said". Clermont was said to have replied "These are the boastings of you English who can invent nothing new but take for your own anything handsome belonging to others" This again illustrates the mindset of medieval man and his attitudes.

King John, wary of the English archers, abandoned the traditional cavalry assault and dismounted all his troops apart from an elite of about 500 fully armoured men, whose role would be to disperse the English archers at the start of the battle. The other men at arms sent their horses to the rear and, as was usual when fighting on foot, shortened their lances to less than 2 metres and removed their spurs. The King armed himself with a battleaxe and dressed in the same "royal armour" or surcoat as 19 other knights, worn to prevent the King being singled out too easily. The Marshal Clermont commanded the the mounted division on the left, supported by some dismounted men at arms. Marshal Audrehem with the Scots Lord Douglas commanded the French mounted division on the right with the crossbowmen behind them ready to counter the English bowmen. The King's eldest son the Dauphin commanded the central division vanguard, the Duke of Orleans the middle and the King himself led the rearguard.

On the morning of the 19th September, The Black Prince gave his final instructions stressing that no prisoners should be taken until the battle was won. At around 9 am the Earl of Warwick's division was seen by the French to withdrawing to the south, this is now thought to have been a feint to provoke the French to attack and, if so, succeeded. Marshal d'Audrehem reported these movements to Clermont, who, observing no movement on his front, accused Audrehem of cowardice and a quarrel ensued. In a rage Audrehem ordered his cavalry forward to attack the archers on Warwick's flank, but they could not reach them due to the marshy ground that the archers had chosen. He therefore headed for Warwick's main body enabling the English archers to open fire on at the charging cavalry. Initially this had little effect. Newer types of horse armour gave better protection from the front than the older padded caparisons and most of the arrows shattered or bounced harmlessly away. As the attackers swept past however, the unprotected flanks and rumps were exposed and more and more animals were wounded, panicked, threw their riders and refused to advance. The attack was badly disrupted before coming into contact with Warwick's men at arms and was broken suffering heavy casualties. The English foot soldiers rushed forward and in Froissart's words "seized and slew them at their pleasure" The French withdrew, both Audrehem and Douglas being badly wounded.. Seeing this,Clermont launched an attack with his cavalry on the English right, but with rather more caution, being sure to retain contact with his supporting dismounted men at arms. His uphill charge was slowed by the hedges and his men were funneled into the gaps only to be met by a hail of arrows from the defenders. Geoffrey le Baker does not record "nor did our archers neglect their duty, aiming arrows which defeated armoured knights while our crossbowmen let fly bolts fast and furiously". The latter being Gascons in the Prince's army. Clermont pressed his attack and vicious hand to hand fighting ensued. The Earl of Suffolk, seeing this sent reinforcements to aid Salisbury and gradually the French were forced back suffering heavy losses including Clermont himself, who Froissart, asserts was killed rather than captured due to the altercation with Chandos the previous day.

The Dauphin now led his vanguard toward the English line. The dismounted force marching up the slope and through the hedge to reach the enemy. The English, who typically, during a lull in fighting, had broken ranks to strip the dead and wounded, were hurriedly called back into line to meet the onslaught. Again the English archers rained arrows on the French who, not only had to protect themselves from this death from the sky, but also had to fight through the retreating troops of Clermont's shattered cavalry. The hand to hand fighting lasted for over two hours with heavy losses on both sides. The Duke de Bourbon being killed and the Dauphin's standard bearer being captured, the loss of the standard would have had a very demoralizing effect on the attackers. Realizising that no progress was being made, the Dauphin began an ordered retreat. Seeing this, it is thought that King John ordered the Dauphin and his two other sons to leave the field, fearing their capture by the English. Whatever the reason, seeing the French Princes leaving the field, the second French division led by the Duke of Orleans, whose purpose was to exploit any English weakness, decided to withdraw also. Much has been made of the misunderstandings that led to this retreat by Orleans who claimed after the battle that King John had ordered it. (Rather conveniently).

Prince Edward now had trouble holding back his forces who wanted to pursue Orleans. Froissart says" they assembled in a body shouting Saint George! Guyenne". Chandos urge the Prince to advance on the French rearguard, but in the event it was King John who moved forward. Le Baker records that the French King states"Forward, for I will recover the day or be taken or slain". The tired English were much dismayed when seeing this new threat approaching. King John's division contained his elite troops and was led by crossbowmen, this time with their pavisses to shield them while loading. They began to fire at the English line while Suffolk passed through each line of his force urging and encouraging not to break ranks and urging the archers not to waste arrows. Meanwhile, Prince Edward sent his Gascon reserve of 60 mounted men at arms and 100 mounted archers under Captal de Buch in a flanking movement around the left flank of the advancing John. When the Black Prince saw de Buch's signal he ordered a charge by his mounted men at arms. He then had his standard bearer Walter Woodland signal a general advance by the infantry, even the unarmoured archers dropping their bows to join the hand to hand fighting. Warwick on the left flank moved forward in support and at the same time the Captal de Buch struck the French rear which almost immediately collapsed. The wounded Douglas, fearing capture by the English more than death, fled the field. The French, under pressure, fell back to a loop in the Miosson River where they were trapped still fighting savagely but were gradually overcome. With their line broken and fighting in small groups they were massacred. One by one the banners fell until at last the sacred Oriflamme was taken. The French King and his household knights fought on desperately but to no avail. The King was taken prisoner by a French knight in the English service, Sir Denise de Morbeke.

With their forces broken, the surviving French could only surrender or flee, those who ran tried to reach Poitiers, but the gates were shut against them for fear of the English taking the city. As a result, large numbers were massacred outside the walls. Back on the battlefield, the Black Prince attached his banner to a large bush to serve as a rallying point for his scattered forces. The French King became the subject of some squabbling among the English and was roughly handled until rescued by Warwick and taken with youngest his son to the Black Prince's tent. The victory had been great, between 500 and 700 French knights and squires had been killed and some thousands (estimates range from 3000 to 6000) common soldiers. Furthermore, over a thousand prisoners of rank were taken with even lowly English archers having 3 or 4 as captives. A French chronicler records" on that day, the flower of French chivalry perished".

With so many prisoners it was decided to ransom most of them immediately, put on their honour to return to Bordeaux the following Christmas to pay their ransoms. On the battlefield, many French knights could not be identified because scavengers had taken their clothing before heralds went around the field identifying the fallen. Only the identified nobles were taken away for a proper burial, the rest were left to rot until the following February when their remains were buried in pits near the Franciscan church in Poitiers.Prince Edward made an almost leisurely return to Bordeaux, arriving there to a great victory welcome in early October. With King John captured and France helpless Edward consolidated his son's victory with the Treaty of London in which a ransom of four million ecus was to be paid for John and the captured nobles. This treaty did not however, ever come into force. Some of John's family were to be brought to England as a guarantee. The territories of Normandy, Brittany, Anjou, Maine and the entire coastline from Flanders to Spain were to be ceded to England, thus restoring the old Angevin empire. John returned to France to raise the ransom money while his relatives, including his second son Louis, were bound on their honour to stay in England. With John's departure however, they took the opportunity to escape back to France. The honourable John, mortified by this stain on French honour, returned himself as prisoner and there remained until his death in 1364, greatly honoured by the English.

In 1358 a peasant revolt in France called the Jacquerie broke out. It was caused by the suffering and deprivation of the English wars, plus hatred of the nobility and resulted in much destruction of property and atrocities against their rulers. King Edward, looking to use this uprising for his own purposes ,invaded France and even though no formally arrayed French force opposed him, was unable to take Paris or Rheims from the Dauphin, who, in his fathers absence was attempting to rebuild the French army and its tactics. The Treaty of Bretigny was signed in 1360 in which Edward gave up his claim to the French crown, plus his claims to Normandy,Brittany,Touraine, Anjou and Maine, in return for the lands of Guinne, Gascony, Poitou, Santonge, Perigord, Limousin, Quercy, Ponthieu and other areas bordering Aquitaine. He also kept Calais together with a payment of 3 million crowns. This treaty marked the end of the first phase of the Hundred Years War. It is interesting to note that between the years of 1357 to 1360 Edward, no doubt fearing that the French might copy the English practice of archery, banned the export of longbows and arrows. Archers were also forbidden to leave England without a Royal license.

From this high point in Edward's fortunes, great victories, territorial gains with ransom monies and a united kingdom, things started to go wrong and he began to lapse into mental and physical decline, withdrawing into himself. He became attracted to, and then besotted by, Alice Perrers, a lady in waiting who began to hold an increasing influence on the ageing king. Promoting her own and her family interests over those of the nobility and Parliament, she ruthlessly exploited her position to her advantage at a time when the country desperately needed cohesion. The growing influence of Parliament, now for the first time with a Speaker of the Commons, the conflict with the church over taxes and Papal influence, the growing power of the French King Charles V threatening all that had been gained in France ,split the English in two factions, the Clerical party of William Wykham supported by the Black Prince. Now returned to England to recover from the illness that had struck him during his campaigning in Spain, and the Court party led by Alice and abetted by the Black Prince's brother, John of Gaunt.

Realizing that he would not live to succeed his father and to ensure the succession of his son Richard, the Prince threw his influence behind the Clerical party and against his brother Gaunt. Under perrer's influence, Edward dismissed his Clerical Council in 1371 leaving the only real power in the hands of his mistress with her sole access to the king.

By 1374 Edward had lost nearly all the territories that he had fought so hard to gain in France except for Calais, Bordeaux and Bayonne. The situation worsened in England until, in 1376, the so called Good Parliament impeached Lord Latimer the Chancellor and his financial agent John Lyons, who were both imprisoned, with Alice Perrers being banished from court despite Edward pleading by letter for her to be treated gently. The death of Edward, the Black Prince in that year was a great blow to the Commons and enabled John of Gaunt, now the senior royal to recall the impeached ministers and also Alice Perrers. Without proper leadership and lacking the victories of earlier years, factioneering and intrigue reigned, the opposing parties of John of Gaunt with John Wyclife and the clerics led by William of Wyckham struggling to maintain stability while Edward drifted further into senility at Sheen, finally dying on 21st June 1377. His death mask shows his mouth twisted from a facial paralysis, probably following a stroke resulting in cerebral thrombosis. He died with only a local priest to comfort him and it is said that Alice Perrers, at the last, stripped the rings from his fingers .He is buried alongside his wife in Westminster Abbey

The Black Prince

Edward, known to history as The Black Prince, was born to King Edward 111 of England and his wife Philippa of Hainault at the Palace of Woodstock on June 15th 1330.There is some dispute concerning the origin of this title, but the current view is that the name was given to him some time later by French historians through his reputation for merciless aggression in war.

His doting father bestowed many honours on him from the start. At the age of three he was created the Earl of Chester, at seven, the first Duke of Cornwall and in 1343, Prince of Wales. He was to become the outstanding soldier of his age and, like his father, revelled in hunting, jousting and gambling, he was known to have had numerous love affairs and fathered several children during their course. Although outlived by his father, and never becoming king, he achieved through his military prowess fame greater than any king of his time. To the people he reflected all the virtues of military and chivalric ideals of his age. His father wished him to be a founder knight of the Order of the Garter, but as the Prince was still only fourteen at the founding, his father waited until the boy was old enough to be armed and thereby qualify for membership. The occasion presented itself when the Prince accompanied his father on the expedition to France in 1346 and was knighted at La Hogue on 12th July 1346. He commanded the right wing of the royal army at the battle of Crecy and distinguished himself in the very close fighting, when his father, refusing a request for support, said "let him win his spurs".

It was in this campaign that the Prince learned the value of strong leadership from his father as well as the overwhelming power of the longbow against armoured cavalry and slower firing crossbows and was to use this knowledge in his great victory at Poitiers.

The vast estates and titles bestowed on him in his youth made him a very rich man and his court was renown for it's brilliance and luxury, both in

Aquitaine, his London home on the Thames at Candlewick Street as well as his country residences at Wallingford and Kennington .For all this he was still a warrior, highly regarded for his prowess in arms as well as his military leadership. In 1361 he married Joan "the Fair Maid of Kent" a renowned beauty who, legend has it, was the lady who dropped her garter in Calais in front of King Edward, prompting the King to remark "evil to him who evil thinks".

Joan had led an interesting life; she was a daughter of Edmund of Woodstock 1st Earl of Kent, a half brother of King Edward 11. When the old King was deposed by Queen Isabella and Roger Mortimer, the Earl was executed. At the age of twelve, Joan went through a form of marriage with Thomas Holland, but while he was away on crusade her family forced her into marriage with William Montecute, Earl of Salisbury and Joan moved into high society. When Holland returned he appealed to the Pope for the return of his wife and when Montacute discovered that Joan supported Holland's case, he kept her virtual prisoner in her home. In 1349 the Pope annulled her marriage to Montacute and she returned to Holland and remained with him until his death in 1360, bearing him four children during the period. Joan had inherited the earldom of Kent when her brother died in 1353 and now at thirty two she was rich and beautiful. The Black Prince had been in love with her for years and was determined to marry her notwithstanding that they were cousins, even the Archbishop of Canterbury cast doubt on the legitimacy of any children they might have, due to her former husband Montacute still being alive.Furthermore, the King hoped that Edward would make a match with someone of royal stock and thereby extend his family's influence and estates. The Prince appealed to the Pope and with an assurance of absolution from him, they were married in October 1361. The family traveled to France where the Prince took up his duties as Prince of Aquitaine, ruler of this vast area of France on his father's behalf. Joan was a devoted wife and bore the Prince two children Edward and Richard. Edward was to die at the age of six and Richard was to succeed his grandfather as Richard 11. The Prince set up his court in Bordeaux and despite some factioneering among the Gascon nobles, ruled the principality justly. For a man of action the life was however stilting and when a request was received from Pedro "the Cruel" King of

Castile for help in regaining his throne from which he had been deposed by his half brother Henry of Trastamara with the help of the French Constable Bertrand du Guesclin, the Prince jumped at the prospect of action announcing" it is not right that a bastard should be king, nor should men agree to the disinheriting of a rightful heir"

Prince Edward collected an army from his provinces and his brother John of Gaunt came from England with 400 knights and a large number of archers. The King of Majorca sent troops and he also hired the services of some of the "Free Companies" that roamed France after the first phase of the Anglo French wars. In February 1367 Edward crossed the Pyrenees at Logrono and learned that a force of some 25,000 under Trastamara was only a short distance away. The usurper had arrayed his army with its back to the River Najarilla which was an unusual deployment. However,Trastamara was a good soldier and with the experienced du Guesclin with him, must have known what he was doing. It is presumed that he felt that with his superior numbers of cavalry, the flat plain in front of the river gave him an advantage. Both sides split their forces into the customary three lines.

Trastamara's front line being headed by du Guesclin himself with 1500 picked men at arms and 500 crossbowmen. To oppose this, Edward put his brother John with 3000 infantry and 3000 archers. Trastamara's second line was two flanking forces of cavalry with himself in the centre supported by 1500 of the cream of his heavy cavalry. Edward led his second line with Pedro together with 2,000 infantry and the same number of archers. Flanking him with similar numbers were the Gascon Captal de Buch and Sir Thomas Percy.Trastamara's third line consisted of some 20,000 infantry while Edward's last section was led by the King of Majorca and Count Armagnac with a force of 3,000 infantry and the same number of archers. In all three of Edward's divisions the men at arms were drawn up in the centre with the archers on either flank. As soon as his forces were in position. Edward ordered his entire army to dismount and sent the horses to the rear.Du Guesclin led his force forward and smashed into John ofGaunt's leading division, the English archers dispersed the crossbowmen, but once the battle started, could contribute little. Gaunt and du Guesclin's forces remained locked in vicious hand to hand fighting for the remainder of the battle. The Spanish flanking cavalry then charged the the wings of Edward's forces who were led by Captal de Buch and Sir Thomas Percy. Such a charge is normally successful against infantry or slow loading crossbows but the Spanish, making the same mistake as the French, did not reckon on the power of the longbow which did the usual job of reducing the charges to shambles. Shocked and surprised, the Spanish cavalry drew back to reform still under the hail of arrows and sufferered still more heavily. The remainder of the Spanish cavalry made a charge but never even reached the enemy lines before being cut down by the arrow storm. The surviving cavalry, now totally demoralized, wheeled about and fled the field leaving their comrades to their fate.

On command of Prince Edward, the flanking forces of Captal de Buch and Sir Thomas Percy now moved forward and joined forces behind the Spanish still fighting in the centre. The men at arms now turned inwards to take du Guesclin's forces in the rear, while the archers faced out against the inevitable counter attack from the remainder of Trastamara's troops. It was not long in coming, three times Trastamara's heavy cavalry charged and each time was beaten back by the firepower of the archers. Sensing the moment, Edward ordered his central division forward to increase the pressure on du Guesclin and seeing this,Trastamara ordered forward his infantry mass. Despite the enemy's superior numbers the archers waited calmly until they came in range and loosed salvo after salvo. This was enough for Trastamara's foot soldiers and they faltered and then fled, their only escape being over the one bridge spanning the River Najarilla. They were swiftly pursued and many were cut down trying to cross the narrow bridge while many others drowned trying to swim for their lives.Trastamara escaped while the brave du Guesclin only surrendered when he realized that he had been deserted. The English had to protect their Spanish captives from the mercies of Pedro looking for cruel revenge although Pedro did begin his usual bloodbaths against his enemies once restored to his throne. His reign did not last long however,Trastamara raised a fresh army and on 13th March 1369 defeated and killed Pedro at Montiel.

Prince Edward was rewarded by Pedro with gifts and lands including the Lordship of Biscay. A rebellion had flared in Aquitaine in his absence and he hurried to return to the principality but seems to have picked up some malady on his campaign and his health was suffering. The costs of the campaign had been high and the Prince lost no time in raising taxes in the principality. Many of the Gascon nobles led by Jean d'Armagnac and Lord d'Albret objected to these demands and soon were appealing to the French King Charles V in open defiance to Prince Edward. Charles relished the prospect of stirring up trouble between Edward and his nobles and, in 1369, duly sent his Seneschal to Bordeaux to demand Edward's appearance at the French court. Edward promptly threw the Seneschal in prison. The situation worsened and war was again declared between England and France on 2nd May 1369. Edward's health continued to decline and he pursued his campaign carried on a litter, his forces being ably commanded by Sir John Chandos until he was killed at Poitou in January 1370.

Taking heart from the disaffection shown by others, many more towns declared their loyalty to Charles V infuriating Edward who, to set an example, had the entire population of Limoges massacred when they also attempted to defect, thus illustrating again the mindset of medieval who ruled the massacre a legitimate act of war. John of Gaunt was sent from England to take command of royal forces in France, but was more concerned with pressing his claim for the throne of Castile following his marriage to the Princess Constanza than regaining English royal possessions in France. In January 1371, Edward, now severely ill, returned with his wife and remaining son Richard to England and two months later, surrendered his French principality into his father's hands. Sickness and the death of his eldest son had taken all the fight from him and by 1374 most of the English empire in France was back in the hands of Charles V. Bedridden with dysentery, cirrhosis or syphilis Edward attempted to play some part in England's affairs by supporting the Clerical party against the Court party of Alice Perrers and brother John in a bid to ensure the succession of his son Richard. His support of the so called "Good Parliament" of 1376 resulted in the downfall of Alice Perrers and Gaunt's dismissal. He demanded and received from Gaunt and the ageing Edward their sworn word to recognize his son Richard as the next King. It is a mark of the Black Prince's high standing that Parliament also formally recognized the succession. Becoming progressively weaker, he lingered on until 1376, when, after making his will in the Great Chamber at Westminster on 7th June, he died the following day. The chronicler Knighton wrote," thus died the hope of the English for while he lived they feared no invasion of the enemy or onslaught of battle". While Froissart declared him "the flower of English chivalry of the entire world" He was embalmed and lay in state at Westminster for the next four months until the meeting of Parliament at Michaelmas in order that he might be buried with greater solemnity in the great Cathedral at Canterbury.

Richard 11

Richard was born in Bordeaux on 6th January 1367, the second son of Prince Edward of Woodstock (the Black Prince) and Joan of Kent. The first four years of his life were spent in the opulence of his father's Aquitaine Duchy where he was educated in the European style. His first language was French but he also learned English, the language that was rapidly becoming the tongue of English nobility.

The declining health of his father resulted in the family returning to England in 1371 and the control of the Duchy being handed back to King Edward. He continued his education under Simon Burley, his father's chamberlain who became vice chamberlain to the young king during his minority. Following the death of his father in 1376 and of his grandfather in 1377, Richard inherited the throne on June 22nd 1377 and was crowned on July 16th of that year at the age of 10.His coronation was such an arduous affair that the young king had to be carried on the shoulders of his tutor to the palace for a nap before the coronation banquet that was to end a day of mass, prayer, sermon, anointing, arming, enthronement and presentation to the people. He was the inheritor of a great military dynasty with titles and estates in England,Ireland,France and Wales. Despite the continuing Hundred Years War, the kingdom was financially sound, the army, through its victories at Crecy and Poitiers.was universally respected. Managed and equipped and his royal authority extended throughout his lands via his sheriffs and local nobility.

The powers of Parliament had grown considerably during his grandfather's reign and it was they who selected a council to rule during his minority. It is unfortunate that no Regency was declared following the death of his grandfather, the result being that ,although government was at first conducted on Richard's behalf by his council and ministers while he himself lived with his mother, no formal decision was ever made regarding the date that he would take over personally.Richard,already in possession of a personal seal, was soon making his wishes felt and by the age of 14 had dismissed his chancellor for failing to obey his commands and at 16 was telling parliament that the choice of ministers was his alone.

 This council had specifically excluded the young king's uncle John of Gaunt Duke of Lancaster and the resulting split of interests between Gaunt, the council and parliament greatly disorganized the government of the kingdom and was made worse by the precocious temper, outbursts of rage and impulsive actions of the young king. Gaunt was by far the most powerful and influential figure of Richard's reign and his forces easily outnumbered those of the crown. He was seen by some to be a potential rival for Richard's throne which is why he was excluded from council although his words and actions were almost always in clear support of the king. Through his portraits we know Richard to have been a tall handsome man, well educated and with an enquiring mind. A contempory description of him states "his hair yellowish, his face fair and rosy", it goes on "extravagantly splendid in his entertainment and dress, timid as to war,hauty and too much devoted to voluptuousness". Many of the political crises in his early reign can be put down to his immaturity and an inflated sense of his royal state, plus his refusal to accept that his rule should be by consent and in partnership with parliament and the nobility. He is said to have started the use of handkerchiefs in England and also the use of spoons.
 He had a love of stylish clothing and fine architecture and commissioned much new works in the minsters of York, Canterbury and the beautiful hammer beam roof in the Great Hall at Westminster. The downside to his character was his belief in his divine right to rule plus a degree of self obsession. Impressed by the images and symbols of authority he sought to raise his position above the constraints of his parliament and surrounding himself with sycophantic followers including Burley,de Vere and Aumerle on whom he would shower gifts of land and titles, revelling in their praises. He was the first king to employ a full time uniformed

bodyguard of Cheshire bowmen who wore the king's symbol of the White Hart and who guarded him at all times.

The first real test of his authority came in 1381 when following the ravages of the Black Death and the imposition of the Poll Tax by the king's chancellor Sudbury which due to its demand of the same payment from all men irrespective of their position, fell most heavily on the poor, the common people rose in what is now called the Peasant's Revolt. An earlier version of the tax had been responsible for the removal of the king's former chancellor Scrope .This tax of three groats (about one shilling) from every person on the tax register was a huge burden to the peasants and when, in May 1381, a tax collector arrived at the village of Fobbing in Essex demanding payment, he was thrown out. Troops were then sent but they too were routed. The villagers were soon joined by others and began a march on London to demand that the king rescind the tax. A similar uprising in Kent, incited by local clerics Jack Straw, John Wrawe and John Ball, led by a certain Wat Tyler attacked Canterbury on 7th June and freed the prisoners in Maidstone jail before heading for London.

Meanwhile other villagers in Kent and Surrey had also revolted and and marched on London where the local people opened the gates and admitted them. The rebels attacked the offices of the treasury and burned the tax registers. On the12th, a mob takes five Flemish whores and thirty five other Flemings and beheads them at St Martins-in-the –Vintry. On the 13th, Richard sails by barge to meet the rebels at Blackheath, but his Chancellor and his Treasurer advice against it. Some verbal exchanges are made between boat and shore and the barge returns to the tower. The mob open Marshalsea prison, force the keeper of London Bridge to lower the span and frees prisoners from Fleet jail. That night Richard addresses a mob on Tower Hill and offers them pardon if they go home. He is ignored and a meeting is agreed at Mile End for the next day. Although the people of London had originally welcomed them, by mid June all discipline had broken down and the rebels took to drink and to looting despite the pleas of their leader Wat Tyler. On June 14th the young king met with the rebels at Mile End where they demanded. Among other things, free labour contracts and that rent for land should be frozen at 4p an acre. The king promised them that all would be put right if they were to go home. Some did, but others returned to the city where they murdered the Archbishop and the Treasurer with an axe on Tower Hill. Richard spent the night in hiding in fear of his life. On June 15th a mob drags Richard Imworth, governor of Marshalsea prison from St Edward's chapel and beheads him at Cheapside, Richard again meets with the rebels at Smithfield who listed their demands which included that there should be" no seignory except the king" and "that there should be no serf in England" During this meeting the Mayor of London William Walworth attacked and killed Wat Tyler. The young king, showing a brief flash of his ancestry, then rode bravely into the mob and shouted "Sirs, would you kill your king? I am your captain and your leader". He promised that all grievances would be addressed and ordered them to disperse. By the end of summer the revolt was over and the ringleaders hanged. Richard reneged on his promises stating that they were made under duress. The poll tax was withdrawn but the peasants were forced back under the control of the local nobility.

In January 1382 he married Anne of Bohemia, the daughter of the late Emperor Charles IV and sister of King Wenzel of Bohemia, who, although impoverished, was thought to be a good dynastic match. Richard was said to have made a loan to Wenzel of some £15000, greatly displeasing many of his subjects. The marriage was a happy one however and although childless, never persuaded Richard to to look elsewhere despite his desire for offspring to continue the Plantagenet line. The couple made a number of royal progresses in the first years of their marriage and the queen became much loved by the people.

Meanwhile, in the north, the Scots had again started to harry the border country aided by the French who also threatened the south coast with their fleet. For the last time in the middle ages, the feudal levy was summoned and Richard led an army of some 14000 to invade Scotland. The Scots knew enough not to tackle an English army head on and wisely withdrew to the hills leaving Richard to burn the abbeys and towns of the border and return to England. Parliament demanded reforms and refused to pay the royal debts. The French meanwhile, raised an army of 30000 men to invade England, but ran out of money and the plan was abandoned, while in Brittanny,English forces on chevauchee in the Duchy had received no pay for over six months The royal court was renown for its lavish entertainments and the richness and opulence of the king and his retinue. All this cost money and parliament was becoming increasingly worried at the king's profligate lifestyle. In 1386 an alliance of the Commons and key lords in parliament investigated the royal finances and in the "Wonderful Parliament", put the Duke of Gloucester in control. Expenditure was cut and grants to the king's favourites were reduced, badly undermining the king's authority.Humiliated, he left London for one of his Progresses around the country, seeking advice from various leading judges that were sympathetic to the royal cause. Unsurprisingly they concluded that it was treason to limit the royal power and, more seriously, only the king could choose ministers or dissolve parliament and that only he could determine its business. Thus empowered Richard now charged his more powerful opponents, known as the Apellant Lords, with treason .These lords now moved against the king claiming to be acting in the interests of the crown. These Apellants represented the traditional noble houses that had been scorned by the young King,

Thomas, DukeofGloucester, Thomas,Earlof Warwick, Richard,Earl of Arundel, Thomas,Earl of Nottingham and Henry,Earl of Derby (the son of Gaunt).Matters came to a head when Robert de Vere,Earl of Oxford and a confidante of the king, raised a force of Cheshire troops and met with the Apellants at Radcot Bridge on 19th December where de Vere was killed and his force destroyed. The Apellants rode to London and met with Richard at the Tower. The king was temporarily imprisoned and his leading councilors tried and executed, among them his favourite,Burley despite personal pleas from both the king and the queen. Richard was never to forget this humiliation.

The Apellants now controlled the government but were failing to unite the various factions. The situation was worsening when in late 1388,the Scots under Sir Archibald Douglas attacked Carlisle while James, the Earl of Douglas led a raiding force of 2300 men into Northumberland the territory of the powerful Percy family. The Earl of Northumberland sent his sons Sir Henry Percy (known as Hotspur) and Ralph Percy to block the Scots at Newcastle. During some skirmishing at Newcastle, James Douglas snatched Hotspur's lance pennon and displayed it in front of his tent as a mocking taunt. When Hotspur vowed to recover it,Douglas taunted him and offered him battle at Otterburn where Hotspur could try to recover it.

Douglas did indeed make camp at Otterburn on the night of 19th August 1388 and was found by Hotspur. The English crept into the sleeping camp and set fire to the tents, killing all who opposed them. Unfortunately the attack had been launched at the part of the camp occupied by the baggage train and not the rich pavilions of the knights and the noise had aroused Douglas and his men at arms who charged at the attackers. A witness talks of Douglas "taking his axe in both hands he entered into the press that none durst approach near him". The brave Douglas was finally killed with three spear thrusts and seeing this, his kinsmen hid his body beneath a bush so as not to dishearten his forces. When the battle was finally won by the Scots and Hotspur taken prisoner, the Englishman was told to surrender his sword to the bush wherein Douglas laid, an event later recorded as "the surrender to a dead man"

The Appellant Lords meanwhile were finding government no easy task and their financial reforms made little difference. Attacks on France led to failure and the commons were becoming disillusioned and Richard's popularity increased. The defection to Richard of two of the chief Appellants, the Earls of Nottingham and Derby in 1389 strengthened the king's hand sufficiently to enable him to declare his own majority and to resume his rule. Speaking before the council at Westminster, he demanded to be given back the reigns of power and insisted upon his right to appoint his own advisors. Their surprising agreement was probably based on the poor performance of the alternative. Gaunt returned to add his weight to Richard's cause and the remaining Appellants were removed from office being replaced by eight new Appellants loyal to the king.

Richard, now in full control lost no time in paying back what he saw as the insults and indignities that had been heaped on him. Injured pride, a desire for vengeance and vindication of his past conduct led him to imprison opponents without trial, to take out loans that he would not repay and to force his richer subjects to buy pardons for their alleged failure to aid the king against the Appellants and to sign so called blank charters, simply fabricated confessions that could be brought out and used at any time that Richard wished and that placed people and goods at his mercy. He further alienated support when, following a dispute between royal officers and London citizens, he suspended the city's liberties and charters and replaced the mayor and sheriffs. A secret list of fifty names was compiled of the people that Richard suspected of treason, clearly designed to make any potential rebel feel vulnerable. One name on the list was deliberately leaked, that of Thomas Arundel, Archbishop of Canterbury, seen by Richard as a particular enemy.

In 1394 he resolved to bring the rebellious Irish to heel and landed a large army at Waterford in October of that year. Ireland had long been a thorn in the side of the English royalty. Successive settlement by the Normans, Scots and the English themselves had not produced the desired effect of pacification. The settlers went native, adopting Irish speech and customs and refusing to acknowledge the authority of the crown. Only an area around Dublin known as the Pale was under royal control. Richard's campaign was successful and he received the homage and submission of eighty Irish chieftans, When Richard sailed for home he left Ireland under the control of de Mortimer whose high handed rule resulted in another rebellion in which de Mortimer was killed and all gains lost. To make matters worse, Richard's faithful wife Anne died from plague and being denied her moderating influence, he again surrounded himself with favourites who would defer to his wishes.

Richard's desire for revenge continued at the parliament of 17th September 1397 when the so called "appeals" by some of the original Appellants were heard. Gloucester did not attend as he was already dead, murdered it was rumoured , by Richard. A further hearing was convened on 20th October where the Earl of Arundel was pronounced guilty of treason and was duly beheaded on Tower Hill and the Archbishop was banished. Richard rewarded his supporters with great gifts and created five new Dukedoms, among them Hereford, given to Henry Bolingbroke the Earl of Derby and Norfolk, given to the Thomas Mowbray, Earl of Nottingham, thus wiping out the tradition set by Edward 111 that Dukedoms should be the sole prerogative of the sons of monarchs. When these two quarreled in 1398 after being accused of disloyalty by some nobles seeking to gain the king's favour, it was decided that the matter must be settled by combat and Gosford Green in Coventry was selected for the venue. Richard however, was aware of the frailty of his position; he was 30 years old with no heir. He had recently married the seven year old Princess Isabella of France and it would be a considerable time before she would be capable of motherhood. He was greatly disliked and there where two strong contenders for the throne, Hereford through his father Gaunt, the brother of Edward 111 and Mortimer Earl of March through his mother Phillipa,granddaughter of Edward 111 by his second son Lionel, Duke of Clarence.

Richard realized that whatever the outcome of the Duke's fight it would split the nobility. He therefore banned the contest and in a typical manner, exiled both combatants, Norfolk for life and Hereford for ten years. Norfolk went on a pilgrimage to Jerusalem and on his return, died in Venice of plague. Hereford was invited as a guest to the court of the French king Charles.

When Gaunt died in 1399, after a lifetime of loyalty to Richard, the king disinherited the exiled Hereford of his father's estates, sharing the vasts estates out among his favourites and extending Henry's banishment from ten years to life. This outraged all nobility. The right of inheritance was fundamental to their way of life. If Richard could do this to a mighty Duke, could he not easily do the same to them? At this time of growing unrest Richard decided to take a force to Ireland to crush the rebels. Earl Henry chose the time of Richard's absence to return to England, landing at Ravenspur in Yorkshire with a small force on July 4th 1399, ostensibly to claim his inheritance, but soon to claim the throne itself. His half brother Ralph Neville, Earl of Westmorland joined him and began a march southwards gathering support as they went and even the Duke of York who had been left in charge in Richard's absence declared for Bolingbroke. Richard, hearing of this and rapidly becoming friendless, hastened to return to England, finally crossing to Milford Haven from Waterford and on to Conway castle. It was here that he met the Earl of Northumberland, head of the powerful Percy clan who had joined Earl Henry's cause and Thomas Arundel the supposedly exiled Archbishop of Canterbury.

Northumberland promised that the king's position would be respected and guaranteed safe conduct to Flint Castle where he was to meet the Henry. Why Richard chose to believe the promises made by the pair is difficult to understand. Perhaps it was due to his continuing belief in his own sanctity and the knowledge that he had bided his time before and eventually triumphed over his enemies. Richard was ambushed on the way however and passed into Henry's custody at Flint Castle from where he was taken, disguised as a friar and lodged in the Tower following an abortive attempt at rescue by the royal bodyguard and a demand that he be executed forthwith from a deputation of London Aldermen who had rode out to meet the party, a demand refused by Henry who declared that Parliament must decide the king's fate.

Earl Henry was aware that Richard, even in captivity, remained a threat to his bid for the throne. The king was fit and healthy and only 32 years old. If allowed to live he might well sire children who would look to regain their right to the crown. A ministerial Committee was established to examine Henry Bolingbroke's claim to the throne as a grandson of Edward 111... The committee agreed that he had a right through default and by conquest, but not by rightful inheritance. The rightful heir, should Richard have no children, was Roger Mortimer through his mother Phillipa, daughter of Lionel Duke of Clarence, second son of Edward 111. Henry tried to argue that Richard's claim to the throne was spurious because Edward 111 had had another son before the Black Prince, but had been born severely deformed. This was not substantiated and further weakened Bolingbrokes claim.

The Earl realized that Richard must be done away with and he was then taken from the Tower of London disguised as a simple forester and on to Leeds castle in Kent. From there he was taken north where Henry's main support was based. He was imprisoned in Pontefract castle where he died on 14th February 1400.There is some mystery surrounding his death.Shakespear has him struck on the head with a poleaxe by Exton the governor of Pontefract, but no wounds were apparent when his body was paraded through the country by Henry. Another tale has him being starved to death but again, his body did not appear emaciated. He is said to have taken 10 days to die and this would indicate poisoning, probably by toadstools, a popular method of the time. The death cap toadstool could be chopped and hidden in food, causing death in the right time span .Henry, aware that any suggestion of his implication in Richard's death could lose him the crown, arranged an elaborate funeral with Richard's embalmed body in an open coffin for all to see, carried from Pontefract to London on a horse drawn carriage with banners of St George and Richard's patron saint St Edward the Confessor at each corner and escorted by torch bearers to St Pauls Cathedral where it was to lay in state for two days.

Richard was buried in the Priory of Kings Langly, probably chosen because of it being the burial place of his brother Edward. On the accession of Henry V, the body was reburied in a grand bronze tomb in Westminster Abbey. Henry V was reputed to be very fond of Richard having spent much of his childhood at court. The tomb was not strongly built and over time the side plates became loose enabling visitors to see the exposed bones. Some of these, including the jawbone were stolen. In 1880 the missing bones were returned and the tomb repaired and sealed.

With Richard's death, the Plantagenet line that had ruled for so long was ended and Henry IV became the first of the Lancastrians.

Henry 1V

Henry was born at Bolingbroke castle in Lincolnshire on April 4th 1366, the eldest son of John of Gaunt and Blanche Plantagenet, heiress to the Duke of Lancaster.

He grew up amid the power and trappings of the mighty house of Lancaster and was clearly destined for high office. He was first cousin and childhood playmate to Richard 11, both being admitted to the Order of the Garter together in 1377. He was 5 feet 10 inches tall, powerfully built and had a love for jousting and the arts of war. His first real jousting contest took place when he was only sixteen and by 1386 he was winning tournaments and in 1390 establishing himself a reputation in Europe at the jousts at St Inglevert in Calais.

In July 1380 he married the Duke of Hereford's daughter Mary de Bohun with whom he was to have five sons and two daughters, The first, Edward, dying in infancy, Henry who was to succeed his father as king, Thomas, Duke of Clarence, John, Duke of Bedford, Humphry Duke of Gloucester, plus Blanche and Philippa. Mary herself died on 4th June 1394 while giving birth to her last daughter.

The circumstances leading to Henry's seizing of the throne began with the high handed Richard surrounding himself with favourites and failing to listen to the advice of his traditional mentors. The loss of Flanders and the attempts to secure peace with France, plus the parlous state of the king's finances and his demands that they be covered by parliament were the final straw and parliament, supported by members of the Lords demanded reforms and the sacking of the king's chancellor de la Pole. Parliament set out to examine the king's finances and put his uncle the Duke of Gloucester in charge of cutting expenditure and blocking grants to favourites. Richard left London humiliated and angry. He sought advice from sympathetic judges who unsurprisingly confirmed his belief that no minister could be impeached without royal approval and that only he could choose ministers and suspend parliament. So empowered, Richard charged his opponents with treason, leaving them little choice but to submit or oppose. The ringleaders in this opposition to Richard were the so called Appellant Lords, comprising Thomas Duke of Gloucester ,the ringleader,Richard,Earl of Arundel, Thomas, Earl of Warwick, Thomas, Earl of Nottingham and the son of the mighty John of Gaunt, Henry Earl of Derby, all claiming to be acting in the interests of the crown and good government.

In late 1387 matters came to a head when de Vere, a favourite of Richard's, raised the men of Cheshire in revolt against the Appellants, but was soundly defeated in battle at Radcote Bridge. The Lords marched on London and temporarily removed Richard from the throne while they tried his leading councilors in what became known as the Merciless Parliament of February 1388. The king's advisors, Nicholas Bembre, and Robert Tresilian, the Chief Justice being charged with "living in vice...deluding the said king...embracing the mammon of iniquity" were hanged at Tyburn immediately.de la Pole escaped into exile while his favourites, Simon Burly, John Beauchamp, James Baret and John Salisbury were tried, found guilty, hanged and beheaded, despite pleas for clemency from Richard, his wife and surprisingly, Henry of Derby.

The Appellants were now in full control of the country but failed to make any serious improvements. The Scots invading the north under the Earl of Douglas and the failed attempts to pursue the French campaigns, plus some disastrous attempts at financial reforms further isolated the Appellants and hastened the drift back to support for Richard who, in 1389,being 22 years old, declared his own majority and resumed his rule aided by the defection to his camp of two of the prime movers in the Appellants ranks, Nottingham and Derby He set out to seek revenge on many who had supported the Appellants, imprisoning many without trial and extorting fines from estates. Henry obviously thought this an ideal time to be somewhere else and traveled to Europe where he was well received. His hosts being most impressed with his handsome appearance, prowess and chivalry. Froissart describes him as "an amiable knight, courteous and pleasant to all".

In 1390 he traveled to Prussia and took part in the storming of Vilnya in Lithuania with the Teutonic Knights and in 1392 went on pilgrimage through Europe and Italy to the Holy Land. Henry's marriage to Mary de Bohun heiress to the earldoms of Essex, Hereford and Nottingham, plus his own considerable estates as Earl of Derby, made him a wealthy man able to dress richly and live in high luxury, but this did not prevent him from being a very grasping landlord to his tenants. Mary died in 1394 and three years later he was granted the title of the Duke if Hereford by Richard as a reward it is thought for his original support of the king in the Duke of Gloucester's uprising and for his attempt to intercede in the execution of Burley. It was also a good way of ensuring Henry's loyalty in any future schism. Henry's co conspirator, Thomas Mowbray Earl of Nottingham was similarly rewarded with the Dukedom of Norfolk and it was while these two were out riding one day that Norfolk told Henry of rumours being circulated in baronial circles to the effect that Henry was plotting to overthrow the king. The impetuous but loyal Henry brought these allegations direct to the king and in turn accused Mowbray of treason. Richard decided that the matter should be settled by trial by combat and the meeting was arranged at Gosford Green in Coventry. Richard however, began to have second thoughts. On the one hand was the son of Gaunt, the greatest and most powerful magnate in the land and on the other was Thomas Mowbray, Earl Marshal of England. Both had their supporters and he knew that whatever the outcome of the fight, the ensuing turmoil could only further destabilize his own rather shaky position. He therefore cancelled the contest moments before the fight was about to begin and imposed his own punishment on the two men. Mowbray would be banished for life and Henry would be exiled for ten years. Richard had finally got revenge for the two's support of Gloucester in the Merciless Parliament. Mowbray travelled on pilgrimage to Jerusalem and died in Venice within a year, Hereford became a guest of the French King Charles at the French court where he was much admired for his chivalry and charm.

Richard became increasingly isolated, conferring only with his favourites and becoming cold and distant with other members of his council. He was protected at all times by his Cheshire archers who, due to their closeness to the king, saw themselves as beyond normal laws and pillaged, raped and burnt without constraint and became feared and loathed by all.

In February 1399, John of Gaunt, Duke of Lancaster died and Richard made the fateful decision to disinherit Henry of his father's estates and to grant them to royal favourites. He also extended Henry's banishment from ten years to life. This was seen as the last straw by many in England. Richard's tyranny had finally gone too far. Inheritance was seen as the bedrock of society and now no man was safe. Henry found an able ally in Thomas Arundel, Archbishop of Canterbury who himself had been exiled by Richard and the two became a focus for many of the discontented English barons including the powerful Percy family and the old retainers of Lancaster all seeking to rid England of the hated Richard.

Henry decided that he was released from all allegiance to Richard and it was probably about this time that he resolved to return to England to "claim his own" although he must have known that any such invasion could never be undertaken for so limited a purpose. It was at this time that Richard decided to make another expedition to Ireland, an odd decision in view of the mood in the country. The king's uncle, Edward Langly, Duke of York was left in charge of England and had consolidated his available forces in the south of the country in anticipation of any attack from Henry which illustrates the belief in England that the exile would return.

The country was awash with rumours with many people believing that only Henry could put right the wrongs that Richard and his hated government had imposed on the country. Henry landed with a small force at Ravenspur in Yorkshire in July 1399 within easy march of his old Lancastrian estates and soon men of all ranks were flocking to his banner. Henry clung to his statement that he only wished to regain that which was his, while shrewdly allowing his followers to promote the popular tide of opinion that Richard must be deposed. He must have known however, that having defied the king's orders, his head could never be safe while Richard lived and probably suited him well to display a reluctance to seek the crown while at the same time bowing to the strident demands of his followers. The Duke of York. Also with an eye on the main chance, did not oppose Henry while he still had the power to do so, probably realizing that Henry was the one person who could perhaps achieve the political reforms so badly needed. The old

Duke chose his moment and declared for Henry and the recruitment of the sole surviving son of Edward 111 added much weight to Henry's later claim to the throne.

Richard meanwhile ,delayed by bad weather, finally landed back in Wales and failing in his attempt to raise forces to oppose the rebels, took refuge in Conway Castle and sent his half brother and nephew the Dukes of Exeter and Surrey to negotiate terms with Henry. These two were promptly thrown in prison and envoys being considered sacrosanct, illustrates how strong Henry felt his position to be. He did need to tread carefully however, if he claimed the crown by right of conquest then all property would revert to him as conqueror and the danger to rights and property was one of the reasons that men had risen against Richard in the first place. Henry also considered claiming his right to rule through his ancestor Edmund Crouchback who, according to legend was passed over for kingship due to his many disabilities in favour of Edward 1st. This claim, apart from being unbelievable, would also put the House of Lancaster in constant danger of upheaval and warfare when all men sought peace and stability. The best course would be to persuade Richard to abdicate. There was a precedent for this from the deposition of Edward 111 in favour of his son in 1327, but the circumstances were very different. With Edward's abdication his rightful heir took over the throne but, should Richard abdicate, his rightful heir was Edmund Earl of March, the descendant of Edward 111s second son Lionel, Duke of Clarence who took precedence over Henry whose father was the third son of Edward.. Edmund was but 8 years old and the country had had enough of a boy king, the results of which, once he had grown up, had been disasterous.Henry was a well respected and popular choice, but had to tread warily. The uncertainty of the times had led to an increase in disorder and crime throughout the country and support could melt away as fast as it had grown. Parliament must be persuaded to accept a Deed of Abdication and Richard must be made to sign it. The clever mind of Thomas Arundel would get to work on parliament while, on the morning of 29th September 1399, 14 magnates led by Thomas Percy Earl of Northumberland and Ralph Neville Earl of Westmorland visited Richard and invited him to sign the Deed of Abdication, details

of which can be read in the Great Chronicles of London and which
starts "In the name of God Amen! I Richard by the Grace of God
Kyng of England and off Ffraunce and Lorde off Ireland,quyte and
assoyle Erchebysshopes,Byshopes,Dukes,Marquys,Barons,Lords and
alle my other liegemen both spyrituelle and secular ffrom her othe of
ffeute and homage,I resigne all my Kyngly Mageste,Dignitie and
Crowne".

The document had been very carefully prepared and contained a
number of admissions by Richard that he was unworthy to be King,
probably drafted by the clever Arundel and in words designed to help
Parliament in its historic decision. Richard can have been left in no
doubt that his life would be forfeit if he did not sign and also realized
that the only people that could guarantee his safety were Earl Henry
and Thomas Arundel. He confirmed that he would sign if the two
would visit him and they came that very afternoon and held a meeting
in private with Richard. We are told that Richard signed the Deed
"with gladde chere" probably after extracting a promise of his personal
safety. Richard removed his gold Signet Ring and handed it to Henry
as a sign that he wished Henry to be his chosen successor and armed
with the ring and the Deed, Henry and Arundel left.

Parliament was set to meet the next day September 30th and we can
only imagine the thoughts that were going through Henry's head the
night before. For the first time Parliament was to be asked to dethrone
an anointed king and to pass the crown to someone other than the
lawful heir. Furthermore, only the king could summon Parliament and
none of the attendees could have been under any illusion that Richard
had done this as a free agent. He was at that moment still king
however, a most important distinction as the rebels could rightfully
claim that the Parliament itself was lawfully summoned. The meeting
was faced with a number of questions. Was Parliament able to sit and
conduct business in the absence of the king? It was the royal
prerogative to set the agenda for all sittings and now the members
were faced with an empty throne. Did Parliament have the authority to
dethrone Richard? This was untried territory and many feared
punishment be it in this world or the next. Was the king not anointed
by God?

In the event, the whole business was completed on one day and indicates the amount of networking that Arundel and his allies had carried out prior to the session and the absence of any constitutional lawyers who had been deliberately excluded. Parliament decided that Richard's Deed of Abdication had absolved them of their oath of allegiance and that the meeting was not therefore treasonable.Furthermore,it was decided that Parliament owed its authority ,in the case of the Lords to the nobility of the land and in the case of the Commons to their elections. It was felt that they therefore had sufficient mandate from the nation and judged that where there was no law or precedent to deal with a question then Parliament was authorized to be the Supreme Lawmaker until such time as Parliament was once again properly constituted in its three elements of King, Lords and Commons. The Deed of Abdication was read out and approved, followed by a reading of some 32 charges against Richard showing the king in the worst possible light. The only voice to be raised against this was from Thomas Merks, Bishop of Carlisle but he was shouted down. Arundel then declared "We pronounce,discerne and declare the same Kynge Richard....to have be and yitte to be...vnsufficient and vnworthy to the Reule and gournenance of the fforsaid Rewmes and lordshippes....we pryve hym of all kyngley dignyte and worship".In the hush that followed, Henry rose to his feet and making the sign of the cross on his head and breast announced" In the name of Fadir,Son and Holy Gost,I Henry of Lancaster challenge the Rewme of Yngland and the corone with all the members that I am disendit be right of lyne of the blod coming from the gude lorde King Henry therde and throgthe that right that God of his grace hath sent with helpe of my kyn and of my frendes to recover". His supporters, no doubt primed for the occasion, shouted their approval and he was led to the royal chair and held up his hand showing the Golden Ring given to him by Richard, thus claiming some sort of support from the deposed king.

It is relevant to note that all this was accomplished in a single day. Parliament had, at a stroke, declared itself the supreme lawgiver, deposed an anointed king and elected another. This was a very brave step for all involved, they had, after all, committed treason, certainly within the terms of the 1351 Treason Act and also under the Common Law. Should by any chance Richard regain the throne, all those involved would be charged with treason and suffer the awful penalty of hanging, drawing and quartering. Not only in this world would they suffer, treason was thought to be a crime against God also and their suffering would therefore continue in the next world. That the participants were willing to go through with it all gives some indication of how badly Richard was viewed. Parliament met again one week later and ratified the decisions made on the 30th. It is surprising that Henry experienced little opposition to his claiming the throne. The rightful heir, Edmund Mortimer, later Earl of March, still lived and could no doubt have become a rallying point for Richard's supporters as could the new king's uncle, Richard, Duke of York. That both supported the Lancastrian cause and served with distinction ,Edmund in France alongside Henry V and Richard serving as the king's Lieutenant General in Ireland, indicates how Henry of Derby was accepted as ruler, it should be bourne in mind however, that they were not completely free agents. Henry took them into his custody "for their safety", as soon as he was crowned. The Barons, Lords and Commons wanted peace and order and as long as Henry ruled fairly he would have their support.

Henry chose the 13th October 1399 as the date of his coronation, being the date of the feast day of St Edward, considered the founder of the English line of kings. It was a custom of the time to knight deserving persons on the day before a coronation and Henry chose the occasion to found the Order of the Bath, investing his four sons into the new order. The new knights, the Lord Mayor and Aldermen led Henry in procession to Westminster. Henry wished to impress all present with his right to the throne and had changed parts of the ceremony to add weight to his regality. When the swords of the three estates were raised aloft, a fourth symbolizing the House of Lancaster was also raised. The oil used to anoint him was said to be that revealed to Becket by the Virgin Mary and its holy properties were thought to add extra sanctity to the blessing. It is known that Henry, previously a healthy and fit man, had began to develop some skin problems that manifested itself in eruptions, flaking and weeping, either a form of eczema or possibly leprosy. When the oil was applied to his head it was recorded that "the same rotting did the anointing at his coronation portend, for there ensued such a growth of lice, especially on his head, that he neither grew hair, nor could he have his head covered for many months".

The coronation was concluded with all due pomp and ceremony, ending with Sir Thomas Dymock, the King's Champion riding into the building and challenging anyone who opposed the new king. Henry began to view his illness as a divine retribution for his usurpation of the throne and in an attempt to appease the Almighty, began to persecute the Lollards, a religious sect founded by John Wycliffe whose views were thought heretical by the established church. Lollards believed that the priesthood should own no property, that the bible was the supreme authority and that there was no basis for belief in transubstiation. Henry issued his first order for the burnings 'de Haretico Comburendo' in 1401. He was most active in his persecutions although one incident did show that he had some sensitivity. He attended a burning and offered one of the victims his freedom if he recanted. The man refused and the fire was lit. The cries of the burning martyrs were so pitiful that Henry ordered the flames to be doused and again asked if the victim wished to recant and be spared. The offer was again refused and the fire relit.

Henry knew that he could never be secure on his throne while Richard lived and it is likely that he ordered the murder of the dethroned Richard following a number of attempts on his own life by supporters of the deposed king, the most serious occurring at Windsor in January 1400 during a Christmas tournament. Henry was told of the plot by Edward Earl of Rutland and escaped with his family to London. It is interesting to note that when he returned to Windsor with a force to engage the rebels, the uprising had already been put down by the local townsfolk, indicating their preference for the new monarch. It was important to appear that Richard had died of natural causes and it seems that poison was mixed in his food over a period of ten days.

Henry made great show of having Richard's body returned to London, ensuring that it was visible to all and that it showed no injury.

Henry now began to suffer blackouts, perhaps some form of epilepsy and his skin condition worsened. Fortunately perhaps, the eruptions were confined to his arms and body which he kept covered and did not spread to his face. Despite this disfiguration, Henry married the widow of the Duke of Brittany, Joan of Navarre In 1402 and no doubt hoped to settle down to a quiet life but it was not to be. For some time the Welsh under Prince Owen Glendower had been harassing the borders and Henry resolved to move against them.Glendower had fallen out with the Marcher baron Lord Grey of Ruthin over his alleged refusal to send troops for a Scottish expedition and Ruthin had then confiscated Glendower's estates as forfeit. This dispute soon escalated into full scale rebellion against English rule and the kings eldest son, Henry, Prince of Wales, although only thirteen was given command of the forces sent by the king to put down the growing unrest in the principality and to assist and guide him, Henry Percy, son of the Earl of Northumberland and known as Hotspur, the most famous knight in the land. The king, struggling to find the money to pay for these endless little wars, failed to pay Hotspur for the costs of maintaining the army and Hotspur in high dudgeon, left for home. When in June 1402,Owen Glendower began raiding into England, it was left to the Marcher Lords to oppose him.Emund Mortimer, Earl of March gathered a small army and moved to intercept Glendower at Pilleth. The morning of the 22nd June found Mortimer facing a Welsh army commanding the high ground before him. His forces were disadvantaged by fighting uphill and there ensued a very bloody battle in which over 800 of Mortimer's troops were killed and he himself taken prisoner.Glendower demanded a huge ransom for Mortimer's release, but the king refused to pay. This further infuriated the Percies who where kin to Mortimer and started the chain of events that would lead to their rebellion. In the north, the Scot Sir Archibald Douglas chose this time to invade the north of England, laying waste and killing everything between the border and Newcastle. Moving north towards the border, Douglas encountered the forces of his long time enemy, Henry Percy the Earl of Northumbria barring his way about five miles north west of the town of Wooler. The Scots were a long way from safety and much wearied by the recent raiding, but had no alternative but to fight and moved their forces to the steep slopes of Homildon Hill and awaited attack. Earl Percy's son, Hotspur, a brave but impetuous knight, argued for an all out frontal attack, but fortunately the old Earl was wiser. His knights and infantry were backed by a large contingent of longbowman whose devastating fire had won so many victories in the previous century and he deployed a large number of them on the nearby Harehope Hill, a feature of similar height just a short distance to the north of Homildon and from which his archers could shoot directly into the Scots ranks yet remain protected from cavalry by the steep slope. Northumberland's remaining bowmen were positioned in front of his infantry on the plain. The English archers on the hill poured arrows which "fell like a storm of rain" on the Scots, provoking fury among the Scots noblemen who felt that these tactics were somehow unchivalrous. One of their numbers, Sir John Swinton raged at his comrades urging them to move forward against the enemy urging them to "join in hand to hand battle and move amongst our enemies to save our lives in so doing or at least to fall as knights of honour". Hearing these words, a rival of Swinton.one Adam de Gordon knelt before him and attested that Swinton was" the bravest knight in the land" and together they marched forward followed by a hundred or so of others vowing to teach the English a lesson in chivalry. Archibald Douglas, seeing this, rode down the hill with a troop of horsemen and tried to ride down the archers who, while retreating, continued to fire at the attackers, killing and wounding men and horses alike. Douglas himself, despite his costly armour, was badly wounded, being hit by no less than five arrows which gives some indication of the ferocity of the arrow storm. The remainder of the Scottish army, seeing the carnage, turned tail and fled only to be trapped by the River Tweed where over five hundred were said to have drowned while the remainder surrendered.

As was customary, prisoners of noble birth could be ransomed by the victors and having captured a high number of knights, the Percies calculated that they stood to collect a fortune from the prisoners. At this point Henry made an error that would result in much further bloodshed. Realizing the size of the potential ransoms, he demanded that all prisoners be turned over to him, a huge break with tradition and one that enraged the proud Percies and was seen as an insult that would not be forgotten, made worse by the king's failure to pay the family monies due for protecting the kingdom's northern and western borders. In July 1402 Henry marched north with an army variously estimated of between 14,000 and 60,000 men to support the Percies against an expected Scottish invasion when he learned that the son of Percy his former friend, Henry Percy, was in turn, marching south to link up with Owen Glendower the rebel Welsh prince. On hearing this, Henry turned eastwards at Burton on Trent to intercept Hotspur and his army also estimated at between 5,000 and 20,000.Reaching Shrewsbury, he learned that the rebels were camped to the north east around Berwick .

Henry was concerned at the prospect of a pitched battle with the powerful Percy family but needed to conclude the matter before Owen Glendower could link up with the Percy's. His forces made camp at Haughmond to the north east and during the night of 20th July began moving his forces across the Severn and took up a position on the wide plain below Haughmond Abbey where his larger force could spread out, leaving Percy to take his position on less favourable ground. He was still insecure in his position as king and feared that such a fight with a leading English baron could open up many old wounds and lead to further rebellion. He accordingly sent a local Abbot to offer "peace and pardon" to Percy if he submitted. Percy in reply sent his uncle Thomas Percy to meet the king with demands for some reformation of government and the king, eager to avoid battle, agreed to the terms. Thomas however, had his own agenda. He was still furious over the ransom money and returning to his camp at nightfall, told Hotspur that the king refused all negotiations and that the matter must be settled by combat.

On the morning of 21st July 1403, Hotspur's forces were lined up in a single division fronted by a line of archers. The front line was commanded by Archibald Douglas who had recovered from his many wounds received at Homildon Hill and, on seeing the king's troops forming up before him, ordered his archers to open fire. Archery had come a long way since the short bows of the Normans and the powerful longbow was capable of killing at ranges of over three hundred yards. For longer ranges the archers used "flight arrows" with elongated shafts for greater distance and when within closer range used "sheaf arrows" with heavier heads for greater penetration. It was boasted that some archers could keep six arrows in the air at one time, a shocking rate of fire which quickly exhausted supplies and special "retrievers" were employed to run forward and gather up undamaged arrows for reuse, a fairly dangerous employment! The English archers responded and an arrow duel took place with the royal archers surprisingly getting the worst of the exchange. Henry moved the main body of his troops forward in support and the two sides met with a clash of arms. Hotspur knew that he would have to kill Henry if he was to win the day and charged forward towards the royal banner with thirty of his best knights. The king, as was usual at the time, had several of his own followers dressed in the royal surcoat and two of these decoys, the Earl of Stafford and Sir Thomas Blount were killed in the attack. On the king's left stood his son the Prince of Wales (later Henry V) with the reserve and seeing his father besieged, moved his troops forward to hit Percy's men from the side. He was struck in the face and hurt badly by an arrow, but bravely refused to retire. Percy's forces were now fighting on two fronts and the battle became a series of individual combats. With neither side wearing uniform it became difficult to recognize friend from foe and in the confusion a cry went up that Henry was dead. The king however, was very much alive and raising his visor, he immediately retaliated with the cry "Hotspur is slain". Hearing no answering roar of denial, some of the rebel troops began to lose heart and drift away but the fighting had become so widespread and the noise so great that many of the combatants. unaware of Hotspur's death, struggled fighting on till darkness fell and men sank exhausted to the ground not knowing who had gained the day. Hotspur had indeed been killed, by an arrow in the face and his father taken prisoner. The battle was won at terrible cost, it is estimated that more than 300 knights were slain in addition to some 20,000 soldiers and archers. This portent of a new kind of warfare was the culmination of the lessons learned in the many battles of the preceding years, both in England and France. The power of the longbow and its rate of fire, plus the developing of fighting on foot in massed ranks protected by the archers was a long way from the cavalry shock charge of old. The improvements in plate armour, both in strength and flexibility had made the use of two handed swords popular again and these, plus other dreadful weapons such as hand axe, mace and Morningstar resulted in greater fatalities at all levels.

Hotspur's body was buried at Whitchurch, but the king ordered it disinterred and displayed to prove he was dead. His corpse ,impaled on a spear and wedged between two millstones was left for all to see in Shrewsbury and later quartered, the parts being sent for display in the four corners of the kingdom. What remained after this time was returned to his family for burial. Henry ordered the building of a church on the site to commemorate the battle. This church, St Mary Magdalen, no longer exists but was thought to have been built over the grave pit that was dug to contain the battle's many casualties.

Henry was to know no peace, increasingly add odds with both church and parliament over taxes to pay for his armies, weighed down with his deteriorating physical condition and the guilt that he felt over usurping Richard all combined to turn this once fine figure into a shadow. In 1404 Glendower captured the strategic castles of Aberystwyth and Harlech with the aid of the French who stationed a fleet in the Irish Sea to prevent reprovisioning by sea. They then attacked and burned Cardiff to the ground.

The French king, ever eager to capitalize on England's woes, plus his loyalty to the deposed Richard his son in law, formally recognized Glendower and sent aid to him (but no troops as yet).Glendower increased his power and by 1405 controlled most of Wales. At Machynlleth he was crowned king of free Wales and began to develop his own foreign and domestic policies knowing that he could not hope to retain power through rebellion alone and needed to bring his kingdom together to withstand any attempt by the English to reclaim it. King Charles of France increased his aid to the Welsh, his fleets protected the Welsh coast and a French force of some 2,800 men landed at Milford Haven, marching to Carmarthen, capturing it, but due to a lack of coordination between them and Glendower's forces, the invasion petered out and the French took ship back to France. Later a similar size force again landed at Milford Haven and this time joined forces with Glendower's army of some 10,000. Together they marched through South Wales into England and met with Henry's forces at Worcester. Both sides, being of equal strength, where unwilling to instigate hostilities and stayed camped near each other for some days. Henry used this time to infiltrate his men behind the invaders, cutting through their supply lines. It seems that at this point Glendower lost his nerve, fearing that his army was overextended and open to counterattack, he withdrew, this moment being seen as a turning point in his fortunes with some historians asserting that, had he continued, he could have forced his own terms on King Henry.

Glendower began plotting with the Percies and Mortimer who was now Glendower's son in law. At a Parliament held in Harlech it was decided that, following King Henry's overthrow, England was to be divided up in three parts, Mortimer would rule the south and west, Percy would have the north and the midlands, while Glendower was to have Wales and the English Marches. Time was running out for the rebels however, a royalist force from Dublin landed at Holyhead and defeated a Welsh force at Ynys Mon and at Crosmont. A further defeat was inflicted on 15th March at Pwll Melyn where the English caught the Welsh unprepared and did much slaughter before capturing some 300 soldiers and Glendower's son Gruffydd.The soldiers were taken to a nearby castle and executed while Gruffydd was taken to London for torture.

 The Mortimers and the Percy's had not been idle during this time, whipping up rebellion and discontent in Yorkshire against the king and gaining support in this from Richard Scrope,Archbishop of York, a former ally of Henry. On the 29th May, the rebels led by Scrope and Thomas Mowbray Earl of Norfolk, with an army of some 6000 men met the much larger royal forces led by Henry Prince of Wales and Ralph Neville, Earl of Westmorland at Shipton Moor. Earl Percy who was having problems of his own abandoned his attempt to join them and left the two inexperienced leaders to their fate. After three days spent eying each other up, Scrope rode forward to negotiate with Westmorland and the two talked and drank together in front of their forces and concluded a truce whereby both would disperse their forces. As Scrope's forces began to retire, Westmorland arrested Mowbray and Scrope and imprisoned them both at Pontefract. The king immediately instigated charges of treason against the rebels, but many felt that Scrope's trial was illegal with even the Archbishop of Canterbury pleading for clemency and Chief Justice Gascoine refusing to participate. It is said that he went to his death," on a collier's sorry mare, bareback with a halter for a bridle". He sang psalms as he went and was beheaded with five strokes in commemoration of the five wounds of Christ. Thomas Mowbray and Sir William Plumpton were also publicly executed and their heads displayed on pikes ,but Mortimer escaped and joined Glendower at Harlech castle.Glendower did all he could to strengthen an independent Wales, he established an independent church of Wales and tried to create Welsh universities free from English domination. He positioned himself closer to the French by supporting the anti pope Benedict X111 at Avignon. His attempts to forge a strong alliance with Scotland were foiled by the death of the Scots king Robert 111, plus the fact that the heir to the Scots throne, James 1st was a hostage in King Henry's court and was to remain so for 17 years, having been captured by the English while traveling to France.

In 1408 Northumberland, who had taken refuge in Scotland, again took up arms against the king and together with his ally Lord Bardolfe, invaded the north of England with a small army. They achieved some modest successes, but were soon faced with a force of loyal Yorkshire knights led by Sir Thomas Rokeby, Sheriff of Yorkshire and on 28th February 1408 at Bramham Moor found their retreat to Scotland cut off by the loyalist forces leaving them no alternative but to fight. The battle was particularly bloody with the rebels being cut to pieces and both Northumberland and Bardolfe slain. Their heads were cut off and taken to be displayed in London. Glendower was faring no better with most of south east Wales retaken by the English and in September Prince Henry recaptured Aberystwyth. In March 1409 after a long siege, Harlech fell and when Prince Henry entered, he found that Mortimer had died and Glendower and his son Maredudd had escaped, leaving his wife and two other children to be taken by the English.

With Glendower now on the run, Henry offered various pardons and bribes to the remaining opposition to desert their leader and the rebellion was effectively over.

Glendower was to rise again briefly in 1410 when he raided Shropshire, but was soundly beaten and his lieutenants executed.

When Prince Henry succeeded to the throne in 1413, he offered to pardon Glendower and restore his lands but received no response. He tried again in 1416 but again received no response and it is thought that Glendower had died. He had waged a war of independence for over ten years and in doing so had lost his family and exhausted his small country. The length of the revolt is a testament to the tenacity of his people as well as a mark of his leadership.

From 1410 the king's health declined further and much of his duty was taken over by his eldest son. There was much friction between them with the prince eager to assume power and the king unwilling to hand the reins over.

Henry was by now, a sick man and was nearing his end. Much had been achieved during his short reign, the subjugation of Wales, the stabilization of the Scottish border and a truce with the French. He had defeated powerful enemies in England and the land was once again at peace. Henry's dearest wish now was to go on Crusade, but it was not to be. While praying at Westminster Abbey at the Confessor's shrine, he was seized with one of his fits and was taken to the abbot's lodging. When he asked where he was, he was told that he was in the Jerusalem Chamber." Praise be to God" said Henry" I know I will die in this chamber according to the prophecy of me aforesaid that I should die in Jerusalem". He called for his confessor John Tiklle who advised that the king repent for three things. The death of Richard, the execution of Scrope and the usurpation of the crown. Henry retorted that he had been absolved of the first by the Pope and had done pennance.As for the third; he did not think that confessing would alter the fact that his children "will not suffer the regalic to go oute of oure lineage".

The chronicler Monstrelet writes that near the end, it was the custom to place the crown near a dying king so that his successor could pick it up the moment the king died. When Henry appeared to have died, a cloth was placed over his face and the young Prince Henry took the crown and left the room. Shortly afterwards, the king recovered and asked where was the crown? Prince Henry returned and explained that he thought his father had died. The king replied "My son, how could you have right to this crown when I have none. And this you well know". Prince Henry replied," My Lord, as you have held it and kept it with the sword, so shall I keep it as long as I live".

Henry died on 20th March 1413, it is thought from an uraemic kidney condition which was made worse by his severe exfoliatuve dermatitis. It is also likely that the many blows to the head he would have received in his years of jousting would have contributed to his failing mental state. His second wife Joan commissioned Richard's architect Henry Yevele to make an alabaster effigy and a beautiful canopy for his tomb in Canterbury. It is interesting to note that in the nineteenth century the coffin was opened and, according to Archaelogia of 1832 Vol XX111, "The face was seen in complete preservation, though on the admission of air it shrank away. The skin was of the consistency of the upper leather of a shoe, brown and moist, the beard thick and matted and of a deep russet colour". This examination would seem to rule out the leprosy that many of the people of the time thought that he suffered as a punishment for his usurpation and for the death of Archbishop Scrope.

Henry V

Henry was born at Monmouth in August or September 1387, the first of the four sons of King Henry IV. A good education enabled him to read and write in English, French and Latin, although his preference was always English. He studied law and theology and was the first king to leave behind official documents and letters written in his own hand.

His childhood was happy and uneventful although it is known that in his early life he did contract some form of serious disease, but apparently made a full recovery thanks to the ministrations of his nurse Joan Waring, who, many years later, was rewarded in his will.

Much has been written regarding his adolescence, the English Chronicle noted that "in his youth, he had been wild and reckless and sparing nothing of his lusts and desires" and his exploits in the taverns and dives of London was said to have infuriated his father, although with the years spent campaigning in Wales it is difficult to see where he found the time!.Shakespeare also makes much of the princes' carousing in his play of Henry's life. What is known for sure is his prowess as a soldier, skilled in Arms and a natural strategist and leader. These qualities were soon to be displayed when in 1400, at the age of thirteen, his father sent him to lead the royal forces, aided by Henry Percy or Hotspur, son of the Earl of Northumberland, against the Welsh rebel Glendower, who, following a feud with the English Marcher baron Lord Grey of Ruthin, rapidly escalated the dispute into full scale rebellion. Henry spent much of the next nine years hunting Glendower in a series of raids and skirmishes during which the English forces cruelly burnt villages, destroyed crops and killed prisoners.

The young Henry, or Prince Hal as he was known, enhanced his reputation as a soldier during the savage skirmishes in the unforgiving Welsh mountains and when in 1403, Hotspur, now an ally of Glendower, rose against the king, he led a division of the royal forces against his former friend at the Battle of Shrewsbury and was badly wounded in the face by an arrow during the fighting. The young Prince owed his life to the surgeon John Bradmore who had devised a tong shaped probe with which he was able to remove the barbed head of the arrow. The dispute between the Percy's and the king gave Glendower time to reorganize and in 1404 he captured Cardiff and Harlech castles. Glendower was no rabble rousing savage, he was well educated and had studied law in London as a young man. He declared himself the true Prince of Wales and received ambassadors from Scotland and France pledging support for his war of independence. He sent his brother in law John Hanmer to Brittany to elicit support from his fellow Celts and sought similar support from Ireland. He entered into a pact with Edmund Mortimer and the Earl of Northumberland whereby, having defeated King Henry, they would divide England and Wales in three parts, Glendower was to have Wales and the West Country, Northumberland was to have Northern England and Mortimer the rest. It is difficult to imagine their plans as anything more than fantasy, but by 1404 the rebellion had gained such support that English landowners in Shropshire, Herefordshire and Mongomeryshire had ceased resistance and were making their own treaties with Glendower.

With every success the revolt grew. Village after village joined him and Royal officials reported that Welsh scholars were leaving Oxford for Glendower, Welsh labourers and craftsmen were leaving England in droves as were many of the Welsh archers and men at arms who had served the English in their French campaigns.
Glendower's diplomacy paid dividends and soon Welsh and Franco Breton forces were attacking English castles in Wales while Scot and French privateers were harrying English settlements around the Welsh coast. In 1403 a Breton squadron defeated the English in the Channel and attacked Jersey, Guernsey and Plymouth while the French made a landing on the Isle of Wight. By 1406 the English were under pressure on all sides. The French invaded Aquitaine and also landed an army at Milford Haven. Joining up with Glendower's forces they took Haverfordwest and besieged Carmarthen and Tenby. They then marched into England where they met with an English force at Worcester.

Strangely, the two armies viewed each other without action for some eight days; finally the Franco Welsh withdrew and moved back to Wales. Some further French troops were sent to Wales later in the year but with some political changes in France the desire to continue aid came to an end.

Throughout this time Prince Henry had been constantly on the move against Glendower in a pitiless campaign where both sides displayed the utmost cruelty. The Prince by now a seasoned warrior continued to hunt down the rebels and at the battles of Grosmont and Usk decisively defeated the Welsh inflicting heavy casualties. It was during the first battle that Glendower's brother Tudur was killed and his son Gruffud captured. It is said that Henry had three hundred prisoners beheaded outside the walls of Usk castle after the battle, a foretaste of his massacre of French prisoners at Agincourt some nine years later.

The young English Prince now showed his mastery of strategy by abandoning his father's method of punitive expeditions and began a policy of blockade. From his bases in the captured Welsh castles he began to retake the Principality by cutting off trade and the supply of weapons. By 1407 this policy was bearing fruit and opposition crumbling with over 1,000 men in Flintshire alone appearing before the County's Chief Justice and paying a communal fine for their support of the rebels. This pattern was repeated throughout Wales as the Prince advanced. By Autumn Glendower's castle at Aberystwyth had surrendered. By 1409 the Prince had besieged Harlech. Glendower sent desperate envoys to the French for help but without result. The castle fell and in the final battle Edmund Mortimer was killed and Glendower's wife Margaret and two daughters were taken prisoner and taken to The Tower where they were to subsequently die

Glendower escaped but was now a hunted man. The revolt was largely over apart from the odd flicker of resistance which was ruthlessly put down. In late 1409, Glendower made a last raid into Shropshire, but it came to nothing with many of his leading supporters being captured including the notorious Rhys Ddu who was taken to London for execution. A contempory account reads that he was "drawn forth on a hurdle to Tyburn and was hanged and let down again. His head was smitten off and his body quartered and sent to four towns, his head being set on London Bridge"

In 1412 Glendower ambushed, captured and ransomed Dafydd Gam a supporter of Henry. This was the last time Glendower was seen alive. Henry IV died in 1413 and his son began conciliatory moves towards the Welsh, offering pardons to some of the Welsh leaders and, as a symbolic gesture, interred the body of Richard 11 in Westminster Abbey. Henry also entered into negotiations with Glendower's son Maredudd but without result. It is thought that Maredudd was unwilling to accept a pardon while his father was alive. He again refused a pardon in 1416 indicating that Glendower still lived. He finally accepted a pardon in 1421 suggesting that his father was finally dead.

The cost in lives and destruction of the rebellion was catastrophic for the Welsh. Already a poor country it was further impoverished by pillage, blockade and fines. Travellers told of ruined Abbeys and Castles, grass grew in market squares and commerce had died. Many of its leading families were ruined including the Anglesey Tudors, although it is of interest to note that one son of the family, Maredudd, moved to London and established a new destiny.

Henry had not spent all his time on his Welsh campaign. His father, much weakened by illness had lost much of the drive that had led to his coronation and from 1410 the young Henry increasingly took over the reins of power, although not without much friction between the two. Having created a majority in the Privy Council, Prince Henry began to dominate policy, not least in his support of the Burgundians in their civil war against the Armagnacs in France. This dispute centered on the rivalry for power between Louis of Orleans, brother of the recurrently insane French King Charles VI and his cousin John the Fearless Duke of Burgundy. Henry was quick to see advantage in this schism of the French nobility. Louis was murdered in 1407 and his cause was taken up by the king's father in law Bernard VII Count of Armagnac .The Burgundians at first held power but were then ousted by the Armagnacs. The Duke of Burgundy allied himself to the English king and when Henry invaded France in 1415 he was supported by Burgundy. Henry continually exploited these divisions within the French nobility to further his own cause while at the same time attempting to gain more power in England. The king's health increasingly prevented him from effective rule and much authority was delegated to Archbishop Arundel as chancellor. By 1409 the prince had replaced the chancellor's authority with his own and that of Henry and Thomas Beaufort, but following suggestions from his followers that he should succeed his father immediately, he and his faction were dismissed and Arundel reinstated. He does seem to have accepted this reverse and became reconciled with his father before the latter's death in 1413.

Throughout the period Lollardy was gaining ground in England, Henry IV had moved against them and sanctioned death by burning on a number of occasions. One of the leaders of the Lollards was Sir John Oldcastle, a Herefordshire baron who had become friends with Prince Hal during the Welsh rebellion. Lollardy had much support on Herefordshire and when Oldcastle married Joan of Cobham he became Lord Cobham and took his seat in Parliament. When it was discovered that Lollardy was being preached in churches in the Cobham area, they were put under interdict for unlicensed preaching and Oldcastle was charged with heresy, but his friendship with the king prevented any action against him until more proof against him was discovered .The king again prevaricated and tried to persuade Oldcastle to recant. Oldcastle promised to submit to the king "all his fortune in the world" but would not recant his beliefs. Oldcastle was convicted as a heretic, but escaped from the Tower and put himself at the head of a Lollard conspiracy to seize the king and his brothers and establish a form of commonwealth in England. He managed to evade capture for some years before finally being cornered in Monmouthshire and taken by Lord Charlton of Powys and on 14th December he was hanged and burned "gallows and all" in St Giles Fields. It is thought that the character of Falstaff in Shakespeare's plays is based on Oldcastle.

Henry now began to mend fences within the kingdom in preparation for his plans to invade France and claim the French throne. Some of the senior Welsh lords had their estates returned and even the Mortimers were brought back in to favour. Events both in England and Europe were to shape his plans however. The Holy Roman Emperor Sigismund of Hungary in 1414 summoned a council, or more properly councils (there where many) at Constance to deliberate on the schism in the church over the true Pope. In 1305 the papacy, under French pressure, had been moved from Rome to Avignon. In 1376 it was returned to Rome, but following the death of the then Pope the Cardinals who were mainly French, wanted to elect a Frenchman to the post. The Italians, fearing that the papacy would be returned to Avignon wanted an Italian for the position. The Cardinals elected an Italian but then fled and elected another Pope, declaring that the first election was made under duress. A council of bishops met at Pisa in 1409 to unravel the problem, but ended up electing a third pope Alexander V. Thus there where now three popes all claiming legitimacy, John XXIII who had succeeded on Alexander's death, Benedict XIII at Avignon and Gregory XII in Rome. The 1409 solution had worsened the problem and Sigismund wanted to restore the one true pope (as he saw it).The outcome was that Benedict and John were deposed and Gregory resigned, thus leaving no legitimate candidate. In true medieval fashion the council ploughed on and it was not until 11th November 1417 that a legitimate pontiff was elected and regarded as pope by the church as a whole, this was Martin V. King Henry had allied himself with Sigismund's efforts to unite the church, seeing in this an opportunity to widen his influence in Europe and the church in general as well as ensuring the Emperor's non interference in his forthcoming French invasion.

Henry had long wanted to reclaim from France all the territory he thought rightfully belonged to the English crown. Further, through the claim of Edward III he considered himself to be the true heir to the French throne. He saw in this venture an opportunity to achieve these aims and with the earlier victories at Crecy and Poitiers in mind, was very aware of the ransoms and plunder that could be made from a successful campaign. He was also no doubt aware that such a course would divert attention from his political problems at home. He knew that the French king was suffering from recurring bouts of insanity and the country was weakened by the civil wars of the French nobility. With the tacit support of the Burgundians Henry made plans and began to marshal forces at Southampton for his expedition. Shakespeare tells of Henry receiving a delegation from France bearing a gift of tennis balls from the Dauphin suggesting that his time would be better spent playing games than taking on the might of France. A furious Henry is purported to have replied that he would turn the balls into gunstones.

It was at Southampton that a plot was uncovered to depose him and set in his place Edmund Mortimer the 5th Earl of March. The scheme was led by Richard, Earl of Cambridge, Henry Scrope and Thomas Grey, who had underestimated the loyalty of Mortimer. Upon hearing of the plot to put him on the throne, he promptly told the king on 31st July 1415, who wasted no time in rounding up the traitors. Grey was executed on August 3rd and the others on the 11th.

Henry, with a force of 8000 archers and 2000 men at arms sailed for France in a fleet variously estimated at between 300 and 1000 ships(the lower figure being far more likely) and landed on the 13th August some three miles west of the town of Harfleur where he laid siege. Harfleur was a strongly fortified town with thick walls, twenty six towers, a moat and three barbicans. Despite the huge cannons used against its walls, the siege took longer than expected and the town did not surrender until 22nd September. The marshy conditions in the area had resulted in much disease among the English forces through sleeping in the open and drinking contaminated water. Harfleur's surrender which according to the laws of war, saved it from destruction, and had cost Henry about one third of his army and many of the survivors were too sick to travel. His plan, to march on Paris and then on to Bordeaux, would have to be modified. Against the advice of his officers he decided to feign an intent to fight the gathering French army and embark on a "show the flag"chevauchee northwards, outmarching his enemies and reach the English held town of Calais 120 miles away.

Abandoning his artillery and much of his baggage train, Henry placed the Earl of Dorset in command of Harfleur with a force of some 500 men at arms and 1000 archers. On October 8th 1415 he left with a force of about 900 men at arms and 5000 archers and headed north carrying provisions for 8 days. As was usual, the force was divided in three, the vanguard commanded by Sir Gilbert Umfraville, and the rearguard by the Duke of York. He himself commanded the main body. Much has been made of Henry's supposed tight discipline of his troops, forbidding looting and hanging some of his soldiers for theft, but French chroniclers report the usual laying waste of the countryside by the

English force. Finding the Bethune River in flood, they marched upstream to find a ford which they crossed on the 11th.They crossed the Breste the next day and had covered 80 miles in five days. On the 13th they turned inland to cross the Somme at Abbeville, but discovered a French force of 6000 blocking the crossing. Henry turned his weary force south east and for five days looked for a suitable place to cross, with the French force shadowing them on the other side of the river. Henry's forces were now growing weak through hunger. Finding a loop in the river which enabled him to overtake the French, Henry finally crossed the Somme on 19th at Voyenes, while at the same time, beating off a French cavalry attack. Henry declared the 20th a rest day and to dry their clothes, but French heralds arrived in the afternoon to issue a challenge for battle." Our lords have heard how you intend with your army to conquer the towns, castles and cities of the realm of France and of the Frenchmen you have destroyed. Many of our lords are assembled to defend their rights and they inform you that before you come to Calais they will fight you and be revenged of your conduct". Henry simply replied "We march straight to Calais and if our enemies disturb our march, it will be at their great peril. Be all things according to the will of God".

The English moved on although many were now weak from hunger and sick from eating nuts and raw vegetables, nevertheless covering a further 71 miles in the next four days and being only two days march from Calais, the advance guard reported on the 24th that they had been overtaken by a large French army which was now blocking the road to Calais. Henry knew that he must now fight or surrender. He moved his forces to a ridge close to the villages of Azincourt (mispronounced as Agincourt by the English) and Tramecourt, protected on both sides by thick woodland and took up battle positions. The French also took up position about half a mile away, but did not attack immediately, having learnt from Crecy.

The French army was reckoned to be some 20000 to 30000 strong led by the flower of French chivalry including the Constable of France Charles de Albret, Marshal, Boucicaut and many Dukes, Counts and Barons. Although these men commanded great numbers, their troops were composed of fiery and undisciplined aristocracy who believed that they were the most efficient fighting force in the world, but were in reality, little better than an armed mob all too eager to be first against what they considered English rabble. Henry, having marched 260 miles in 17 day, realizing that his forces were heavily outnumbered and much weakened, offered to return to Harfleur and pay damages in return for free and safe passage to Calais. The French however, with their superior numbers, demanded that he also give up all claim to the French throne and to all French territory apart from Guyenne .Negotiations were broken off as night fell and both sides returned to their camps. Henry ordered silence in the camp on pain of a loss of horse for a knight or a right ear for a person of lesser rank. The English sat in the dark thinking of the coming battle and Henry moved among his troops talking and giving words of comfort to all.Shakespeare makes much of this in his tale of Henry, giving the king his famous monologue of "we happy few" and there are some references to him making a speech from various contempory sources, perhaps the most reliable being those of a priest stationed with the baggage train who wrote two years later of the battle and tells of Henry giving words of encouragement, plus another reference from a Jean de Fevre,a French squire who also wrote of the battle and tells of Henry addressing his troops. The French camp was full of drinking and gambling with knights boasting of how many English they would kill or capture .One can imagine how the English felt, cold, hungry and with the hundreds of French campfires lighting up the woods before them. It rained heavily later in the night, turning the ground sodden with mud and adding to the English misery.

Both armies rose early and prepared for battle. They were about 1000 yards apart and separated by a ploughed field with a slight dip in the centre which ensured that both armies were in full view of each other. Thick woodland pressed in from both sides of the field which was about 1200 yards wide where the French assembled and narrowing to 900 yards where the forces could be expected to meet. This would greatly restrict the movement of the French preventing them from outflanking the smaller English force. It is thought that some English archers were positioned in the thick woods behind the French lines to harass the enemy and divert troops from the main battle. What is known is that Henry arrayed his forces in a single line of three divisions. These divisions, four men deep were commanded by the Duke of York on the right, Lord Camoys on the left and Henry in the centre. It was originally thought that wedges of archers were placed between the divisions, but we now know that they were stationed on the two wings of the English army, angled slightly forward to allow converging fire on any attack to the lines centre. Sharpened stakes were set in front of their positions as a defence against cavalry. The English stood, waiting to meet the French onslaught.

The French formed in three lines, men at arms with some cavalry on the wings in the first two and cavalry in the rear ready to roll over the English once their line was broken. The first French line alone contained 8000 knights and how feircesome they must have looked in their bright armour, their banners and standards flying and the huge purple flag with the white cross of the French patron Saint Denis and the long, bright red Orriflame indicating that no quarter was to be given. The English must have looked a sad sight to these flowers of French chivalry. The two sided waited unmoving for four hours between 7am and 11am.De Albret had cautioned the French to wait and let the English come to them where superior numbers would win the day. In fact it was argued that they should not attack at all, but let the English starve and be defeated without the bother of battle. The French troops spent the wait in jostling for position, eating and hurling insults at their foes. Henry new that he must fight today as his troops, without food, could only grow weaker and, after consulting his senior captains, ordered the English advance.

The English, with full knowledge that they were probably going to their deaths, knelt and kissed the ground, each taking a morsel of soil in his mouth in the old earth housel of the Saxons and took the next ten minutes, quietly and steadily advancing to within extreme longbow range (approx 250 yards).Should the French have decided to charge during this time, they would have simply rolled over their adversaries, but they stayed in position. The English archers reset their stakes arranged like a thicket in front of their positions, enabling them to move about but presenting a fearful obstacle to cavalry and, on the command from Sir Thomas Erpingham, Marshal of the Archers, fired a volley. It is recorded that "the sky was darkened by the arrow storm "fired high to drop vertically on the French with a thunderous crash as broad bladed clothyards struck armour and mail. The Longbow, drawn back to the ear, could, at 200 yards, produce wounds through chain mall to a depth of more than 6 inches. The arrows struck with an impact of more than 90 Joules of energy, greater than many modern bullets and, due to the habit of bowmen of sticking arrows in the earth before them for quick use, normally resulted in infection in the target. The arrows, being barbed, were difficult to remove and death was the normal result. A second volley was in the air before the first struck and one can only imagine the shock and confusion among the French as the shafts struck home injuring both men and horses. Stung by this attack, the French cavalry on both wings charged the English line followed by the first line of men at arms. The success of a shock charge by cavalry depends upon their arriving at the point of contact together, but due to lack of control, many French cavalry had been allowed to wander off and, as a result, the charge did not have its intended power. As the distance closed, the English archers were able to fire directly into the flanks of the cavalry firing shorter arrows with the deadly bodkin pointed heads able to pierce armour and the field was soon strewn with wounded and dying men and horses. The wet ground being churned up turned into a sea of mud which suffocated many of the fallen and wounded horses, mad with pain, charged into others or impaled themselves on the English stakes. The survivors, desperate to escape, retreated and crashed into the advancing men at arms, breaking the line and slowing the advance. The French, wanting to get at the English men at arms whom they saw as equals and not get involved with the archers seen as their inferiors, narrowed ranks as they approached and this was compounded by those on the flanks pressing inward to avoid the storm of arrows from the sides. Consequently, when they arrived at the English line, they lacked sufficient room to fight freely and had little momentum left. Even so, when the two lines met the English line buckled, but did not break. The English knew that they had to stand and fight as any retreat would result in annihilation. King Henry had dismounted for the advance and fought in the front rank and it was here that he received the blow on his helmet that may still be seen hung in the Abbey at Westminster. The French front line, being pressed back by the English and pressed forward by those behind eager to join the fight, found themselves increasingly hemmed in and unable to move freely. Further, as the desperate English continued their slaughter, the piles of bodies were creating further obstacles to the French advance. This caused a tumbling effect whereby French men at arms, pushed back from the English and forward by their own advancing troops, began to fall and drown in the morass underfoot. This created a surge outwards towards the archers, who seeing the confusion, dropped their bows and threw themselves at the confused and shaken French. The French men at arms would not normally be concerned at attacks from such lightly armed foes, but the archers, operating in twos and threes, slashed at any unprotected parts of the French who, once down, were an easy target for a dagger through the visor or a joint in the armour.

Thus the first French line were either totally destroyed or taken prisoner and the second line upon arriving at the battle suffered the same fate, but with many quitting the field after seeing the carnage among the first rank. Arriving late, the Duke of Brabant threw his troops at the English but the charge was quickly broken up and he himself killed. The action had taken less than thirty minutes and the English had broken the might of the French army. The threat of the French third line still remained however and events now took a different turn. Henry had forbade the individual collecting of prisoners for ransom and all French prisoners were herded to the rear, guarded by the few English troops as could be spared. These prisoners greatly outnumbered the entire English force. Henry realized that should the French attack again, there was a great risk of the still armoured prisoners picking up the many weapons scattered on the field and attacking from the rear. At this moment he received reports of an attack on his baggage wagons by a force led by the Lord of Agincourt. The wagons being only lightly guarded were an easy target for what was probably no more than an opportunistic foray by a small force of locals. They made off with their spoils including one of the royal crowns. At the same time, the Counts of Marle and Fauquemberghes launched another attack on the English line. This was defeated as bloodily as the others, but made Henry aware of the possibility of being attacked from front and rear. Accordingly he gave orders for all prisoners to be killed, but his men at arms refused, possibly because it would be dishonorable to kill an equal after surrender, but more likely the thought of the ransom money they stood to lose .Henry then ordered his personal guard of archers to do the job, these men being outside the bounds of chivalry and being a long way down the pecking order for any ransoms. Various chroniclers have made much of Henry's decision and his reasons. It may have been revenge for the baggage train attack or simply Henry's hard edged view that they were too much of a potential threat. How many were killed is not known but contemporary observers say it was more than were killed in the main battle. Interestingly, although modern scholars have condemned Henry for this act, observers at the time considered his actions justified in view of the potential attack from the French third line and it was only when this line dispersed that the killing stopped. Various figures have been recorded for French losses, but most are between 8000 and 12000 with the English losing between 100 and 500. It is known that some 2000 prisoners of rank were returned to England and many being unable to pay the required ransom, remained in captivity thereafter.. This, together with the numbers killed, resulted in the loss of over half the French nobility and greatly weakened the French king's support base and made easier Henry's future victories. Yet again the English had shown that a regular, trained and disciplined army will always defeat one that is poorly led and without discipline.

The return crossing to England was made in terrible weather, but Henry was not seasick although he did have certain medicines sent out from England for "the King's person". His reception on landing was tumultuous and he and his troops were feted throughout their journey to London.

The campaign however, despite the resounding victory of Agincourt, had done little more than give the English another foothold in France. Henry set about rebuilding the damage to Harfleur and had shipped in immigrants to Anglicize the town. In January 1416, the Earl of Dorset arrived with a force of 900 men at arms and 1500 archers and in March led them on a raid towards the Somne. Marching back, loaded with plunder, his force was intercepted at Valmont by a French army of some 5000 under the new Constable of France, Bernard, Count of Armagnac. Dorset deployed his small force in a single line in the hedges and ditches, supported by his archers. The Count, having learned nothing from Agincourt, threw his cavalry against the English line and many were duly brought down by the arrow storm and the English men at arms. Some French riders, having broken the English line, made no attempt to exploit their success, but rode on to plunder the English baggage park, thus enabling the English to reform and await the next charge. The English withdrew to a small orchard and slipped away after darkness fell. By daylight he had reached the woods at Etretat where they waited for a further French attack. At dawn the English set off along the beach and had reached Cap de le Havre only 10 miles from Harfleur when the French advance guard appeared on the dunes above the beach and charged down on them, The English, strung out along the shore, turned and greeted the French with an arrow storm and then charged with axe and sword, destroying them with this aggressive response. They began stripping the dead for plunder when the main French force appeared on the dunes. So confident now where the English of their superiority that they simply charged up the dunes, scrambling on all fours to get at the French, who simply turned and fled. During this time, Sigismund, Holy Roman Emperor offered to mediate between Henry and the French king, but by August 1416 gave his support to Henry's claim to the French throne in the Treaty of Canterbury. Henry also enjoyed the support of John, Duke of Burgundy who saw in Henry a way to defeat his Armagnac opposition. John met with Henry and Sigismund at Calais in October 1416 where attempts were made to have him accept Henry as King of France. John would not commit that far, but promised that, if Henry made good his claim, he would have the support of Burgundy. Thus encouraged, Henry set sail for France in August 1417 with a force of some 12000 and landed on August 1st near Trouville. leaving his brother John Duke of Bedford in charge of England. Henry's plan was to conquer the old Duchy of Normandy and use this as a base to conquer France. Securing his base, Henry set out with all his forces to besiege Caen and using his royal artillery train to bombard the walls, finally breached them in two places on 4th September. His assault on these breaches was repulsed with crossbow bolts, buckets of hot lead, lime and boiling water being poured on his troops and it began to seem that the assault would fail. Henry's brother the Duke of Clarence was however having more luck on the far side of the town where his forces had succeeded in forcing a breach and attacking the defenders in the rear. The defence crumpled and the English, furious at their losses, rampaged through the town pillaging and burning. While Henry tightened his hold on Normandy, the Duke of Burgundy had not been idle and took the opportunity to attack the Armagnacs and occupy Pontoise to the north of Paris and Chartres to the south. Henry was reluctant to move directly on Paris for fear that this might unite French forces against a common enemy and instead, marched on Falais, which surrendered in February 1418.

In May 1418, the citizens of Paris rose against the hated Armagnacs and murdered Duke Bernard. John of Burgundy then entered the city and allied himself with Queen Isabeau who ruled France in the name of her demented husband. John ordered his forces to contain any further English advances. English and Burgundian forces clashed at Pont de l'Arche, with the English having little difficulty in brushing their opponents aside and besieging the heavily fortified walls of Rouen. So thick were the walls that Henry could make no headway and the siege dragged on until 1419.During the winter of 1418, in an attempt to conserve their dwindling food suppliers the defenders expelled some 12000 people the so called bouches inutiles-, useless mouths. Henry refused to let them pass through his lines and most of them died from cold and hunger between the walls and the English forces. An Englishman John Page recorded that" Here and there were children of two or three begging for bread and starving, their parents dead…there were ten or twelve dead for everyone alive, many dying quietly and lying between the lines as if asleep". It is unclear why Henry refused to aid these starving people, while his ruthlessness in battle is well known, these refugees were non combatants and it must be presumed that he wanted to instill fear into the French and to signal that he would go to any length to achieve his aims.

The French, it seemed, could do nothing positive to save their country from the English. Since Agincourt they were in the grip of some trauma, unable to act against their enemy, but ever eager to squabble with each other. Burgundy controlled the mad King and Queen Isabeau, while Armagnac controlled the Dauphin Charles. When Henry had advanced to the Ile-de- France and was threatening Paris, both sides began to realize that their squabble was helping to deliver their country to the English. They therefore made an uneasy truce, but the Dauphin, trusting neither sent word to the English proposing a joint alliance against Burgundy which the English rejected. The Dauphin finally met John of Burgundy on 10th September 1419 at Montereau. The meeting was a stormy one and, following a scuffle, one of the Dauphin's knights Tanguay de Chatel killed Duke John with a battleaxe. Duke John's skull may still be seen at his ancestral home in Dijon and it is said that through the hole in it, the English came to France. The new Duke, Philip of Burgundy immediately threw in his lot with the English and with his help; the English began their inexorable advance. With the Dauphin having fled, it only remained for Henry to negotiate with King Charles and Queen Isabeau and in the Treaty of Troyes in 1420; Henry became heir to the Throne of France. The Dauphin Charles was declared a bastard and a rebel and Henry was betrothed to the king's daughter Catherine, younger sister of Isabella who had married Richard 11.Henry was named Regent of France while retaining all his lands in Normandy by right of conquest, plus all his ancestral territories in Aquitaine. Henry swore to uphold all the rights and customs of France and on 14th June 1420, married the French princess. In July the English Parliament endorsed the treaty with the caveat that no French customs were to be imported into England. Henry's entrance into Paris with his new Queen, his father in law King Charles and the mighty Duke of Burgundy marked the high point of his ambitions. He seemed to have achieved all his aims.

Henry returned to England with his bride who was crowned Queen in December 1420, leaving his brother Thomas Duke of Clarence in charge of his forces in France. Thomas led a force of some 3000 men on a chevauchee south towards Orleans. The raid was successful and on their return journey, camped overnight at Bauge. It was here that they were found by a Franco Scottish force under the command of the Scot the Earl of Buchann and the new Constable of France the Sieur de Lafayette. The Scots had, for some time, been sending troops to aid the struggling French and it has been said that it was only through this aid that France could resist at all the English advance in the years following Agincourt. The English forces were dispersed with most of the archers away foraging and Clarence had a problem. The next day was Easter Sunday and a battle on a holy day would be unthinkable. A two day delay would be out of the question and he therefore resolved to attack at once without waiting for his archers. He was advised against it by Sir Gilbert Umfraville who had been at Agincourt, but the Duke would not wait. Clarence had only 1500 men at best against the enemy's 5000 (mostly Scots) and set out in the dying light to attack. He sent some troops over the bridge while he led others through the river in a flank attack which was at first successful against the Franco Scots vanguard, but when the main force arrived they were greatly outnumbered. Full of confidence the English charged uphill at the French line, but the French charged down to meet them. In the fighting, Clarence, together with Gilbert Umfraville and Lord Roos were killed together with many of their troops. The battle lasted less than an hour and the Franco Scots, after having stripped the dead of any valuables, moved on. Later that night, The Earl of Salisbury arrived with the archers and spent a sad day burying the fallen and removing the bodies of Clarence and other knights for return to England. This small victory greatly heartened the French who until now had felt incapable of standing up to English arms.

Henry returned to France in June 1421 with a small army of about 4000, intent on attacking the Dauphinist strongholds on the Seine and Loire while his ally Burgundy was to deal with the Dauphinists in Picardy which bordered his own lands. Henry pursued the Dauphin's forces eastwards and by October 1421 had laid siege to Meaux. It was here that, just as at Harfleur, dysentery broke out among his troops. and this time, Henry himself was taken ill. The siege dragged on, but nearing Christmas, Henry received news of the birth, on 6th December, of his son Henry, heir to the two kingdoms that his father had fought so hard to unite. The king knew he had no choice but to continue the struggle, all depended on him and his fighting reputation. He could only retain his claim to France with the aid of the Burgundians and by defeating the Dauphinists. His hold on Normandy and Aquitaine was only as strong as his garrisons. Plantagenet power in France depended on him uniting his lands across the Loire with his territories in the north. It was not to be, on 31st August 1422 in the castle of Vincennes, Henry died. Thomas Walsingham wrote "The King from having an old distemper fell into an acute fever with violent dysentery". Modern opinion leans towards him having cancer of the rectum. His physicians made no attempt to treat him, implying that his condition was thought incurable although it is known that dysentery was curable at that time.

Henry's body was not embalmed, but boiled down with the bones being taken to England where Catherine commissioned a silver effigy for his tomb in the Henry V chapel at Westminster Abbey where his sword, shield and battered helm are still displayed. Within a month, the mad French King was dead. If Henry could have lived a little longer he would have achieved the throne of France the prize for which he had fought for so long.

King Henry V1

Prince Henry was born on 6th December 1421 at Windsor Castle, the only child of King Henry V and Catherine of France. He never knew his father, being just 9 months old at Henry's death and was brought up by his mother and later by his guardian Richard Beauchamp, Earl of Warwick.

Because of his religious fixation and increasing depressive psychosis, this chapter must concentrate more on the great events that occurred during his reign rather than on his shaping of them.

By his inheritance and also the Treaty of Troyes he was heir to the dual kingdoms of England and France for which his father had fought for so long and when his father died in 1422 the weight of maintaining this huge inheritance was borne primarily by his uncles John, Duke of Bedford, acting as Regent in France and Humphrey, Duke of Gloucester, styled as Protector of the Realm in England. This arrangement had been deliberately planned by the old king before his death. He knew that he could rely on Bedford and in his will charged the Duke with carrying out his wishes in France. He was to retain Normandy at all costs, continue the war against the Dauphin and offer the Regency of France to the Duke of Burgundy(knowing that it was unlikely to be accepted all the time the Dauphin lived)

Humphrey, a brave and chivalrous man, but often hot headed and quarrelsome was given the rank of Protector in the absence of Duke John, but the Regency was put in the hands of a council of ministers led by the new king's great uncles Henry Beaufort,Bishop of Winchester, John Beaufort Earl of Dorset and Thomas Beaufort,Duke of Exeter. It would not be long before Humphrey quarreled with all three. Friction existed between the parties from the start. When the Chancellor as was customary, formally surrendered his seal of office following King Henry's death, the ceremony was performed in the prince's nursery while the child slept, making it clear to Humphrey that he was not the acting head of state that he thought himself. When Humphrey complained to Parliament, they were more concerned about who was to occupy the main offices of state, Chancellor, Treasurer and Lord Privy Seal and when they were told that the present incumbents were to remain, they showed no further interest.

Humphrey appealed to the Lords, who also backed the dead king's wishes.

The Duke of Bedford, ever faithful to his dead brother's plans, wasted no time in having prince Henry proclaimed throughout occupied France, King of England and of France immediately on the death of the mad King Charles. To understand Henry's formative years and the subsequent effects of the Wars of the Roses, it is necessary to look at the situation in France in 1415.

France at this time was divided roughly into three parts. Duke John of Bedford ruled Normandy, Aquitaine and other such parts of France that his forces could occupy. The north and East of France, plus Paris was ruled by Philipe, Duke of Burgundy in the name of the English monarch, while south of the Loire most areas remained loyal to the Dauphin Charles who held his court at Berri.The borders between these areas was by no means absolute and were the subject of frequent changes of ownership as skirmishes ebbed and flowed.

The English had a force of only some 15000 soldiers in France and therefore relied greatly on the support of Burgundy. The Dauphin remained at Berri, biding his time and gathering his forces, waited for better times. Steady trickles of knights from France and increasingly Scotland swelled his forces while he waited for Burgundy and the English to fall out.

Duke John was astute enough to rule France wherever possible, through native Frenchmen and strove to maintain all rights and customs in the land. He faced many problems however, King Henry had ravaged and laid waste much of northern France causing the terrified population to flee and settle elsewhere, taking their skills with them. Much of the land grew wild and untilled yielding little sustenance and could not produce tax revenues needed to pay for the cost of maintaining the English army in France, whereas in more peaceful times, Normandy alone could yield as much as 20% of the total English revenue.Furthermore, the raising of taxes in England was in the hands of Parliament and the convocations of Canterbury and York. This was gladly forthcoming while Henry fought for his right to the French crown, but now that this issue seemed to have been resolved the desire to continue to contribute was declining. The result of which was that the English garrisons in France were not being paid and the soldiers, as usual, resorted to taking whatever they needed at the point of a sword, further alienating them from the local population. It has been said that Henry's soldiers won the war but lost the peace. The contempory writer Deschamps wrote early in the 14th century"England,the heart of a rabbit, the body of a lion" and went on to describe the English as "Poltroons,cowards,skulkers and dastards"

The Duke of Bedford, faithful to his dead brother's wishes, continued to consolidate English influence. In April 1423 he signed a concordat at Amiens with Philippe of Burgundy and John, Duke of Brittany, confirming their acceptance of Henry Vls title as King of France. Their joint fortunes were further bound together by the marriage of Philippe's daughter Anne to Bedford. The alliance was put to the test when troops from both Dukes gathered at Auxerre to meet a Dauphinist army marching on Burgundy from Bourges. The armies met at Cravant on the banks of the Yonne on 31st July 1423. The Dauphin's army of some 10000 French and Scots were commanded by Sir John Stewart and were drawn up on the eastern bank. The Anglo Burgundians with some 4000 troops were commanded by the Earl of Salisbury and formed up on the western shore.
Neither side wished to attempt an opposed river crossing and stood facing each other for three hours or more until Salisbury ordered the advance. The Yonne is waist deep at this point and is about 50 yards wide and the English archers gave their usual covering fire as the men at arms waded across. Meanwhile another English force under the command of Lord Willoughby, forced a crossing over the only bridge and split the Dauphin's forces in two. The French front buckled and crumbled under the onslaught, but the Scots refused to retreat and were cut down by the hundred with over 3000 being killed on the bridge and on the river bank with a further 2000 taken prisoner, including Sir John Stewart and the French Count of Vendomme. Encouraged by this victory, Salisbury headed west clearing Dauphinist resistance south of Paris and began plans to retake the old Plantagenet lands of Anjou and Maine.
The Scots, ever willing to aid England's enemies, continued to send men and material to France and in April 1424 a complete expeditionary force of 6000 Scots, led by the Earl of Douglas, arrived on the Loire. The grateful Dauphin rewarded Douglas with the Duchy of Touraine. Bedford also had been strengthening his forces in France and when he heard that a Franco Scottish army of 15000 was in the field, he gathered all available forces from his Normandy garrisons

and marched south from Rouen to intercept them. He was joined by Salisbury and some Burgundians under the command of Lord de L'Isle Adam, whom Bedford promptly sent off to Picardy saying that he had no need of numbers to crush the French. The two armies met on 17th August 1424 in open country south of the town of Verneuil. The French force was composed of Scots and French knights, cavalry, men at arms and Italian crossbowmen. Bedford's forces, wholly English since he had sent the Burgundians off to harass Picardy, numbered some 10000 including a strong contingent of archers. Bedford deployed his forces astride the Verneuil to Damville road in Agincourt formation, dismounted and with archers on the wings, each archer with his stake to ward off cavalry. Bedford, with memories of Agincourt, stationed a force of 1000 archers to defend the Baggage Park and horses. The Dauphinists also arranged their forces astride the road with the French under the Duke of Aumale in the centre and on the left, while the Scots held the right flank. Cavalry and crossbowmen were sited on both flanks. Douglas took much of the day deploying his forces and it was the English who started the battle by advancing on the enemy at around four o clock. At that moment, the less disciplined French cavalry decided to charge and managed to get among the English archers before they could plant their stakes, scattering them and exposing Bedford's centre. If they had continued, the outcome could have been very different, but, true to type, the cavalry, more interested in plunder, galloped on to attack the English baggage park where they were met by a storm of arrows from the defending archers.Bedfords men at arms formed a new front to cover their right and rear while the archers reformed and rained death on the French line. Bedford line pushed forward and after half an hour's fierce fighting, the French broke and fled. Meanwhile the English left flank led by the Earl of Salisbury was attacking the Scottish position who, before the battle, had sworn that they would give no quarter and ask for none. They stood their ground when the French fled even when the remaining cavalry and crossbowmen, skirted the main battle and went for the baggage train where the English archers again made them suffer terribly. The Scots were thus fully exposed and as the English finished off the remaining French and turned to add their weight to Salisbury's attack they were increasingly beleaguered. An English force crashed into the Scots flank while Salisbury's men, having driven off the French, charged forward and crushed the Scots

211

between them. The Scots were massacred, stubbornly refusing to flee and were almost slaughtered to a man with a mere handful being taken alive.

It was another great victory for the English. The French lost the Duke de Aumale, the Counts of Narbonne,Ventadour and Tonnerre, plus the Duc d'Alencon and the Marshal Lafayette were made prisoner. The Scots Earls of Douglas and Buchan and Douglas's heir Lord James were killed along with fifty other Scots knights. The Franco Scottish casualties amounted to 8000, a terrible blow when added to the dead at Cravant.The English had again decimated French armies far larger than their own, truly, God must be an Englishman!

During this time, the young prince was being raised by his mother at Wallingford where she had been sent following King Henry's death. Being the daughter of a French king she was still regarded with some suspicion by the English. Prince Henry received a formal education and became fluent in French and Latin. The sons of other nobles were brought up with him and they were tutored in arms, horsemanship and hunting as befitted their rank. By the age of ten the increasingly arrogant Henry was demanding the respect and subservience due to a king, signed his first warrant at fourteen and at fifteen was attending Council meetings regularly. He was also beginning to show signs of piety, spending much time in prayer and devotions. His religion was to become an obsession and he was soon attending all church services and even acting as server to priests at Mass. John Blacman, a Carthusian monk in Henry's service wrote a memoir of Henry describing an intense lay piety which would be bliss in a monk, but a disaster for a king. In matters of state he grew to be dictatorial and rode roughshod over his opponents, not through any particular conviction in his own decisions, but rather that he found the whole business of kingship tiresome. Although. Ever ready to forgive or reward his friends, he became surrounded with a coterie of sycophants and self seekers. He was crowned King of England in Westminster Abbey on 6th November 1429.

Against this background the war in France continued under the tireless hand of the Duke of Bedford and while the English and their allies continued to achieve dominance over the French, the rewards were increasingly flowing into the coffers of Burgundy. Things may have dragged on this way forever, but new phenomena now appeared, one that would help the French to regain their confidence and begin the long decline in the English hold on French land. In the small village of Domremy in Champagne, on 6th January 1412 a daughter was born to a peasant farmer. Her early years were unremarkable although she was considered fairly religious even for the time. This daughter, Joan, soon to be known as 'La Pucelle', at the age of thirteen, began to hear voices and have visions, convincing her that she was destined to carry out God's work by clearing the English from France. In 1428 at the age of sixteen, she traveled to Vaucoeleurs to meet the Dauphin's lieutenant for the area, Robert Bauricourt and to request to be taken to the Dauphin. After questioning her, he decided that she was mad and should be sent home and suggested a good whipping. The visions persisted and in January 1429 she again traveled to meet Bauricourt.Her passion and obvious conviction this time persuaded Bauricourt that there was something special about her. He was finally convinced when she announced on 17th October that the English had won a great victory at Orleans (the Battle of the Herrings). This news was confirmed some days later and greatly strengthened her standing. She was allowed to travel to Chinon to meet the French king who to test her, had disguised himself, but she at once saluted him among a crowd of attendants. She also confided in him a "secret sign" given to her by the voices, which convinced the king of her legitimacy. She was sent to Poitiers to be questioned by a committee of clergy and doctors. They found, after questioning her simple and ardent faith that she was not heretical. It is a pity that none of these records survived, she was to make reference to this questioning in her defense at her later trial. Returning to Chinon, the king offered her a sword, but she refused and asked that a search be made for an ancient sword, buried behind the alter in the chapel of St Catherine de Ferbois.The search was made and the sword found. There was then made for her, a banner, bearing the words Jesus,Maria and God, with angels displayed presenting fleur de lis.Her fame was growing and when a letter, sent on 22nd April 1429 by a certain Sire de Rotslaer was received in Brussels stating that Joan had foretold that she" would save Orleans, raise the siege, be wounded by an arrow, but would recover, and come summer, the king would be crowned on Reims, more and more people came to believe that she was indeed being spoken to by God." Before starting out for Orleans, Joan called upon the English king withdraw all his troops from French soil. Her demands infuriated the English. Joan arrived in

Orleans on September 30th, her presence greatly heartening the besieged garrison. By the 8th May, all the English forts surrounding the city had been captured and the siege raised although, as predicted, not before Joan was wounded in the breast by an arrow. She knew that she must maintain pressure on the enemy as her voices had often told her that she would have but one year to carry out her mission as commanded by God, Her forces continued campaigning along the Loire and achieved a series of successes culminating in the battle of Patay where the English army was defeated with great loss. Joan's forces had recaptured the bridge at Meung sur Loire on the 17th and English forces were making preparations to counterattack. The French, knowing the power of the English in open battle, were anxious to take their enemy by surprise. The English had formed up in open country just outside Patay when a stag wandered across their front. The English raised a hunting cry and chased it, revealing their position to the French. The French vanguard attacked immediately, giving the English archers no time to erect their anti cavalry stakes and their defence collapsed and the English were routed. Anyone with a horse fled while the archers and men at arms were cut down with Lord Talbot and the Earl of Shrewsbury being captured. The loss of two experienced leaders, plus many trained soldiers greatly weakened the English and the French exploited their ascendancy and marched on to Reims where Charles was crowned on 17th July 1429. Joan stood with him at the ceremony and carried her banner stating" it has shared in the war and it is just that it should share in the victory"

Having achieved her aims, Joan wished to return to her home. The newly crowned Charles was engaged in reconciliation talks with Burgundy and her leadership had empowered the French enough to believe that the English could at last be defeated. She herself was disillusioned at the French king's apathy and negotiations with the traitor Burgundy. The army wished her to remain however and she was persuaded to lead an attack on Paris itself. On the 8th September, having regained St Denis, she was leading her troops in an attack on the capital when she was wounded in the thigh by a crossbow bolt and the attack was abandoned. This setback was a blow to her prestige and, following a political truce agreement of two years agreed with Burgundy, she lay down her arms at St Denis... She was not happy with court life even though the king ennobled her family as a sign of his gratitude and in reference to the lilies on her new coat of arms; the family adopted the name Du Lis. It was not until April following the end of the truce that she again took to the field and on the 24th May arrived at sunrise in the besieged Compiegne to help defend it. In the evening she attempted a sortie with a force of some 500, but were surprised by a greatly superior force. Fighting desperately, they retreated into the town, but the the town commander Guilliame de Flavey, either through error or panic, closed the gates trapping her and her forces outside. She was pulled from her horse and became prisoner. Why Charles did not make a greater effort to free her remains a mystery. He had many important prisoners, for whom he could have negotiated an exchange, but he did nothing and Joan was sold by her captor, John of Luxembourg to the English. To them, she was indeed a prize. The English leaders feared her power of self belief and the effect she had on French troops, while the ordinary soldier believed her a witch. The English had the very man in their pay to convict Joan. Pierre Cauchon, Bishop of Beauvais was a Burgundian, self seeking, unscrupulous and very much in the pay of the English. He summoned clerics and lawmen from the University of Paris as well as the Vicar of the Inquisition to assess her case and it was not until 21st February 1431 that she was stood in front of her judges. She was allowed no advocate and although being tried in an ecclesiastical court, was held in a secular prison, and guarded by the roughest of English soldiery. It was probably for the better protection of her modesty that she remained dressed in male clothing, her requests to be kept in a secular prison with other females was refused. She attempted suicide on one occasion by trying to throw herself from a window. Thereafter she was detained in an iron cage, manacled by her hands, feet and neck. She was allowed no spiritual comfort because of her alleged crimes of heresy and the wearing of men's clothes.(difformitate habitus). Joan was very fierce in her defence, swearing that all her instructions came from God and referred to her examination by clergy and lawyers from the University of Paris who cleared her of heresy when she first came to the Dauphin. As none of these records still existed, they were deemed inadmissible. She told the court that the voices had foretold her that" within seven years, the English will lose far more than Orleans". It is interesting to note that Paris was lost to the French on 12th November 1437, just six years and eight months afterwards.

The court was packed at all these hearings and Joan gained much sympathy from the people. The Bishop, intent on gaining a guilty verdict, moved the court to a private room inside the prison and with a small committee of judges, who listed 70 propositions on which she was to be charged. When Joan was called, she replied to them all in repudiation.

The judges then came up with 12 more, this time accusing her of having visions and voices from the devil and on 9th May a further 42 judges from the same University of Paris that had once cleared her, declared her a heretic and if she would not recant, was to be handed to the secular authorities. On the 22nd May, a stake was erected in St Oeun and she was again solemnly admonished for her crimes and threatened with torture. Worn out and weary, Joan signed a retraction which, when published later, was very long and very humiliating to her. It would seem however, that the retraction she signed was very different from the one published. Jean Massieu.the man who read her signed document stated later that it" was but a few lines long". She also stated that she only retracted "in so far as it was God's will" and was returned to prison. The English and Burgundians were furious. as was Bishop Cauchon. He ordered that her female clothes were to be taken away and her male clothing left for her, forcing her in modesty to wear them. On the 29th May, 37 judges ruled her relapsed heretic and sentenced to death by burning. On the 30th May, having now been allowed confession and communion, she was led to the stake. She asked for a cross and when it was given, she hugged it to her. As the fire was lit she asked that the cross be held before her and as she burned, continuously called on the name of Jesus "until the last" said the Recorder Machon, her final words being that "her voices came from God and he had not deceived her". The English threw her ashes in the Seine.

Wither or not Joan was divinely inspired, she had had the effect of galvanizing French opposition to English rule and the Dauphin never again doubted the ultimate victory.

Meanwhile in England, Henry continued his education under the guidance of Warwick while Duke Humphrey continued to create divisions in the country, often making it necessary for the Duke of Bedford to return from France to give rulings in matters of contention. The situation was further aggravated when, in 1423, Humphry married Jacqueline of Hainault a niece of Philippe of Burgundy and she endowed Humphrey with the county even though it was currently ruled by Burgundy. She urged Humphrey to lead an army across the Channel and repossess it, thus bringing him into direct conflict with Burgundy, an ally of the English in their war with France. Humphrey landed at Calais, prompting Philippe to advance on Hainault and captured Countess Jacqueline. Humphrey and Burgundy exchanged heated letters and challenged each other to single combat. The new Pope Martin V declared Jacqueline's marriage To Humphrey invalid and in great rage he returned to England, bringing with him the beautiful Eleanor Coahoma lady in waiting to Jacqueline. On his return he accused Beaufort of not supporting him and worse, plotting to overthrow Prince Henry. Humphrey was popular with the people of London and could always raise a mob to demonstrate in his favour, much to the fury of the Beauforts.On the 29th October 1425, having been accused of treason by Beaufort, Humphrey, with the aid of followers, attempted to seize the Tower, but failed. It took the tactful and diplomatic Duke of Bedford a great effort to placate all concerned. The price of harmony with Burgundy was to let Philippe retain his hold on Hainault, although he did allow Jaqueline, half the revenue for her lifetime. With the growing French confidence, the Duke of Bedford needed some assistance in maintaining the loyalty of the people in occupied territories and began arrangements for Prince Henry to come to France and show himself to his new subjects. He also needed reinforcements for the army. On the 23rd April 1430 a force of 1200 men at arms, plus some 3500 archers were landed and with them, the young Prince Henry and many notables including the Duke of York, the Duke of Norfolk, the Earl of Huntingdon and the prince's mentor, the Earl of Warwick. The fortunes of the warring parties ebbed and flowed, but now strongly reinforced, the English launched further campaigns with some success.

In June 1430 Chateau Gaillard was retaken and in July the English recaptured Aumale and Etrapagny and in August the stronghold of Torcy was captured and the way to Paris was now clear enough for Duke John to appoint Lord Roos governor of Paris. His rule lasted but two days however as, shortly after his arrival, he fell into the Seine and was drowned. Humphrey Earl of Stafford was sent to replace him and was announced as Constable of France. The situation was still not safe enough to bring Prince Henry to Paris although the English continued to enjoy some military gains. Warwick roundly defeated the

French at Savignies and the besieged town of Louviers capitulated in October 1431. The situation was now considered safe enough to bring Prince Henry to Paris for his coronation. He entered Paris on 2nd December 1431 together with a large number of English nobles especially sent to pad out the numbers as most of the French aristocracy stayed away ,understandably unwilling to be seen too close to the English king. On 16th December he was crowned King of France by Beaufort in the cathedral of Notre Dame

It is thought that Henry had no wish to be king; he became a kindly and gentle soul, ill fitted to the demands of court intrigue and the rigors of the French wars. He was also naïve and trusting of his friends and could see no malice in the many that took advantage of his nature for their own gain. He hated excess of any kind and his views on chastity are exampled when, at a Christmas revel, a courtier introduced a dance by young women naked from the waist upbringing down the full, although unusual wrath of the king. The king was reputed to have said, "Fy fy for shame, Forsothe on ye be to blame", before leaving. While riding through Bath, he observed men bathing naked in the warm springs and condemned them all for their shameful nudity. On another occasion, when riding across London Bridge, he saw a grisly object impaled on a pike and asked what it was. When told that it was a quarter of the body of an executed traitor hung there as a warning to others, he commanded that it be pulled down and given proper burial because such a thing was unworthy of a Christian society. His devotion to religion was evidenced by his habit of demanding that a certain dish depicting the five wounds of Christ, due to its red color, be set on his table before any other whereupon he would contemplate it with great fervor and praise God before commencing to eat.

The war with France wore on and both sides were exhausted and running short of money to continue. The ultimate defection of Burgundy to the French king, plus the death of the brave and loyal John, Duke of Bedford would soon shift the power struggle in favor of the French although by 1435 it is true to say that English territories in France were larger than had been the case in 1415 after Agincourt he French now had the measure of their opponents.A diplomatic attempt at a peace was attempted at the Congress of Arras in 1435 when the English, French and Burundians met in an attempt to negotiate a treaty. The English proposed a marriage of Prince Henry to a daughter of the French king but would not give up Henry's claim to the French throne. The negotiations were suspended when the English left the meeting to put down a raid by the French captains La Hire and Potton de Xantrailles. During this break, the French urged Burgundy to give up their support of the English and defect to them and when the English returned, they found that Burgundy had switched sides. Duke John died on September 14th 1435, one week before the conclusion of the Congress. His role as protector of English interests in France was taken over by Richard, Duke of York appointed as the King's Lieutenant in France. The Duke, being a descendant of both Lionel, Duke of Clarence, the second son of Edward 111 and, through Edmund, Duke of York, the fourth son of King Edward, had a claim to the throne that was superior to King Henry, whose descent was from John of Gaunt, the third son of the old king. With the growing dissatisfaction at King Henry's weak rule, there was talk that Richard should claim the crown, causing the pro Lancastrian Beauforts to "keep him out of the way". York swept south and took Dieppe before being recalled to England and then being dispatched to campaign in Ireland, and was replaced in France by the King's old tutor, Richard, Earl of Warwick.

The Duc d'Orleans ,still a captive in England and well versed in English politics, attempted to bring the warring parties together by proposing that a marriage between Henry and the 15 year old Margaret d Anjou could be the centerpiece of a comprehensive peace plan. He knew that if Henry was not to produce an heir, Humphrey of Gloucester might succeed to the English throne and Humphrey was no friend to the French. The two sides were far too wary of each other to accept the arrangement in toto, although the idea of the wedding itself was not rejected. Margaret was a pretty 15 year old, the daughter of Renee Duc de Bar and Lorraine and titular King of Sicily,Naples and Jerusalem. The titles were very grand but, following his capture by Philippe of Burgundy at the battle of Bulgneville and the payment of his ransom, was impoverished although of sufficiently high position to be considered by the English king.

King Charles therefore rejected any proposals for a peace treaty, but cleverly agreed to a truce. A treaty would have entailed concessions of territory to the English, but a truce would give him breathing space to revitalize his exhausted forces. Furthermore, he knew the rowdy

English soldiery would inevitably break a truce and give Charles the choice of compensation payments or to reopen hostilities.

Another attempt to end the fighting took place at Oye in 1439. This meeting was convened by the formidable Duchess of Burgundy who, heeding the complaints of the Flemish wool merchants whose trade had suffered badly due to the wars, looked to arrange a truce between England and France. The English delegation was headed by Cardinal Beaufort who had been given a fairly wide remit, but refused to accept Henry renouncing his claim to the French throne. The French demanded that Henry give up his claim and in return would accept English dominion over the occupied territories as long as Henry paid full homage to the French king for these lands. This was flatly refused despite many attempts at compromise. The Duchess looked for some movement from either side and suggested a long truce. The French agreed but on condition that, during the truce, Henry must not style himself King of France and that the Duc d'Orleans be released. Beaufort sent the Bishop of York back to England to explain the French offer to Henry who, under the influence of his uncle Duke Humphrey, refused. Why Beaufort did not travel to England himself with such important decisions is not known. In the event, the Duchess was only able to agree a commercial truce which did at least open the door to the wool trade again.

In England feelings were divided, State finances were in a parlous position, Royal purveyors were not paying bills, judges were threatening strikes as they had not been paid for months and many yearned for an end to the war. Only Duke Humphrey and his followers still believed in ultimate victory, although any moves towards giving up title to the French throne was seen as a betrayal of King Henry Vs legacy by much of the populace. Humphrey was popular and seen as more accessible to the lesser nobles. He was also a survivor of Agincourt and brother to the venerated Henry V. Beaufort had, on the other hand, made substantial loans to the crown to continue prosecution of the war and, in doing so, had advanced his families interests considerably. The friction between Beaufort and Humphrey brought the country to the verge of civil war. A stronger king could have stamped his authority on the situation, but the saintly Henry was content to let things drift. So immersed in religion had he become that all else seemed but a distraction. During the years 1440/1441 he founded Eton College and Kings College Cambridge and poured time and money into their design, planning, pupils and staffing. They were built for the "Glory of God" and to ensure that hymns and prayers were offered daily by their choirs. The war was costing some £170000 per year, more than twice the royal revenues and Parliament was grudging in its contributions. More unrest was caused when the Archbishop of York was offered a cardinalship by the Pope and Humphrey made much of the situation by denouncing the influence of the Pope and, by implication, his old enemy Beaufort, who had been similarly honored earlier. An opportunity came for Beaufort to discredit Humphrey when an obscure priest Roger Bolingbroke (no relation) was charged with casting a horoscope for Humphrey's wife Eleanor Cobham to determine wither she would ever be queen. This was probably no more than an innocent parlour game designed to amuse, but was seized on by Beaufort. Roger found himself placed on a stage in St Paul's churchyard, dressed in mystical garb and surrounded by the "tools of his craft". A large crowd led by the Archbishop of Canterbury, together with the Bishops of London, Salisbury and Rochester exhorted him turn his back on sorcery and accusing him of "missownyng the Cristen faith". Eleanour, seeing where this was leading, fled to Westminster Abbey for sanctuary, but was refused as no protection could be offered for sorcery. She was brought before an eccliastical court on 25th July 1441, where Roger and others, no doubt following torture, gave evidence against her. She was found guilty of 28 charges of treason, heresy and sorcery and was sent to Leeds castle to await further examination.

The Beauforts gathered support against her and Henry was persuaded to commission a further examination, but, typically, stipulated that she was not to be tortured. The Commission managed to find a flimsy connection with a Marjery Jourdemain the so called "witch of Eye". The truth was that Marjery sold cosmetics and Eleanor had bought from her from time to time. This was enough for Beaufort however and Eleanor was again brought to London and charged with plotting the king's death by magic and was found guilty. In November 1441 she was forced to walk barefoot through London to St Paul's to beg forgiveness. The populace was encouraged to line the streets and, as was the practice, throw noxious things at her. It is interesting to note that the people were recorded as standing silent as she passed which indicates where their sympathies lay although her plight had undoubtedly weakened Humphrey's standing in some circles.

The Duc d'Orleans, the last prisoner still in captivity from Agincourt saw an opportunity to mediate between England and France. His captivity was not as bad as it sounds. While nominally a prisoner in the Tower he led a life befitting a person of rank, spending his time being entertained as an honored guest among the English nobility. He had gained much insight into English politics and attitudes during his time in England and saw himself as just the man to reconcile the two factions. Negotiations were restarted with a view to Henry's marriage to Margaret, plus whatever the English could salvage from the agreement. The English delegation was led by William de la Pole, Earl of Suffolk. He was charged with reaching an accord with the French, becoming betrothed to Margaret by proxy for Henry, extracting a promise of Normandy and Guienne being ceded to England and in return, Henry would give up his claim to the French crown and free the Duc d Orleans. Suffolk must have had some misgivings regarding his task because he insisted on being given an indemnity before leaving England; absolving him of any blame should the arrangements go wrong. The proposed agreement made no mention of Maine, a territory that had been earlier promised to Edmund Beaufort and this was to be a trigger for further unrest in England later. It became clear that the French were not very interested in the English offer; the success of French arms in recent encounters had made them confident that the English power in France was waning, especially as they no longer had the support of Burgundy. Suffolk' tried in vain to impress the French, but the only offer on the table was a betrothal and a truce.

The betrothal took place on 14th March 1444. Edmund Beaufort, angered at the promised Maine being given to the French, opened hostilities in the county to reinforce his claim, but the French pressured Suffolk to withdraw under the threat of cancellation of a truce. Suffolk was forced to agree and the treaty was signed on 25th December 1444.

Margaret sailed for England in March 1445 on the Cock Johan, a great storm blew up in the channel and the ship was dismasted, swamped and finally beached near Porcester where she was forced to take refuge in a peasant's hut until arrangements could be made to get her to London. Many English, still suspicious of France, viewed the storm as a bad omen. Parliament, still short of money, refused to pay for all the royal wedding, forcing Henry to pay half the costs from his own pocket. The couple were married on 23rd April 1445.

Trouble flared again when the question of the return of Le Mans and Maine became due in April 1446 under the terms of treaty. Humphrey used his position to oppose the return and raised the spectre of all of the old king's French gains being meekly handed back to the French. The king however, had signed the necessary orders and Humphrey's opposition was denounced as treason by Beaufort.Parliament was commanded to meet at Cambridge (later changed to Bury St Edmunds) on 10th February 1447, where Articles of Impeachment were to be read against Humphrey. Eleanor was sent to the Isle of Man as a hostage for Humphrey's attendance. Humphrey, at last sensing what was in store. Appealed to the City of London to supply him a bodyguard for protection and a force of 80 men were assembled. Humphrey set out with his retinue to attend Parliament, but was accosted on the way by the king's messenger ordering him to go directly to his arranged lodgings at St Salvatores and await instructions. He arrived at St Salvatores and settled in while his men were lodged elsewhere and disarmed. He was visited by the Duke of Buckingam and other nobles and placed under arrest. He was to remain under guard until called for. The shock of his arrest stunned him, he is reported to have "fell into a stupor" and rallied only to receive the last rites before dying on 23rd February 1447, probably of a stroke, although some think he was poisoned. Thus died the last hero of Agincourt and loyal brother to the old king. There is no doubt that, while often wayward and quarrelsome, he had, like Bedford, the best interests of the Plantagenet dynasty at heart and fought hard to retain all that Henry V had won and against what he saw as appeasement with the French.

The Treaty of Tours, agreed in 1446 had some years to run but was repeatedly broken by skirmishes and raids on both sides. In England and in Normandy the rule of law was breaking down with the king quite unable and unwilling to show firm leadership. With Humphrey dead, Queen Margaret came more and more under the influence of the Duke of Suffolk who was increasingly unpopular as the blame for French ascendancy was placed on him for his poor diplomacy. It was rumored that the pair were lovers and this rumor was strengthened when, as part of a new truce to run until 1450, the English were obliged to give up Maine and hand it over to the Queen's father Renee.

In 1449, some English mercenaries led by the Aragon knight Francois de Surienne, wantonly burnt the town of Fougeres on the Breton March. This gave the now stronger French king the excuse he needed to break the truce and his armies, over the next twelve months swept the English from all of lower Normandy. Treachery and self interest were the order of the day with many English nobles making separate deals with the French so as to hang on to their Norman estates. In October the French besieged Rouen, but after three days the townspeople rose against the English garrison and opened the gates to their countryman. The English retreated to the castle but surrendered after a few days. England's most experienced general John Talbot was captured and later released under promise that he "would never wear armour against the King of France again". The bulk of the English force was allowed to march back to Caen under the Duke of Somerset. By December, even Harfleur, the first town to be captured by Henry V, was back in French hands.

The Duke of Suffolk, following the death of Cardinal Beaufort, stood alone at the head of government. Henry, becoming more and more preoccupied and vague,

Drifted into melancholy and would sit for hours, staring into space saying nothing. This is now thought to be the beginning of his decline into the intermittent madness that had for so long plagued the French royal family and had passed to him through his mother

In 1450, Suffolk sent a force of some 3000 men under Sir Thomas Kyriel to stem the tide of French success. Linking up with the 2000 remaining garrison of Somerset's forces in Caen, he advanced on Bayeux. On the 15th April he confronted a smaller French force commanded by the Count of Clermond near the village of Formigny. Clermond sent riders to contact another French force some distance away, while the English formed in the usual Agincourt formation of dismounted men at arms, interspersed with archers. At three in the afternoon the French attacked, but were three times driven back by the archers, suffering heavy losses. They then brought up 2 cannon to fire from the flanks, causing much distress to the archers who, breaking ranks charged the cannon intending to pull them back to the English line. They had almost reached safety when the reserve French force of 2000 mounted men, summoned by Clermond appeared on rising ground to their left. Kyriel desperately tried to regroup his forces to meet this new attack. Clermond's troops rallied and struck back while the mounted men ploughed into the side of Kyriel's force. It was a complete rout many of the archers, fearing slaughter or the loss of fingers, fought to the last man in a little walled garden of the village church, while all over the field archers and men at arms fought to the finish. By nightfall it was over. Nearly 5000 English were killed and Kyriel taken prisoner.

The news of such a disaster plunged England into yet more misery, common people rose in protest at the losses in France, the demands for yet more taxes and the incompetence of the king's advisors. They found a leader in Jack Cade, a man of Kent, who met King Henry on Black heath and demanded redress for the people or they would sack London. Henry agreed to arrest the particularly detested Lord Saye and then fled to the midlands for safety. Cade's band entered London and beheaded Lord Saye and the Sheriff of Kent who had tried to resist them and then began to pillage the city. The citizens who had first welcomed them now turned on the rebels and civil war broke out with hundreds being killed before the rebels were finally ejected. Cade was eventually killed and the king, like Richard before him, reneged on the promises he had given. None of these events seemed to touch Henry, he was content to return to his devotions and let others do what they would in his name. The country needed a scapegoat however, and, following news of the Formigny disaster, the Duke of Suffolk was impeached by parliament who wanted him executed. The king reduced punishment to five years exile and on 25th April, Suffolk sailed for Brittany. He was not to escape however. On 30th April, his ship was intercepted by an assortment of ships, at least one of which was the royal vessel 'St Nicholas of the Tower'. Suffolk was bundled into a rowing boat and his head struck off over the gunwale. His body was thrown into the sea.

In the midst of this unrest, Richard, Duke of York had been relieved of his command as King's Lieutenant in France and sent to Ireland in the same rank. His enemy Edmond Beafort, Duke of Somerset took over his role in France and it was clear that those in power wanted Richard away from England for a long time. Instead of the normal five year stint, Richard was given a ten year commission. Richard, who was heir to the throne unless Henry had children, was rightly concerned at the Beaufort family having so much power and influence

225

over the king. Although in 1406, a statute had been specifically precluded the Beauforts from claiming the crown, Richard knew that the statute could be rescinded at any time and he could find his claim usurped. He resigned his commission and in September 1450 landed in Wales and was met by the young Richard of Warwick who had gathered the nucleus of a force to build an army in York's support. Richard preferred to try gentler means to curb the Beauforts and set out for London to seek audience with Henry. On learning this, the Chancellor, fearing civil war, ordered the King's men to arrest York, but either through cleverness or, more probably, the connivance of ordinary folk who saw Richard as the man to ease England's problems, they failed and Richard duly arrived in the presence of Henry. Richard, becoming heated, described the government as a shambles, demanded that a parliament be summoned, cited Cade's rebellion and the loss of Normandy as evidence of Beaufort mismanagement and demanded that Edmond Beaufort be impeached. The king listened to all and promised to appoint a substantial government in which Richard would have a role. Richard traveled to his friend Mowbray's estate in Norfolk and awaited the summoning of the new parliament which met on 6th October 1450.

Richard again demanded Somerset's impeachment and while the Commons was clearly with him, the Lords sided with Somerset and no decision was reached. Richard attempted to seize Somerset and rioting broke out in London. Somerset was taken to the Tower "for his own protection" and then, following Margaret's persuading, was sent by the king to take up duties as Captain of Calais. The next parliament was convened on 24th April 1451 and among other reforms agreed was the Statute of Resumption which did much to increase royal revenues as well as reversing the effects of some nobles profiting from remaining in England while others served the crown in France during the war. By the end of 1451 Somerset was back and to rub salt in Richard's wounds was made Constable of England. The furious Duke issued a proclamation blaming the Beauforts for all the country's ills, the loss of France and Cade's rebellion. He insisted he was loyal to the king and asked only for the removal of the Beauforts and their followers who he accused of being responsible for the mismanagement of the country. On 3rd February 1452, he called on the men of Shrewsbury to raise a force and help him remove these bad advisors. He thought that folk would flock to him but, while Somerset was hated by most Englishmen, they were not ready to rise against the king and it is a pattern of the remainder of Henry's life that he became a cipher and an easy rallying point for whichever side held him captive at the time.

It is ironic that, if Richard had asked this in 1450, the people would have risen without hesitation. In the event, a modest force was raised and was supplemented by other small detachments on the journey to London. The government understandably viewed this as rebellion and dispatched a force to intercept the rebels. York sidestepped them and camped near Dartford to await what he confidently expected as a rallying of Londoners to his banner. The royal forces arrived shortly after and the two sides faced each other without attacking. The king sent Warwick and some other old friends of York to negotiate a peaceful solution. Richard explained his grievances and believed that assurances were received as to the justice of his complaints. In the meantime, the Bishops had been prevailing on the king to have sympathy for Richards's grievances. They felt that, on balance, Richard had a better chance of uniting the country than the Beauforts. Henry agreed and sent his officers to arrest Somerset and take his sword. On hearing of this, Richard went to the king to assure him of his loyalty and was shocked to see Somerset sat at the king's right hand again. Thus showed the influence of Margaret whose hatred of Richard knew no bounds. When she heard of Somerset's arrest, she flew into a rage and shrieked at the king, did he not realize that York wanted the throne? Did he not see that Somerset was the only true friend? The king, like all meek men wanted only a quiet life, could not say no to his wife and in his weakness asked Somerset's forgiveness and reinstated him. Richard was arrested for treason, but stood and, looking the king straight in the eye, stated that he was no traitor and his only crime was to place too much trust in the king's word. The king set great store in his personal integrity and the accusation touched him deeply. Margaret was screeching for York's execution, but the king, for once overriding his wife, pardons Richard and his followers, promising no action would be taken against them and begged them to disperse to their homes. Somerset had one more humiliation to place on York and Richard was made to walk through the city to St Pauls and swear on the Host that he would never take up arms against his sovereign, sending a clear signal to the people that Richard was a lost cause. In his later rebellion, he was to renege on his oath by declaring that Henry was not the true king and that his own lineage was senior to the throne.

Throughout this period Aquitaine remained relatively peaceful with King Charles' attention focused on ridding northern France of the English. Having achieved this, he now set out to recapture this huge southern duchy that had been in English hands for three hundred years, His forces arrived outside Bordeaux in April 1451 to lay siege. The commander of Bordeaux, the Gascon Captal de Buch agreed that, should the city not be relieved by 14th June, it would surrender. No English relieving force arrived and Bordeaux duly surrendered .French forces entered Bordeaux on 30th June. The French then spread out throughout the duchy and, by August, Bayonne was captured and the fighting was over. King Charles allowed the Gascon lords to retain all titles and lands, but must swear an oath of loyalty to Charles. English citizens were allowed to depart without ransom and were also given six months to sell up their properties. The French king has however, underestimated the residual loyalty many felt for their long time English masters. The people also had little time for Frenchmen north of the Loire. Furthermore, he installed his artillery commander as Mayor of Bordeaux and made a Breton the Seneschal of Aquitaine. Meanwhile the wine trade, on which the economy of the region depended, had virtually stopped and in a very short time rebellion was in the air. In October 1452, the English sent an army of 5000 men under the old warrior John Talbot, and landed in the Medoc. People flocked to join them and overthrow the French. Bordeaux opened its gates and in towns across the region the people evicted the French garrisons from the castles. Everywhere the people rejoiced at the return of the English. The French king, when told, was furious and by April 1453 had sent a huge force into Aquitaine. The force was too large for Talbot to venture an attack, but when it split into smaller units to besiege various towns, Talbot marched from Bordeaux with a force of some 6000 including his son Lord de Lisle, intending to attack the French force besieging Castillon.

The French, having had word of his coming had built strong defences of ditches and barriers of tree trunks, backed with a large range of cannon. Talbot, seeing a large cloud of dust over the French position, thought that the enemy was retreating although the truth was that the

French were merely rounding up their horses in readiness for the battle. Talbot did not hesitate, keeping to the terms he had agreed for his release at Falaise,where he had vowed never to wear armour against the French king again, he rode into battle unarmed and unarmoured on a white pony and hurled wave after wave of his troops at the French positions. The French artillery broke up these attacks easily and as the English faltered, the French rushed forward to slaughter the dazed attackers. Talbot sat on his pony, urging his troops on until a cannonball killed his horse, whereupon a French man at arms rushed from the barricades and killed him with a battleaxe. The English forces were pushed back to the banks of the Dordogne and made a final stand. Many were drowned in their panic to escape. On the following day, the French let the English heralds roam the battlefield to search for Talbot's body which was returned to England and lies buried at Whitchurch in Shropshire.

The French army was once again at the gates of Bordeaux and, following a three month siege, the city surrendered on 19th October. King Charles was not to be so generous and lenient with the defenders as before. He demanded a fine of 100,000 crowns and banished the Gascon lords who had opposed him. The war which had started over control of Aquitaine had finally ended in the duchy in 1453, 116 years after it began.

Henry's mental condition, meanwhile, was steadily worsening. On 10th August 1453, he suffered a major attack that was to last until Christmas 1454. During these attacks he would sit without moving, paying no attention to anything going on around him. The squabbles between York, Exeter and Somerset over the succession were ended when on 1st January 1454 Queen Margaret gave birth to Prince Edward. It was thought that the sight of his son might bring the King out of the attack, but when Buckingham presented the infant to him, Henry took no notice and did not speak. The queen then came in and "toke the prince in her arms and presented hym,desiring that he should blisse it,but alle their labour was in veyne for they departed thens without any answer sayving only that ones he loked on the Prince and caste dounne his eyene without any more".

In England York, who had been made Protector of the Realm during the king's illness, continued to cause unrest, presenting himself as the alternative to the "evil rule" of the Duke of Somerset and the King.

229

Posing as a reformer, he used every opportunity to further his own cause, becomimg ever more arrogant, not even accepting the king's veto. He remained however, popular with the Commons due to his support of proposed financial reforms. Most lords initially supported neither Somerset nor York and gave loyalty to the king. With the king making a brief recovery, York lost his position as Protector and began, with his friends the Nevilles, to gather forces in the north to prevent Somerset from resuming his old position of power. His forces moved south and by the middle of May had reached Ware. The Lancastrians gathered a force to oppose York and the two armies met at St Albans on 22nd May 1455 in the first battle of what was to become the Wars of the Roses. The Duke of Buckingham as Constable of England had been given command of the royal forces and with Somerset, plus their two heirs, the Earls of Devon and Stafford, plus three other earls, six barons and the king, entered the town at 4am. York's men had camped in Key Field which lay behind the houses of St Peters Street and Hollywell Street. The royalists rode into the town and set up barriers across the roads into town and placed detachments of troops at each roadblock. York sent an emissary to the Duke of Buckingham demanding that Somerset be handed over, but the king refused and for once and uncharacteristically, damned the rebels, saying "By the faith that I owe to Seynt Edward and to the Coronc of England, I shall destroy them every moder sone". York's forces then advanced and the king raised his banner at Goslawe in St Peter's Street, an act of great significance as any who fought when the royal banner was displayed were ipso facto traitors. York's ally Richard Neville the Earl of Warwick led his men behind the rows of houses and, bursting through them to the main street, came face to face with the royal forces. The Steward of St Albans, Sir William Stonor was an eye witness to these events and records that Warwick's men "ferociously broke in by the garden sides between the Sign of the Key and the Sign of the Chequer in Hollywell Street and when in the town set up a great cry of "A Warwick, A Warwick". In the general fighting that followed Yorkist soldiers cast down the royal standard that had been left unguarded. Buckingham was hit in the face by an arrow while another grazed the king's neck. The remainder of the royalist leaders made a defiant last stand until Somerset was mortally wounded at the door of the Castle Inn and with his demise the fight was over. With York's army numbering around 3000 and the king's around 2000, this was not a battle on the scale of the French wars, but was significant as the opening battle of the very bloody Wars of the Roses. York immediately rushed to the king who had taken refuge in a tanner's house and asked forgiveness, saying that Somerset's death would be a joy to all the people. The unruly Welsh elements of York's force sacked the town while York and the king went in procession together to attend a thanksgiving service in St Albans cathedral. York was again back in charge and Warwick was made Captain of Calais, a shrewd move by York as Calais garrison contained the largest force of professional soldiers available to the crown.

Henry's failure to punish York for his earlier rebellion led to the duke becoming even more demanding . York's protests and obstructions soon made government virtually impossible and by 1460 was forcing a choice between himself and royal favorites and then between himself and the king. In parliament, a certain Thomas Yonge, a lawyer, proposed that a successor should be nominated to stabilize the kingdom and suggested York. Henry was quite unable to stand up for himself and when York renounced his allegiance and claimed the crown by heredity right, the country was divided. In 1459 queen Margaret managed to wrest control of the king from York and gathered a force at Coventry to attack York's castle at Ludlow. They were met at Bloreheath near Market Drayton by a Yorkist army led by the Earl of Salisbury. On the 23rd September, the two sides met and the Yorkists, using the Agincourt tactic, arranged themselves behind sharpened wooden stakes and used their archers to repulse three attacks. The Lancastrians pushed on and would have overwhelmed their enemy, but the usual medieval mixture of treachery and betrayal in their ranks enabled the Earl to emerge the victor. The battle was also notable for the appearance, due to unusual atmospheric conditions, of "three suns" in the sky and it is said that York's son Edward took his emblem of the Flaming Sun from that day. The Yorkists moved on into Ludlow and met up with the Duke of York and Warwick who had brought with him 200 men of the Calais garrison all wearing the red coat of Warwick with the Bear and Ragged Staff badge on the shoulder. They constructed a fortified camp outside the town and cut a moat from the nearby River Teme as a further defence. A Lancastrian army arrived on the other side of the river on October 12th and the Lancastrians called across the river offering free pardon to all who would leave the Duke of York and rejoin the royal army. Many of the Calais men who had served under Somerset in the past, defected, causing York to lose his nerve and ordered his army to disperse. He fled to Ireland while Warwick and York's son Edward went to Devon and from there, on a boat hired by their squire John Dinham for £73, returned to France. It is said that Warwick had to act as Steersman due to the inadequacies of the crew. This reverse strengthened queen Margaret's hand and she decided to attempt to dislodge Warwick from Calais. The fleet she sent were driven however, by contrary winds into the Calais roads and under the guns of Warwick. The troops sent emissaries ashore to bargain with the duke for their lives, offering all their supplies and their services. Warwick was pitiless, on landing; the invaders were divided on Calais pier between those who were the queen's men and those who had deserted him at Ludlow. The former were forced to swear allegiance and don the Bear and Ragged Staff livery of Warwick, while the rest were butchered on the pier.

On the 26th June, Warwick landed at Sandwich and was joined by many Kentish men tired of the Lancastrian misrule and marched on London where he was welcomed by the inhabitants. The Lancastrian forces retreated to the Tower and an artillery battle began. Warwick moved north, intending to bring the royal forces to battle. The two groups met at Northampton on 10th July. Warwick sent heralds three times to Buckungham's camp, requesting audience with the king, but all were refused. Warwick swore that he would speak to the king that day or die. The royalists, under Buckingham, had built fortifications with earthworks and cannon and had the River Nene at their backs. Buckingham rightly thought that, even though outnumbered, his position gave him the advantage, but he had not reckoned with the treachery of Lord Grey of Ruthin, who had changed his allegiance. Ruthin's men pulled down the barricades in front of their positions and allowed the Yorkists to stream through. The Lancastrians were now in a death trap and the Yorkists wasted no time in completing their victory. Buckingham and most of his force was butchered and the king captured. Warwick brought the sad and disorientated Henry to London as a captive and awaited the return of the Duke of York from Ireland. York delayed his journey and dragged his feet on the way to London and arrived without having spoken to his allies since Ludlow. He then amazed them by claiming the throne and declaring Henry unfit to rule. Arriving at parliament, York walked straight to the chamber and placed his hand on the cushioned throne. He stayed there for some moments and then, standing beneath the canopy, he turned to the people to await their applause and acclamation. Thomas Bouchier, Archbishop of Canterbury rose and asked York to come and see the king. York replied, " I know not of anyone within the kingdom whom it would not befit to come sooner to me than I should go and visit him" York then went to the king's private chambers and, smashing the locks and flinging open all doors, he lodged there, " more like a king than a duke". Warwick was furious. To support the dismissal of the self servers was one thing, to depose an anointed king was another. York had himself proclaimed Protector again and with the king in his hands, forced parliament to pass the Act of Accord, allowing Henry to live out his life as monarch, but passing the throne to York and his heirs on his death, thus disinheriting the seven year old Prince Edward. Queen Margaret and the Lancastrian supporters were naturally furious at this turn of events, fled north with the prince and a lowly squire John Combe and wasted no time in summoning those nobles loyal to the king to join her. York, aware of the armies being raised against him, collected a force of around 8000 men and marched north, leaving his son Edward and Warwick to continue recruiting in Wales and the south. He arrived at Sandal castle near Wakefield on 21st December 1460. The Lancastrians, led by the new Duke of Somerset with some 15000 men were at Pontefract some nine miles away and devised a plan to lure York from the safety of the castle. A force of Lancastrians moved forward to the open ground that bordered the banks of the River Calder. What the Yorkists did not know was that a much larger Lancastrian force was hidden in the woods either side. . Seeing this array and not waiting to receive the reinforcements that were on their way, York ordered his forces to leave the castle and attack The Yorkists advanced and the trap was sprung. In the ensuing battle, York, together with many of his nobles was killed. The remnants of York's army fled but were pursued and killed by Somerset's men. York's son Edmund, the 17 year old Earl of Rutland was captured on Wakefield Bridge by Lord Clifford. The boy pleaded for his life, but Clifford would not listen. "By God's blod" he said, "thy father slew myne and so wil I do the". With that, he stabbed the boy in the throat, thrusting so hard that the tip appeared at the back of his neck.. Edmund's head and that of his father York were placed on spikes at the gates of Wakefield. York's being decorated with a paper crown. York's ally the Earl of Salisbury (Warwick's father) was caught in the woods near the town the following day and was dragged to Pontefract and beheaded.

Warwick and York's eldest son Edward, Earl of March hastily began to recruit more troops to defeat the now stronger Lancastrian forces. London contributed 2000 silver marks to Warwick's campaign and also released men from jail to enlist. In Wales, the Lancastrian Owen Tudor, lover and reputed husband of Catherine, the wife of the old king Henry V, had raised an army and was marching to join up with other Lancastrians. He was intercepted at Mortimers Cross near Wigmore in Herefordshire and on the 2nd February 1461 was defeated by the Earl of March. Tudor believed that he would be pardoned due to his close relationship with the old royal family, but the war by now had dispensed with any concepts of chivalry or leniency. He was taken to Haverfordwest for execution and when it finally dawned on him that he was to die, was reported to remark, "This head that once lay in Queen Catherine's lap will now lay in the executioner's basket". His head was placed on the top of the market cross where a local madwoman combed the hair and washed the face, lighting a hundred candles in his memory. His son Jasper escaped from the battle and in the strange twists of medieval history his other son Edmund, who had married Margaret Beaufort, descendant of John of Gaunt, was the father of that Henry who was to defeat Richard 111 at Bosworth and become Henry V11 and thus unite the houses of Lancaster and York..

The main Lancastrian force under Queen Margaret continued to move southward and Warwick moved an army northwards to intercept them. On 12th February 1461, he occupied the town of St Albans and blocked the roads to London. He stationed two divisions of his army at Barnards Heath north of the town and waited for Margaret's coming. The chronicler Gregory described the preparations that Warwick's men made, " They (the hand gunners) had such instruments that would shoot both pellets of lead and arrows of an ell in length, with thee feathers in the middle and three at the end with an iron head and wildfire withal." He went on to describe the nets with sharp nails attached which were laid before their positions "so that no man could walk on them without being injured". The gunners and archers also had pavis shields studded with nails to defend themselves while loading which could also be laid before them, nails uppermost to create an obstacle for cavalry. The careful Warwick also placed a company of some 200 archers further north at Dunstable to give warning of the enemy approach. A traitor in Warwick's ranks however, a certain Lovelace, described as a' captain of Kent', got word to the queen's army who sent a detachment to Dunstable and massacred the archers. On the 17th February, the Lancastrians advanced up Romeland Street to be met by a withering arrow storm. They circled around the side streets and came up behind their foe, forcing them back to the main body of some 6000 men under Warwick's command. The queen's forces, under Somerset numbered some 9000, each wearing the ostrich feathers on a black ground, being the arms of King Henry's son, Edward, Prince of Wales, marched forward in a snowstorm. The wind and snow, blowing into the faces of Warwick's archers and gunners, played havoc with the spluttering matches, some of the guns blew up, killing eighteen gunners. The archers too, firing blind into the wind, fell short and in a moment the Lancastrians were on them. Some of the Kentish men broke and ran, causing a general panic, following which, the Lancastrian cavalry charged in and swept the field. During the ensuing massacre, King Henry was found sitting under a tree, accompanied by the Yorkists Sir Thomas Kyriel and Lord Bonville. Henry had promised them their lives if they stayed to protect him. They were executed later however; some say on the order of the eighteen year old Prince Edward.

From St Albans the queen and Somerset withdrew northwards to gather more forces for a final assault on the Yorkists. On 26th February the Earl of March and Warwick, "with many men but few of name" entered London amid much pomp with some 8000 men and at Moorfields on 4th March, a great crowd heard heralds proclaim the young Earl of March, King of England. This had the effect of rallying many nobles who had hitherto been unsure as to who to support and they now flocked to Queen Margaret whose forces were now around 26000, a huge army for the time. Warwick and March had not been idle, with a force of some 20000; they marched north to confront Margaret. The two forces met at Towton on 29th March in what was to become the bloodiest battle ever fought on English soil. At 9am the two armies advanced on each other in a snowstorm. The Yorkists fired a volley of arrows which, carried by the wind, struck hard at the front rank of the Lancastrians. Believing the enemy to be closer than anticipated, Somerset ordered return fire into the snowstorm but all fell " 40 taylors yards short". The Yorkists ran forwards, retrieving the enemy arrows and fired back causing much slaughter. A general bloodbath took place and when the Duke of Norfolk arrived with reinforcements for Warwick, the Lancastrians broke and fled, being pursued by the Yorkist cavalry. Many where trapped on the banks of the River Cocke which was in spate and were massacred in what is still known as Bloody Meadow. Corpses were said to have so filled the river that some troops escaped by walking across them. It was said that the river ran red for three days. Casualties in the battle have been estimated at 28000, one chronicler gives a precise figure of 26777, but medieval estimates should always be suspect. Even so, a figure of around 20000 is probably close. Poor King Henry fled to Scotland with Queen Margaret. York returned to London in triumph and on the 28th June 1461, was crowned King of England. The country now had two monarchs. For the next two years Margaret plotted, offering the Scots Berwick and Carlisle in return for their support, but the Scots were more interested in talks with Edward and she eventually went to France with the Prince of Wales and took refuge with her Burgundy kinfolk.

In early 1464, Warwick's brother, the Marquis of Montagu was on his way to Newcastle negotiate a treaty with the Scots, the Yorkist star was rising and many former Lancastrians flocked to his banner. On 25th of May, he met with a Lancastrian force at Hedgeley Moor led by Somerset, Ralph Percy of Northumberland and the Lords Hungerford and Loos. Somerset arranged his troops in the familiar three divisions and after an exchange of arrow fire, the Yorkists advanced, but as soon as contact had been made, the left flank of the Lancastrians under Hungerford and Loos, faltered, broke and scattered. The remaining royalists vainly tried to readjust the line, but Montagu's forces swept forward and overcame them. Ralph Percy made a gallant last stand with his retainers, but was killed as the Yorkists swept the field.

In June 1464, the Scots concluded a fifteen year treaty with King Edward and Henry was forced to take refuge among his supporters in the wild country of the Lancashire/Yorks borders. He was recognized by a monk called Cantlow while sitting at dinner in Waddington Hall at Ribblesdale, who notified the Yorkists

Of his whereabouts. Henry did manage to escape from the Hall, but was captured at Clitheroe by a Thomas Talbot of Bashal. He was escorted to London by Sir James Harrington, his only companions being a monk, a doctor and a servant and was met at Islington by Warwick who paraded him through the city to the Tower with his legs bound underneath his horse by leather throngs and a straw hat on his head. The Londoners hooted and jeered him on the journey. The Yorkists made much of his capture and swore that the old king was treated with "humanity and reverence", but Lancastrians believed that he was starved, beaten and insulted throughout his captivity. Henry himself professed himself indifferent to the loss of his earthly kingdom, wishing only to continue his religious devotions and the sacraments of the church. His religion became even more intense and was reported to have visions and utter prophecies. There are a number of contempory references to him being Dirty, ill dressed and neglected, but it was clearly not in King Edward's interests for him to be killed all the time that the Prince of Wales was alive. Henry's jailors would cruelly taunt him and reproach him on his usurpation, to which Henry was said to have replied "my father was King of England and his father before him and I, as a boy, crowned almost in my cradle and wore the crown for nearly forty years, with every lord swearing homage and fealty as they had done to my forefathers"

Meanwhile, on 21st May 1464, King Edward secretly married Elizabeth Woodville, much to the disgust of Warwick, who had been negotiating for the king to marry into the French royal family and whose Neville dynasty feared that they would now take second place to the new queen's family. Warwick felt that his family had worked and fought hard for York's cause, and while the family had certainly received large grants of benefits and titles from Edward, the king had made sure that they would never become the power behind the throne as had the Beauforts with Henry. He was also annoyed over the king's refusal to allow George Plantagenet, Duke of Clarence to marry Warwick's daughter. His fears were soon realized and the Woodvilles quickly became favored in the king's court. Warwick, no longer the king's favorite, had a number of disagreements with Edward and 1469, traveled to Calais where he was joined by the George, Duke of Clarence, Edward's brother Together they plotted to overthrow the new king.

A number of small rebellions still stirred in the north and King Edward took a small force northwards to crush them. Warwick, having finally secured an agreement from the Pope for the marriage of his daughter Isabel to Clarence, wasted no time in summoning the Archbishop of York (another Neville) to Calais to perform the ceremony which took place on the 11th July 1469. With the king out of the way, Warwick returned to London and began to stir up feeling against Edward by suggesting that Edward was bastard born and that Clarence was the true heir of York. Upon learning that the rebels had amassed an army bigger than his own, he resolved to wait in Nottingham for reinforcements from the south led by the Earls of Pembroke and Devon. On the 12th July, Warwick declared his support for the rebels and collecting a large army, moved north. The rebels moved south to join with Warwick, bypassing the king's army, but met Pembroke and Devon at Edgecote Moor on 25th July. On the morning of the 26th, the rebels attacked Pembroke's forces. The contingent under Devon had camped a few miles away and had not yet reached the battle. Pembroke, although forced back, held his line until 1pm when he was joined by Devon. His relief was short lived however, when a new force appeared on the hill behind them. This was no real army but a force of local villagers gathered together by one of Warwick's captains, a certain John Clapham. The band holding aloft a motly collection of banners, one of which was mistaken for the Bear and Ragged Staff emblems on Warwick's troops, Pembroke's men presumed that the whole of Warwick's trained professional army was on them. They broke and fled. By the time Warwick arrived, the battle was over. Pembroke and his son Sir Richard Herbert were hustled into Nottingham and executed. Richard Woodville and his son were captured at Chepstow and executed at Kenilworth, probably in the presence of the king himself.. Edward was placed in the custody of Archbishop Neville of York. Having disposed of his enemies, Warwick was again in control. With two Kings of England imprisoned however, things were never to run smoothly. Unrest and disorder was rife throughout the country as it descended into anarchy. Warwick realized that without a royal figurehead as a puppet for him to control, he could not continue and Edward was released. A reconciliation of a sort was made between the two, but Warwick continued his plotting and in early 1470, some local disturbance, instigated by Warwick's supporters Lord Welles and Thomas

Dymmoke in Lincolnshire , escalated into a full scale rebellion when the rebels began to demand the reinstatement of Henry. Edward wasted no time and summoned the two to London on promise of safe conduct to explain the reasons for their rebellion. He then gathered an army, reckoned at 15000 men and marched north. In the north, the rebels, now led by Welles son Robert, stopped north of Slamiord and took up positions across the road between Empingham and Pickworth. Edward's forces took up station opposite and the furious king brought Welles and Dymmoke to the front and executed them in full view of both armies. His army then commenced a heavy artillery barrage against the rebels, to which they had no reply, snd therefore causing much slaughter and when his army advanced, the Lancastrians broke and ran, tearing off their livery coats with the ostrich plume emblem of the Prince of Wales as they fled, thus giving the name Losecoat to the battlefield .

Warwick fled to Calais with Clarence and, following a rapprochement with Margaret, landed back in England on 8th September 1470, now supporting the reinstatement of Henry. The country, although deeply divided, still had a large Lancastrian following and these flocked to Warwick's cause. King Edward, alarmed at the scale of the uprising, fled to Holland without a fight on 3rd October. Warwick was once again Lieutenant of England and began to reestablish his old friends in positions of favor. On the 5th October, Warwick sent Archbishop Neville and Bishop Waynefleet to the Tower to release poor Henry, where they found him in a sorry state. The unworldly Henry had never been particular with his personal habits even for the standards of the age. The priests reported that Henry was "noght worschupfully arrayed as a prince and noght so clenly kepte as schuld seme suche a prince". He was taken to Westminster, bathed and dressed in finery although it seems that he was hardly aware of anything that occurred around him. Contempory reports describe him as "a woolsack, a shadow on a wall, a crowned calf". Warwick had much to do, in the kings name he issued warrants for the summoning of Parliament, appointed George Neville as Chancellor, arranged for the reappointment of judges and for the striking of new coinage with King Henry VIs head on it. Rioting broke out in London on the news of Edward's flight and the gates of London's prisons opened releasing all manner of criminals onto the streets. Whole areas were devastated by looting and killing. Warwick reacted ruthlessly and soon gibbets

239

appeared in the streets festooned with robbers, looters and rapists captured by Warwick's men

King Edward IV was declared a traitor and all his lands confiscated. All his statutes were revoked. Henry was declared the rightful king and should the young Prince Edward die without issue, then Clarence and his male heirs should succeed. The country settled into a surly acceptance of the status quo, with many still favoring one side or the other it was realized that the weak Henry and the strong Edward were alike in their disregard of the common folk who only wished for a period of peace after the widespread corruption and collapse of law and order so evident in the previous years. The French king Charles watched these events with unease. He refused to assist the exiled Edward IV and favored Lancastrian rule, stating that he only wished to maintain the existing peace treaties. He mistrusted Warwick and sent his Emmisary Commyngs to Calais to report on the situation. Commyngs reported that all the garrison wore the Bear and Ragged Staff livery of Warwick, but also reported that the sign of the White Cross was displayed everywhere in the city, a token by Warwick of his unity with France. Since the days of the Maid of Orleans the white cross had been the symbol of French unity and, even earlier, had been the badge of French crusaders. Thus Warwick continued to seem a friend to all in his grasp for power.

Warwick continued to rule in Henry's name, playing nobles off against each other and trying to neutralize the influence of Clarence, who he recognized as another serious contender for the throne. The Earl needed queen Margaret in England to lend authority to his rule, but she did not trust him enough to bring herself and her 17 year old son under his control. Henry, nominally in charge, had little input and was content to drift in his dreams and devotions until 14th March 1471 when Edward landed at Ravenspur with a small force. The local people were not friendly, they had suffered much in earlier years and while they would accept his coming to claim his title of Duke of York, they were not disposed to support his claim to the crown. On 15th March a council was called and a decision made that, until he had gathered sufficient forces to bid for the crown, he should seem only to seek his inheritance as Duke and" shud noyse and say openly where so evar they came, that his entent and purpose was only to claime to be Duke of York". Supporters rallied round his banner and the threat of civil war was again in the air. He marched north to challenge

Warwick, who retreated behind the walls of Coventry. The Earl was expecting reinforcement from Clarence who had written urging that Warwick should not join battle until the two forces had united. Clarence however, playing his own double game, had also written to Edward suggesting a reconciliation.. Edward, with his brother Richard, Duke of Gloucester, met Clarence at Warwick and the three brothers clasped hands as a sign of their new found unity. Clarence ordered his men to remove the Lancastrian SS collars they wore and replace them with the Yorkist rose. It can only be wondered what their feelings were at the change, but in view of the large force behind Edward, perhaps this was the safest option.. With no forces blocking them, Edward's army marched on the Capital. Warwick, still at Coventry and learning of Clarence's duplicity, wrote to Edward offering his surrender in return for the gift of some high office. In London, the Archbishop of York, George Neville paraded the sad King Henry through the streets urging the citizens to arm themselves in defense of the sovereign. Some did and manned the walls of the city until Urswyke the Recorder of London, plus some other Yorkist Aldermen, persuaded them to return home for dinner. During this time, on 11th April, the Yorkist army entered the city unopposed. Edward went straight to the palace of the Bishop of London and arrested king Henry and the Archbishop, who were placed in the Tower as soon as it was captured. No doubt poor Henry was only too pleased to return to his introverted solitude.

Warwick, now fully aware of Clarence's duplicity, marched south and arrived at Chipping Barnet on 13th April 1471 and later that day heard that Edward was approaching from London. There was a brief skirmish between scouts, but both sides knew that a battle was inevitable on the morrow. Warwick knew that queen Margaret and the Prince of Wales were soon to land in Devon and would march to join forces with him. If he had waited for them his army would have hugely outnumbered the Yorkists, but he felt confident enough with his force and a victory without the queen would put him in good standing with her. It was dusk before Warwick had formed his army into the customary three divisions with the Earl of Oxford on the right, Warwick in the centre and the Duke of Exeter on the left. King Edward formed his forces in the dark, a difficult feat and confirming the professionalism of his commanders. It is known that Lord Hastings led the left division; Edward himself commanded the centre, while his brother Richard of Gloucester held the right. Edward commanded his army to move forward during the darkness so that they were within striking distance of the enemy. No sound or fire was to be made and the troops lay on the damp ground to await the morning. At first light, the field was covered in a thick ground mist. Edward ordered his troops forward under its cover and the two forces clashed as the sun rose on Easter Sunday 14th April. Because of the mist, the two armies had not met in the correct alignment, the Yorkist forces outflanking the Lancastrian right and the Lancastrians outflanking the Yorkists on their right. Oxford was the first to take advantage and swiftly enveloped Hasting's forces who panicked and began to run. Oxfords men pursuing them and striking them down before commencing the usual search for plunder. Oxford and some of his officers remounted and hurried after their men, beating them with the flat of their swords and urging them to return to the fight. The tragic outcome of the chase became apparent when Oxford and his men returned to the field. Oxford's banner, a radiant star, in the poor light looked just like Edward's personal banner of a flaming sun and its rays. The Lancastrian army, who had been getting the better of their opponents, mistook the Earl's banner for a fresh contingent of Yorkists, or, worse still, treachery by Oxford's me. The word quickly spread and panic resulted in the Lancastrians fleeing for their lives. Warwick, realizing that the battle was lost, retrieved his horse and attempted his escape, but the Yorkists were upon him and he was hacked down and killed, thus dying a man who had controlled the destinies of two monarchs and had, for a while, ruled the whole of England. By the middle of the morning it was all over. Edward's forces marched back to London to give thanks for their victory and poor Henry was again put in the Tower. On the 13th April 1471, Queen Margaret landed at Weymouth, together with Edward, Prince of Wales, Lord Wenlock and John Beaufort, Marquis of Dorset. When she heard of the defeat at Barnet, the queen resolved to return at once to France, but was persuaded to stay by her supporters who no doubt realized that, should she leave now, they must all return to poor exile in France. When Edward learned of Margaret's arrival, he began to recall his army which had been in the process of disbanding. He knew that he had to finish the Lancastrian cause once and for all if he wished to be secure. His troops were again ready by the 24th April and moved westward to seek Margaret's forces. Margaret intended to head for Wales to meet up with troops being gathered there, but also sent scouts to Shaftsbury and Salisbury who openly negotiated for billets for her army, a ruse to convince Edward that she intended to march on London itself. Edward knew that if she reached Wales her army would be greatly strengthened and sent word to the city of Gloucester to close its gates and to prevent Margaret from crossing the Severn. Her army arrived at Gloucester at 10 am on the 3rd May and seeing the bridges denied to her, moved towards Tewksbury where there was a known ford. Edward followed and on 4th May the two armies faced each other. Margaret's forces led by Somerset, Devon and the Prince of Wales were positioned on a ridge with their flanks protected by a wood on one side and the River Swilgate on the other. Edwards's forces advanced to within 400 yards of the enemy and opened up an artillery barrage. Somerset on the right of the Lancastrians led his division into the woods with the intention of outflanking Richard of Gloucester, but misjudged his distance and emerged at exactly where the Yorkist left and centre divisions met. Gloucester had seen Somerset's intention and had planted a force of spearmen on the edge of the wood and, on the command, they charged forward into Somerset's flank while Gloucester's left division attacked the front. Somerset's men broke and attempted to escape, but Gloucester ordered the pursuit and would not call it off until all of Somerset's troops were cut down in what is still known as Bloody Meadow.

It only remained for Edward to order a general advance and the Lancastrians were overwhelmed by the sheer ferocity of Edward's men who were determined to totally finish the business. Both Devon and Somerset were killed in the battle and it is probable that the Prince of Wales was also killed although the chronicler Fabyan reports that the Prince was captured alive and was brought before Edward who asked him why he waged war against his king? The young prince replied with the same question to Edward and was then cut down by the Yorkist Lords.

This is where we leave the enfeebled monarch whose birthright was to rule two great kingdoms, but who lacked the leadership and fire needed to bring his father's dream to fruition. With the Prince of Wales killed at Tewkesbury, it was no longer necessary to keep the old king alive. It is thought that he died in the White Tower from a blow to the head struck by Richard of Gloucester. A contempory, a Dr Warkworth states that he died on 21st May " between x1 and xii of the clocke" It is easy to blame Richard for the deed as history often portrays him as an evil deformed monster, but in truth he was known to have great regard for Henry, having served him for many years and was later responsible for having Henry reburied at Windsor. Either way, it is accepted that Henry's death was ordered by Edward.

His body was displayed in St Paul's Cathedral and later at Blackfriars before burial at Chertsey Abbey, but later, on the orders of King Richard, was brought to Windsor and reinterred. In November 1910 his tomb was opened for examination and was found to contain " a decayed mass of human bones" the skull was described as "much broken and to the skull was attached some hair of a brown color which in one place was darker and apparently matted with blood"

Edward IV

Edward was born on 28th April 1442 in Rouen, the eldest surviving son of eight boys and five girls born to Richard Duke of York and Cecily Neville. He was nursed in his infancy by Anne of Caux, who came with him to England and who, in later life, was gifted a pension of £120 per year by him. She must have been well regarded for on Edward's death, his brother Richard 111 continued the pension.

From the age of five he lived in Ludlow among his large family and at the age of ten was created the Earl of March, He developed into a strong, athletic and attractive adult, 6 feet 4 inches tall and with the red gold Plantagenet hair of his forefathers. Thomas More wrote of him that "he was a goodly personage and very princely to behold, of heart courageous, politic in council, in adversity nothing abashed" he goes on, "he was of visage lovely, of body mighty, strong and clean made. This was a man who, unlike his predecessor Henry, looked like a king. He was direct and straight in his dealings, energetic in pursuit of his goals and was raised to fit easily into the nobility of which his family was part. He loved hunting, drinking, fighting and was a serial womanizer, in short, an ideal candidate for the crown after so many years of the faltering Henry.

His later childhood was much disturbed by the actions of his father, Richard, Duke of York and from the age of eleven on, was swept up in the Duke's efforts, first to reclaim his rights and later to claim the throne. Following his father's humiliation at Ludlow he fled to France with Warwick but on 26th June 1460 they returned to England, supported by the Neville family and Lord Fauconberg , headed for London where they were welcomed by the citizenry.

The king's forces led by Buckingham had meanwhile moved north to intercept an anticipated invasion from Ireland by the Duke of York and had camped at Northampton. By the 10th July, Edward decided not to wait for his father's reinforcements and moved north to challenge the Lancastrians. His forces outnumbered Buckingham's but the Lancastrian leader felt well protected by the strong defensive position he had chosen, with log and earth ramparts to his front and sides as well as the River Neme to his rear .He had reckoned without the treachery of his ally Lord Grey of Ruthin whose troops manned part of the barricades. Grey had turned his coat in favor of York and knowing this, Edward charged his troops at the defences where Grey's "men met them and seizing them by the hand, hauled them into the embattled field". The shocked Lancastrians found that their walls had become a death trap and were quickly destroyed, Buckingham slain and King Henry captured.

 The Duke of York was now back in control and forced through parliament the Act of Settlement which declared him King Henry's heir, thus disinheriting the king's son Edward Prince of Wales. Queen Margaret was understandably outraged at this turn of events and stormed through Wales and the West Country raising a force to challenge the Duke. York's son Edward meanwhile went to the Welsh Marches to watch the border and to recruit more troops while his father led a force of some 8000 north to intercept Margaret. The two forces met at Sandal Castle near Wakefield on 21st December 1460. The Lancastrian Duke of Somerset lured York into leaving his castle and attacking by hiding a number of his troops in the surrounding woods and sprung the trap once York was committed. In the ensuing battle York was killed and when his forces broke, they were pursued and slaughtered. York's 17 year old; son Edmund, Earl of Rutland was captured on Wakefield Bridge by Lord Clifford. When the boy pleaded for his life Clifford cursed him and murdered him on the spot. His head, together with that of his father, was placed on spikes on the gates of Wakefield; his father's being decorated by a paper crown.

With the Lancastrians again in the ascendant, York's son Edward began to raise another army. London contributed 2000 marks to his costs and also opened the jails to release men to join his forces. He was aware that the Lancastrian Jasper Tudor was raising troops in Wales and moved north to prevent him linking up with Queen Margaret. On 2nd December 1461, the two armies met at Mortimer's Cross in Herefordshire and following a crushing victory by Edward, Tudor was captured and beheaded in Hereford.

Queen Margaret's forces were meanwhile moving south heading for the capital, pillaging and sacking along the way. With Edward still on the

Welsh border, Warwick moved a force to intercept Margaret at St Albans and they met on 12th February in a snowstorm. Warwick had carefully set up his defences in the town and also stationed a force of archers at Dunstable to attack the Lancastrian flank. The treachery of a certain Lovelace, described as a "Captain of Kent" warned Margaret of Warwick's plans and she sent a force to destroy them. Knowing Warwick's dispositions, Margaret maneuvered her troops around the town and attacked from the rear. This also had the effect of Warwick's archers firing blind into the teeth of the wind, causing their shafts to fall short. The Kentish contingent of the Yorkists broke and ran causing a general panic. Margaret's troops moved in and victory was complete. The sickly King Henry was found sitting under a tree reputedly singing to himself and was reunited with Margaret.

Instead of consolidating her victory by marching on London, Margaret's forces moved northward to gather yet more forces allowing Edward to enter London unopposed where he was welcomed on 26th February 1461 and a few days later was proclaimed at Moor fields as the true King of England with much pomp and rejoicing. This proclamation had the effect of rallying many nobles who had hitherto been uncommitted to either cause and who now rallied to Henry the anointed monarch. Margaret's numbers swelled to 26000, a huge army for the time. Warwick and Edward, sensing that things were coming to a head and realizing that their own could not be safe while Henry lived, also raised a force of 20000 and these two groups met at Towton on Palm Sunday, 29th March in what was to be the bloodiest battle so far in the civil war that had ravaged the country for so long.

Edward gave orders that" no prisoners be taken nor one enemy saved". The Lancastrians, led by the twenty four year old Duke of Somerset, were the first to advance with the wind full in their faces and heavy snow falling. The Yorkist Lord Fauconberg in charge of the archers ordered a volley to be loosed which, with the aid of the wind, traveled unseen through the snow until struck the advancing troops, causing much damage and leading them to believe that the enemy were much closer than thought. Somerset ordered his archers to return fire, not realizing that firing into the wind, the arrows would fall short of the enemy line. His troops fired volley after volley, all of which fell short enabling the enemy to move forward, pick up the spent arrows and fire them back into the packed Lancastrians. Stung by the arrows, the main body of Somerset's men charged and crashed into Edward's left flank which buckled and broke. If Somerset's other division had attacked at the same time on the other flank, the battle would have been over, but they remained in position enabling the Yorkists to stabilize.

 Edward moved his banners to the front and dismounting, joined with his troops, stating that "this day would he live or die with his men". The battle raged for hours, but when the Duke of Norfolk arrived with reinforcements for Edward, the Lancastrians's finally broke and streamed back towards Tad caster only to find their way blocked by the River Cock and here the slaughter was horrendous with the retreating Lancastrian troops caught between the freezing water and the swords of the enemy. It was said that so many dead were in the water that a man could later pass across the river on their backs. Edward rode with his victorious army to York where he replaced the rotting heads of his brother and father with that of the newly cut head of the Earl of Devon, to be joined shortly after by that of the Earl of Wiltshire's

Henry and Margaret escaped to Scotland while Edward and Warwick returned to London and forced through the Act of Attainder imposing the charge of treason on one hundred and thirteen of their Lancastrian opponents. Corruption was rife as many of Edward's supporters looked to further their own cause by laying claim to forfeited estates. The Italian ambassador Coppini reported that Edward and Warwick needed "advice and comfort" and also warned that the opportunistic French were preparing an invasion during this troubled period.

To add to Edward's troubles, a plot by the Earl of Oxford was discovered. Oxford had ordered a servant to take some secret letters to Henry and Margaret in Scotland, but the servant brought them first to Edward who, having read them, instructed the servant to complete his mission, but to bring Edward the old king's replies before taking them to Oxford. The plan was to intercept Edward on his forthcoming journey northwards and kill him and his retinue. At the same time, the Duke of Somerset would descend on England while Henry would invade from Scotland. The conspiracy was suppressed and the leaders executed.

Margaret however, continued in her aim of restoring Henry and therefore her son also, to the throne. Traveling to France she obtained some mild support from Louis XI who provided her with a small force of some four hundred men and thus supported, she traveled to Scotland where she managed to add a small number of troops before moving into England and began ravaging southwards. Margaret had already given Berwick to the Scots and in May 1461 offered Carlisle to them as a further bribe to aid the Lancastrian cause. The citizens however would have none of it and drove the Scots out. King Henry who had led another force raiding the border was also driven back.

Intrigue continued with Warwick writing to John McDonald, Earl of Ross, an enemy of the Scots King James, offering English assistance if he were to start a rebellion with the aim of seizing the north of Scotland. Both the French and the Scots were lukewarm in their support for Henry and tried to play a double game so as to gain some advantage from whoever became the final winner in the Lancastrian/Yorkist struggle. Edward in turn, was keen to woo his opponents and give himself time to gather strength. He made a great show of forgiving the Duke of Somerset and also concluded a treaty with France.

Edward was now focused on his coronation. On Friday 26th June 1461 he rode from Lambeth to the Tower, being met at the city gates by the Lord Mayor and Aldermen in their scarlet robes and together in procession moved through the city. The London crowds turned out to witness and cheer this brave sight of Edward, looking every inch a king and so very different from the feeble and bowed figure they had previously seen as their monarch. Once in the Tower, Edward began the process of rewarding his loyal supporters and dubbed thirty two of them Knights of the Bath. It is ironic that this order was created in 1399 by Henry IV, a king that Edward was about to have declared a usurper. Edward's coronation took place on Sunday 28th June and was conducted by Thomas Bourchier, Archbishop of Canterbury, assisted by William Booth, Archbishop of York. At the coronation banquet held afterwards, the king's champion, Sir Thomas Dymock rode into the hall fully armored and, throwing down his gauntlet, challenging anyone who disputed Edward's right to the throne to do battle with him. The Scots border raids, plus Margaret's arrival with her French forces sent the aggressive Edward north with a great army to oppose her.

On the 13th November, Margaret learned of the great force advancing on her and she fled to the coast and took ship on a carvel with her goods and possessions. A great tempest blew up and the carvel was swamped and sank while Margaret was brought to shore at Berwick in a rowing boat. Her French troops too suffered a similar fate; the storm drove their boats on to the beach at Bamborough. They burned the boats and moved into Northumberland where they were attacked and captured by a local chief known as the Bastard of Ogle. King Edward intended to pursue Margaret, but a bout of measles laid him low. The Scots, taking advantage, attacked the castles of Alnwick,Bamborough and Dunstanborough, but Edward's forces prevailed.. Edward had pardoned the Duke of Somerset and made him a close aide. He also appointed some of Somerset's men to his bodyguard and Somerset and his men were with Edward on a journey through Northampton where the people recognized this force as enemies of Edward and would have killed them all if Edward had not spoken for them. To thank the Northampton citizens for their concern he presented them with a tun of wine which was drunk in the market place with everyone bringing some kind of vessel to drink from "For some fette wine in basins, and some in cauldrons, and some on bollys(bowls) and some in pans, Lor, the great treasure that they scheuyd (obtained) that time".

 The treacherous Somerset, with Ralph Percy and other disaffected northern lords continued to foment trouble while the Scots also harried the borders. Edward sent Lord Montagu (Warwick's brother) to settle the region. In the ensuing events Percy was slain and Margaret and her supporters fled to Sluys in Flanders, leaving poor Henry in Scotland. The Yorkist forces continued to harry the northern rebels and on 14th May 1464, met with the turncoat Somerset at the battle of Hexham. The Yorkist John Neville had gone north ahead of King Edward's larger force and was deployed on high ground to the south of the town. The Lancastrians, led by the treacherous Somerset and Lord Roos, arrayed their troops in a meadow near Devils Water. They formed their usual three divisions, but hardly had they settled before the Yorkists charged down the hill. The right division of Somerset's force, led by Lord Roos threw down their weapons and fled before a single blow had been struck, leaving the remainder of the rebels hemmed in the meadow and unable to manouvre. Resistance collapsed and many tried to escape but were trapped by the river and killed. Neville was pitiless and executed thirty of the Lancastrian leaders that evening, including Somerset and Roos. The Lancastrian Sir William Talboys was captured the next day whilst trying to escape northwards with £2000 of Henry's war chest. He too was executed. The old king was finally captured in June 1464 at Ribblesdale and was brought to London and shamefully paraded through the streets by Warwick before being placed in the Tower.

Hitherto, Warwick and Edward seem to have been in accord, but Edward was now to embark on a course that was to drive Warwick into Margaret's camp. While on a journey north, he secretly married Elizabeth Woodville, the widow of Sir John Grey who had been killed at Towton. It is said that he had first met her shortly after the battle while passing through Grey's demesne of Stoney Stratford and she waylaid him to plead that she be allowed to keep her title and estates to support her two sons. The womanizer Edward was immediately attracted to her and courted her, but she refused to become another mistress, insisting on marriage. She must have been special for Edward, with a string of mistresses, eventually agreed and on 1st May 1464 they were wed at her family home in Northampton with only her mother present, plus two gentlewomen, a priest and a young man to help the priest in the singing. Edward kept the union a secret until September. Warwick, who had been conducting secret negotiations with the French regarding a marriage between Edward and the French royalty, was outraged. Not only had he lost face with the French, his Neville family, hitherto the king's closest advisors must now compete for favor with the greedy Woodvilles.

 The new queen wasted no time in advancing her families interests and quickly married her 20 year old brother John to Lady Katherine Neville, daughter of the Earl of Westmorland and Dowager Duchess of Norfolk who was 80 years old but very wealthy. Her sister Catherine was soon married to the 11 year old Henry Stafford, Duke of Buckingham. Another sister, Mary was then married to the Earl of Pembroke. Two other sisters were also married off advantageously. With the Woodville influence growing and increasingly gaining the king's ear, Warwick was further put out when in March 1466 he relieved Warwick's friend Walter Blount, Lord Mountjoy, of the office of Treasurer of England and put another Woodville, this time, Richard, Lord Ryvers in his place. The greed of the Woodvilles and the even greater greed of Lord Ryvers became the subject of many jokes within Edward's court. A squire, one Woodhouse, came before the king dressed in a short coat "cut by the points" and a pair of boots upon his legs as long "as they might be tied to the points of his hoses, and in his hand, a long marsh pike" The king asked why such long boots and long staff. Woodhouse was said to have replied, "Upon my faith sir, I have passed through many counties of your realm and in places I have passed, the Rivers have been so high that I could hardly scrape through them".

The scheming Queen Margaret, learning of a diplomatic conference to be held in St Omer between England France and Burgundy, traveled to the continent with her son the Prince of Wales, arriving at Sluys in July. Her state was much diminished and folk marveled at the poor turnout of her own and her followers clothing. She met with Burgundy to beg assistance in restoring Henry, but he, while being friendly enough, was still keeping his options open and denied her aid. She petitioned King Louis, explaining that, with Warwick and King Edward at loggerheads, now would be a good time to regain her husband's kingdom and begged for his help or, failing that, permission for any French Lords who wished, be allowed to help her. He too turned her down, remarking, "look how proudly she writes"It is a mark of the uncertainty of the outcomeYorkist/Lancastrian struggle that, even though offered Calais as a bribe, Louis would still not support Margaret fully.

By 1467, both France and Burgundy were eager for a marriage alliance with England as a way of increasing their power over the other.. Warwick supported an alliance with France while Edward was for Burgundy. This issue became the cause of much friction between the two and when Edward's sister, Margaret of York finally married Charles, Duke of Burgundy on 9th July 1468, an even deeper wedge was driven between Edward and Warwick. The wedding was extravagant even by the standard of the sumptuous Burgundian court. The streets were hung with bright tapestries, feasting and dancing went on for days in a celebration known as the" Tournament of the Golden Tree", a detailed allegory designed to honor the bride. She wore a magnificent crown adorned with pearls and enameled white roses intertwined with red and green enameled letters of her name which can still be seen in Aachen Cathedral. Much malicious gossip and rumour was circulated in Burgundy regarding the bride's virtue. It was said that she had had many love affairs and that she had even given birth to a son. These rumours, no doubt spread by the French, became so open that the Duke of

Burgundy issued a public decree that no person was to speak of the rumours on pain of being thrown into the river.

Edward continued his diplomatic onslaught on Burgundy and Brittany much to the annoyance of Louis, who feared an Anglo Burgundian alliance against France. The French king gave some modest support to Jasper Tudor in June 1468 by giving him money and three ships to journey back to Britain and attempt to raise more rebellion. Tudor landed at Dyfi near Harlech and traveling across Wales gathering troops as he went, he arrived at Denbeigh Castle, captured and burned it. Edward was incensed at yet another challenge to his rule and sent Lord Herbert with a force to attack the Lancastrian held Harlech Castle, which surrendered on August 14th 1468. Jasper Tudor managed to escape, but was further humiliated when Edward gave Jasper's Earldom of Pembroke to Lord Herbert as a reward.

Warwick, following his disagreements with the king regarding the alliance with France, the king's secret marriage, plus the king's refusal to allow the Duke of Clarence to marry Warwick's daughter Elisabeth, was moving closer to outright rebellion against Edward. In defiance of the king, Clarence was married to Elisabeth Neville on 11th July1469 and the stage was set for an out and out confrontation. A rebellion flared up in the north, led by the self styled Robin of Redesdale, actually a trusted ally of Warwick, named Sir William Conyers . King Edward raised a small force and moved to crush the rebellion, but discovered that the rebels were much too strong for his modest force and retreated to Nottingham to await reinforcements from the the Earls of Pembroke and Devon coming from the south. Edward attempted to raise more troops in Nottingham, but his waning popularity resulted in only a few joining him. The rebels sped south to rendezvous with Warwick, bypassing the king and meeting with Pembroke's and Devon's forces at Edgecote Moor. The two Earls, never the best of friends, had fallen out with each other the previous day and, as a result, Devon had made camp in a village a few miles from Pembroke's men. As a result, when the rebels attacked on the morning of 26th July, Pembroke, on his own, was hard put to oppose them. Under heavy pressure, he retreated and regrouped, holding off the numerically superior rebels until 1pm when Devon's forces arrived. Unfortunately, the advance guard of Warwick's forces arrived at the same time and, seeing Warwick's livery on the newcomers, Pembroke's men, fearing Warwick's highly trained Calais men, broke and fled. Lord Herbert, Earl of Pembroke was executed and the Earldom again became vacant.

In May 1470, Warwick and Clarence went to France to meet Queen Margaret and plan to reinstate King Henry on the throne of England. Clarence, rather naively, had believed that Warwick would proclaim him king following the defeat of Edward, but Warwick, determined to keep all options open, suggested to Margaret that her son Henry, Prince of Wales, should marry Warwick's daughter Anne. Clarence, seeing Warwick's duplicity, began to make overtures to Edward.

Warwick, accompanied by Jasper Tudor, landed in the West Country, Jasper heading for Wales to recruit more forces and Warwick to London. King Edward was in York and too far away to reach London before Warwick. The king had sent Lord Montague with a force to arrest Warwick and Clarence, but Montague changed his allegiance, stating that Edward could not be trusted. Many of the English nobles were uncomfortable at having previously supported Edward against Henry and, sensing a sea change in the country's mood, held back from joining in. Edward, now isolated, deciding that discretion being the better part of valour, rode to Lynn in Norfolk and took ship to Flanders to seek help from the Duke of Burgundy.

Warwick raced to London and sent the Bishop of Winchester to the Tower to free the frail Henry and bring him to Westminster so that he may be restored to the crown. Parliament met in December 1470 and dismantled much of Edward's rule, restoring Henry to his rights and also returning the Earldom of Pembroke to Jasper Tudor.

Warwick's return to England had been financed by the French king Louis, who, as a payment, had demanded Warwick's help in an invasion of Burgundy. Warwick had therefore instructed his Calais garrison to join with Louis in an attack on the duchy. The Duke of Burgundy, on hearing this news, resolved to help Edward regain his English throne. With a force of some 1200 men, Edward landed at Ravenspur on the 14th March. His brother, Richard, Duke of Gloucester, with about 300 men landed some four miles further up the coast. They joined up on the 15th and began to seek recruits for their challenge to Henry. The local people however, where lukewarm to him and, while accepting his right to reinstatement as Duke of York, did not support his claim to the throne.

He met with varying levels of support as he moved south. Beverly admitted him, Hull did not. The city of York would at first not admit him, but showing much courage; Edward went into the town and addressed the burghers, stating his claim and his case. So forceful was he that he won them over to his side.

News of his coming had reached London and Warwick's man Sir Thomas Cook made plans to keep Edward out. He arranged for King Henry to be conveyed through the city carrying a sword and supported by a band of followers carrying a pole with two fox tails attached(a sign of defiance) to encourage the populace to support the old king. This stunt did little more than amuse the people. The writer William Commynes states"three things especially which contributed to his reception in London, the first was the birth of a young prince of whom the queen was there brought to bed. The second was the great debts which he owed in the town which obliged all tradesman and creditors to side with him, and the last was the ladies of quality and rich citizens wives with whom he had formerly intrigued, who forced their husbands and relations to declare for him"

Warwick moved south from Coventry with an army of 15000 men, hoping that London would have kept out Edward or that he would not expect an attack on Easter Day.. Edward learned of the approach and raised a force of around 10000 and marched to Barnet on 13th April 1471. The scouts of both armies made contact just before dusk and preparations were made for battle the next day. Edward moved his troops as close as possible to the enemy and they lay silent in their three divisions throughout the night. Warwick fired a heavy bombardment throughout the night, but overestimated the distance of Edward's forces, the shots landing far behind the hidden divisions. Easter Day, the 14th dawned and the field was covered in a heavy mist. Both sides had adopted the usual three divisions but Edward, in the darkness, had misaligned his troops so that his right overlapped Warwick's left.

Edward's left division, commanded by Lord Hastings, made contact first, attacking Warwick's right commanded by the Earl of Oxford. Oxford's archers loosed volleys into the mist and his hand gunners fired at the advancing troops. The Yorkists faltered and Oxford ordered the charge which crashed into Hastings's forces and sent them reeling back.

On Edward's right wing however, his brother Richard failed to make contact due to the misalignment. Taking advantage of this he swung round and attacked Warwick; s left flank. This flank began to buckle and was pressed back towards the centre where Edward's main division was pushing forward. The battle now spun on its axis and Warwick was forced back into some low ground known as Dead Man's Bottom where much slaughter began. Oxford's division, now chasing the fleeing remnants of Hasting forces, instead of returning to the main battle, rode on to Barnet and commenced the usual medieval armies habit of looting. Oxford managed to rally about 500 men and returned to the fight, but in the confusion of the fighting, Warwick and Oxford mistook each other for the enemy, probably due to the similarity of Oxford's livery of a "star with streamers" to King Edward's "Sun in Splendor" design. Treachery and defection were not unknown in these troubled times and it only took a small incident or error to set off a panic. A commentator of the time states, "The Erle of Warwikes men schott and faught ayens the Erle of Oxenfordes menne and anone the Erle of Oxenforde and his men cried treasone! And fledde awaye the field". Sensing the moment, Edward sent in his reserve, pushing Warwick's centre into Dead Mans Bottom. Warwick tried to rally his men, crying out, "This is the moment!, If we withstand this charge, the day is ours". His troops had lost heart however and a general panic to the rear began. Warwick had no choice but to run with them and, as he attempted to recover his destrier, he was recognized by his livery and attacked by some Yorkist men at arms. Brave to the last, Warwick stood alone as his enemies closed in on him, fighting on until he was struck down, his visor torn open and a dagger thrust into his face. Thus died the mighty Richard Neville, Earl of Warwick and forever dubbed "The Kingmaker". The chronicler Hall records that "the common people thought that the sun had gone out of the heavens". He did not die alone however, over 1000 of his men, as well as more than 500 Yorkists died with him at Barnet.

Edward returned in triumph to London and displayed the corpses of Warwick and Lord Montague in St Paul's Cathedral to forestall any rumors that the pair still lived. On the very day of the Barnet battle, Queen Margaret landed at Weymouth. Edward sent scouts to observe her movements and, when he learned that she traveled north westwards to join with her supporters in Wales, he set off in pursuit on 24th April

1471. She had reached Cerne Abbas when she learned of Warwick's death at Barnet, but was determined to link up with Jasper Tudor's forces and continue the fight. Edward wanted to prevent her from crossing the Severn into Wales and the race was on to reach Gloucester first. Margaret's troops were forced to divert to Bristol for supplies and more weapons and the delay was to prove fatal. Edward ordered the Governor of Gloucester to hold out as long as possible and led his force of 5000 towards Tewkesbury, knowing that, if Gloucester held out, the Lancastrians would need to move further north to cross the river. The Lancastrian army of 7000, finding the gates of Gloucester closed against them and, knowing that Edward was close, had no time foe a siege and moved on towards Tewkesbury to attempt a crossing of the Severn at a ford a mile south of Tewkesbury Abbey. The exhausted Lancastrians with Edward in close pursuit knew that the only option was to stand and fight and they deployed on 4th May 1471 just south of the abbey in an area known as Paynes Place. Edward's force was also tired having marched thirty miles in a day to catch up. The Lancastrian force, led by the Duke of Somerset, Lord Wenlock and the Earl of Devon, had chosen their ground well. Before them were, "fowle lanes and depe dikes and many hedges". They deployed into the usual three divisions with Somerset commanding the right, Wenlock the centre and Devon the left. Edward, knowing his army to be outnumbered as well as tired, advanced cautiously, sending a force of 200 mounted spearmen forward into the trees beyond his left flank as a precaution.. He then arrayed his forces in three divisions opposing the enemy's dispositions with his brother Richard commanding the left, Lord Hasting, the right and himself commanding the centre. The nobles of both forces dismounted to fight on foot, to reassure the cynical foot soldiers that they would not ride off to safety if the battle was lost.

Edward's archers and gunners opened the battle, concentrating their fire on Somerset's division. The arrow storm, plus the stone cannon balls smashed into the Lancastrian ranks causing carnage and prompting Somerset to order his division to charge. His plan called for Wenlock to move his own division forward in support, but Wenlock did not move. Richard of Gloucester's division met Somerset's charge and the king's centre force, seeing that Wenlock was not advancing, turned and attacked Somerset's flank. At this moment, Edwards's spearmen burst from the trees behind Somerset and the route was complete. This final shock was too much for the Duke's troops who "greatly dismayed and abashed, toke them to flight" Edward now moved his main body forward and attacked the Lancastrian centre. Somerset, who had survived the route of his force, made his way back to his own lines with a score to settle with Wenlock, whose loyalty was always under suspicion, having fought for the royalists at Towton. Somerset accused him of treason and" strake his braynes out of his hedde" with his battleaxe. Lancastrian resistance collapsed and the usual flight and pursuit followed with no quarter being given by Edward's forces. The defeated army was trapped on the banks of the Severn and butchered. The scale of the slaughter was such that the area was ever after known as "Bloody Meadow". Somerset himself escaped and tried for refuge in the abbey, but was dragged out and executed as was Edward, the 17 year old Prince of Wales. Margaret, on hearing of the defeat and the death of her son, fled but was captured and brought before King Edward at Coventry. She was held captive for four years until ransomed by King Louis.

Edward's troubles were not yet over. Warwick's lieutenants in Calais, sent Sir George Broke with 300 soldiers to Kent to unite with Thomas Neville, known as the Bastard of Fauconberg and attack London with the intention of meeting up with Margaret, freeing King Henry and deposing Edward. Fauconberg had been hitherto patrolling the channel to prevent aid being sent to Edward by Burgundy. Fauconberg sailed some of his ships up the Thames and fired on the city. Being denied entrance to London, Fauconberg's forces moved west over Kingston Bridge, looting and causing general mayhem. Edward's supporters managed to divide Fauconberg's forces by bribes and promises and they were persuaded to disperse. Fauconberg was quietly captured later and was executed in September 1471.

Edward returned to London and, with the Prince of Wales now dead, had no reason to prolong the life of King Henry. On the night of Tuesday 21st May 1471 he was murdered by order of the king. It is known that Richard of Gloucester was in the Tower that night and it is thought that he organized the deed. Henry's body was displayed in St Paul's "so that every man might see him" and later, taken by boat to Chertsey Abbey where he was buried.

With his enemies defeated, Edward was now able to turn his attention to more personal matters and began to pursue the good life, wearing all the latest fashions, holding great state banquets and spending vast sums on fine clothes, silver and gold plate. He was determined that his court should be seen as the centre of his glittering and powerful kingdom in contrast to the bare Puritanism of Henry. He began to put on much weight and took a number of mistresses. His years of struggle had made him an astute politician as well as a warrior and he quickly realized that he could not rule successfully through the narrow clique who had helped him to the throne and he set out to attract many of his old opponents to court. He reversed more than fifty attainders between 1470 and 1475, including even some of his oldest enemies such as John Morton, a prominent supporter of King Henry who was made Master of the Rolls and who later became Archbishop of Canterbury.

He was careful not to alienate his nobles by oppressive tax demands but raised the huge sums necessary for his sumptuous life style by vigilant care and exercise of royal rights which fell more heavily on the lower classes. He tightened up the administration of the customs system, forced economies on the royal household (although not on himself). He strengthened administration on crown lands and enforced his feudal rights of escheat, wardship and marriage. He also began work on the great St Georges Chapel at Windsor and became influenced by the chivalric tales of the legendary King Arthur. The Round Table that can be seen in Winchester today was the result of his desire to create his own Camelot.

While he was engaged on these domestic distractions the French and Burgundians had not been idle. Both King Louis and Charles of Burgundy had kept up a complicated series of negotiations with Edward, vying for any advantage they could find. Trouble also began brewing at home when Warwick's brother George Neville, Archbishop of York, who had made his peace with Edward the previous year, was suddenly arrested for treason and all his goods seized. The charge would seem to have been completely in character for the Archbishop who had turned his coat a number of times during the previous decade and had accumulated great wealth thereby. The chronicler Warkworth commented "wherefore such goods were gathered with sin, were lost with sorrow".

The king's brothers Richard and Clarence now began to quarrel over Warwick's estate. Clarence had previously married Warwick's eldest daughter and now Richard looked to marry Anne Neville, the widow of King Henry's son Edward who was slain at Tewkesbury. Richard hoped to get his hands on the vast estate of Warwick, as did Clarence. Clarence went so far as to have Anne concealed in London and there is a story that Richard found her disguised as a cookmaid and removed her to sanctuary at St Martins. He duly married her on July 12th 1472. The quarrels between the brothers grew in intensity and Edward had to frequently intervene. In September 1472, the exiled Earl of Oxford landed in Cornwall hoping to raise yet more rebellion against Edward and place Clarence on the throne. He took over St Michaels Mount, considered impregnable to attack, and began looking for allies. The King's Sheriff of Cornwall, a certain Bodrugan, was commanded to arrest the Earl, but secretly aided him. The King angrily dismissed Bodrugan and appointed Richard Fortescue as sheriff, ordering him to arrest Oxford. Much fighting broke out between Bodrugan and Fortescue, but the Earl was eventually persuaded to surrender with promises of pardon. In the event he was arrested and imprisoned at Hammes in France.

Edward, with all this turmoil around him, still had time to think of his own glory. His political scheming with Burgundy had resulted in a plan for them both to invade France, together with the King of Aragon The plan was to divide the country between them. Edward raised an army of 10000 men and landed in France in July 1475. Burgundy however had embroiled himself in another squabble in the Swiss town of Nuz and did not meet up as planned. King Louis feared resurgence of the Hundred Year War and with a large English force in his country, set out to sue for a treaty with Edward. At the Treaty of Picquigny, the wily Louis agreed a seven year peace with Edward and paid him 75000 crowns for his" expenses" in mounting the campaign, plus 50000 crowns per year thereafter, a good result for Edward. A further 50000 was paid for the release of Margaret of Anjou, still in captivity in England and promises made of a marriage between Edward's eldest daughter and the Dauphin. These arrangements were concluded in a remarkable manner. With the English army close to the walls of Amiens, Louis ordered that the gates be opened and inside had arranged for a huge feast for the English. Great tables were set out in the street, piled with food and wines, with French noblemen on hand to serve. Taverns were charged with providing free drinks to the invaders and, not surprisingly. the English were blind drunk by 9 o clock in the morning. Many feared that the English would turn violent and commence their usual looting and raping, but Louis' policy seems to have worked and on Edward's command, his forces withdrew without trouble.

Back in England the king's brothers continued their battle for Warwick's estate. Both were skilled orators and well versed in the law which made Edward's interventions more difficult. Eventually Edward personally decided on the division. The Countess of Warwick was to remain out of the way in sanctuary, Clarence was to receive the greater part of the old Earl's estate, Richard to have the rest, but in return, was to give up the office of Great Chamberlain. The quarrel continued to flare up from time to time and was made worse when the Countess was released from sanctuary as it threatened to depose Clarence of some of his estates. Losing patience, Edward finally created an act of resumption which effectively took from Clarence everything he had gained. Faced with a choice of rebellion or submission, Clarence submitted, paving the way for a new act which allowed the brothers to divide Warwick's inheritance more fairly between them and exclude the Countess.

In December 1476, Clarence's wife Isabel Neville died, probably of TB . A short time later Charles of Burgundy was killed in battle with the Swiss and Clarence resolved to marry his daughter. Edward, alarmed at the power this would give Clarence, banned the marriage, much to the fury of Clarence. From that time on, Clarence changed. He left the court and retired to the country. If ever he went to see Edward for any reason he would not eat or drink at court for fear of poisoning. It is said that he had no kind word for anyone, but met all with a scowl. When Edward proposed that the avaricious Lord Ryvers should marry Burgundy's daughter, Clarence snapped. He accused his dead wife's servant Ankarette Wynho and a servant John Thursby of murdering Isabel and poisoning his infant son. Brought before the Warwick justices, they were found guilty in a rigged trial and executed. In what seems like retaliation, Edward had one of Clarence's servants, John Stacey and an esquire Thomas Burdet accused of witchcraft and executed. Clarence appeared in council at Westminster and insisted that they listen to a priest read out a declaration of Stacey's innocence. Edward, in a rage, had Clarence arrested. The situation worsened when another servant of Clarence was tried and executed for necromancy on Edward's order, a signal to Clarence to behave. Clarence did not heed and began to circulate stories that Edward was bastard born and that his marriage was not valid. He was summoned to appear before the king and then imprisoned in the Tower.

In 1478 parliament convened to try Clarence on the charge of treason. It is said that nobody accused the duke but the king and nobody answered the accusation but the duke. On the 7th February, the death sentence was passed, but the king still stayed his hand, probably to let the furor subside. On the 18th February Clarence was put to death. It has become legend that he was drowned in a vat of malmsey wine, but there is no proof of this. It is known that Clarence was a prodigious drinker of wine and it likely that someone had commented that he" drowns himself in wine" and the story stuck. It is more likely that he was drowned in his bath, leaving no sign of violence.

By 1480 Edward had grown soft and corpulent. His love of the good life became even more marked as did his love for food. It was said that he would use an emetic after a banquet so that he could immediately gorge again. His sexual appetite had not dimmed with his advancing years; in fact it seems to have increased. He had often taken mistresses in his life, but now took three. One was reckoned to be the merriest, one the wisest and one the holiest. Probably the merriest was Jane Shore the strikingly beautiful wife of the London merchant William Shore and her story does not end with Edward. After the king's death, she became the mistress of Thomas Grey, Marquis of Dorset and later of William, Baron Hastings. She was imprisoned for a while during the reign of Richard 111 for misconduct and during that time, so captivated the king's solicitor that he actually entered into a contract of marriage with her. It is believed that Edward had two illegitimate children. By Elisabeth Lucy he had a son, named Arthur Plantagenet who was later created Viscount Lisle by Henry VII. A second child, a daughter, was brought up in the Woodville household. Edward's health was declining by 1481 and he was not fit enough to join his brother Richard in an attack on Scotland which they had jointly planned. He was further disillusioned by the Treaty of Arras in which Louis of France arranged a marriage between the Dauphin and

Mary of Burgundy's daughter. It was a bitter blow to Edward that France had made peace with his old ally Burgundy.He had become obese and could not exercise. He moved from place to place seeking relief and in March 1483 he visited Windsor and returned to Westminster on the 25th. Some days later he was seized with a violent illness with chest pains and prostration. These became worse and none of his doctors could diagnose the cause. Theories abounded that he had been poisoned, or that he had caught a cold while fishing in the Thames, or that he had apoplexy due to the bad news from Arras, or that he simply had malaria. The Croyland Chronicle reported that the king was "neither worn out with old age, nor yet seized with any known kind of malady" The possibility of having caught a cold is the more likely; a chest infection in the obese could lead to pneumonia, which in turn could lead to pleurisy. Edward lingered for another five days and lapsed into unconsciousness, dying shortly thereafter on 9th April 1483. After his death, he was washed and left naked for all to see before being moved to St Stephen's Chapel in Westminster where he lay for a further eight days. After his funeral service, his body was interred in the tomb that he had prepared at Windsor.

Edward had not made proper plans to ensure that his son ascended the throne. He probably felt that he could trust his faithful brother Richard to ensure the young Edward's succession. In this he was to be proved very wrong.

Edward V

Born on 2nd November 1470 at Westminster where his mother, Elisabeth Woodville, was in sanctuary taking refuge from her Lancastrian rivals during the turbulent years of his fathers bid for the throne, His father, temporarily exiled in Flanders, was gathering forces to return to England and depose the feeble Henry and it was to be five months before the two met. He was created Prince of Wales in June 1471.

The young prince spent his early years very much under the care and influence of his mother's Woodville clan who had established themselves in many of the offices of power under King Edward. In 1471, the king had established a Council of Wales and the Marches based at Ludlow castle, with similar arrangements being made for the Duchy of Cornwall and the County of Chester.

In 1473, the king created the prince President of the Welsh Council and he was duly ensconced in his official household in Ludlow. More importantly, we find Earl Rivers, Sir John Scott and Sir John Fogg , all Woodvilles or related to them, appointed, not only to the Council, but also to the prince's household. Contemporizes refer to "a wall of Woodvilles" surrounding the prince and vetting all access to him. Thomas More wrote "everyone as he was nearest kin to the queen so was planted next unto the prince".

It was at Ludlow on the 14th April 1483 that the prince learned of his father's death five days earlier and arrangements were made for his return to London. His Woodville guardians staying close to him and swiftly announcing the date of his coronation as May 4th. His uncle, Richard, Duke of Gloucester, having been a loyal and constant supporter of the dead king, claimed that he had been appointed Protector in the dead king's will and, on learning of the death of Edward, immediately ordered a priest to say a requiem mass before riding with a retinue of knights to York, where he performed a solemn funeral service for Edward, exhorting all the nobility to swear an oath of fealty to the new king. He himself being the first to take the oath .He then rode direct from York to intercept the prince's party at Northampton on 29th April and escort them to London.

The royal party was escorted by 2000 mounted men at arms, to ensure, it is thought, that the Woodvilles, clearly intending to keep all power in their hands, would meet no resistance when entering London with their royal charge. The prince, however, had been sent on to Stony Stratford and it was here that Richard arrested Earl Rivers, Sir Richard Grey (the prince's half brother) and Thomas Vaughan for treason... Despite young Edward's protests the three were sent to the Richard's powerbase in the north and later executed. So swift were Richard's actions that the escort were taken by surprise and seemed to have accepted the change of events with equanimity. The prince, with Gloucester and another relative, Henry Stafford, Duke of Buckingham, continued on to London. News of the events at Northampton had gone before them and Queen Elisabeth, much agitated, fled to sanctuary in Westminster Abbey with her daughters and younger son Richard of York, taking with her a substantial part of the royal treasure.

Edward Woodville, the queen's brother, who had been appointed as Commander of the King's Fleet, also took part of the treasure and sailed with the fleet of twenty ships, ostensibly to deter French pirates, but, in reality, as a show of Woodville force. Richard of Gloucester sent Edward Brampton, a godson of King Edward, off to sea in two ships with orders to "take Sir Edward Woodville". An offer of pardon was made to all sailors on Woodvilles ships and all but two responded and returned to London. Woodville and his two ships landed in Brittany to join the exiled Henry Tudor. Thomas Woodville, Marques of Dorset, as Deputy Constable of the Tower, also took part of the treasure which also found its way to Henry Tudor. When the prince's party entered the city, together with this large force of armed men, there was much talk of a coup-de-etat, but Gloucester calmed the situation, explaining that he was foiling a Woodville conspiracy against him and "the old nobility of the realm. The young king was lodged in the Tower, which, at the time was a royal residence in addition to its role as a prison. The people, having little love for the grasping Woodvilles, accepted his explanations and were reassured. The business of government continued in the name of Edward V until June the 8th when the issue of writs in Edward's name stopped. On the 16th June, the coronation, set for the 22nd, was suddenly postponed until the 9th November.

On the 22nd June 1483, Robert Stillington, Bishop of Bath, announced to the Council that Edward IVs claim to the throne was not lawful. Within days, sermons were preached in London, alleging that Edward IV was not a true king on account of his being born illegitimate. Further, his sons could not inherit the throne because they too were bastards. It is not clear on what grounds Edward IVs legitimacy was questioned, but the sermons also claimed that the old king's marriage to Elisabeth Woodville was invalid due to his having previously married an Elisabeth Lucy. She was known to have been one of Edward's many mistresses and had borne him a son, but no record exists of a marriage. A further claim was that he had precontracted a marriage to an Elisabeth Butler, daughter of the Earl of Shrewsbury. If a precontract had in fact taken place, then in law, his marriage to Elisabeth Woodville would indeed have been unlawful, thus making his offspring illegitimate and Gloucester the true heir to the throne.

Shortly thereafter, the young Richard, Duke of York was taken from his Westminster sanctuary on Gloucester's orders on the pretext that" his brother required his company" and both children were lodged in the Tower The two boys were seen on occasion, playing on the tower green, but these sightings became fewer until they ceased altogether. Many theories have been put forward to explain their fate. Were they murdered and, if so by whom? History tends to favor Richard of Gloucester as the culprit, certainly his friend and ally the Duke of Buckingham, as Constable of England had access to the Tower and he could have arranged the murders on Richard's orders or to remove two more obstacles to his own claim to the throne. Gloucester had reputedly sent a John Green with a letter to the Tower's Constable, Sir Robert Brackenbury, exhorting him to kill the princes, which would seem a fairly foolhardy thing to do. Brackenbury refused and Gloucester later chose Tyrell for the deed. John Howard, later to become the Duke of Norfolk could also be regarded as a suspect. He was, quite unusually, given custody of the Tower on the night that the children were supposed to have disappeared, but it also known that Sir James Tyrell was sent by Gloucester to Sir Robert Brackenbury, with a demand for the keys to the fortress. Sir Thomas More, quoting from contempory hearsay states that the princes were smothered by pillows in their beds by Sir James

Tyrell, John Dighton and Miles Forest. Tyrell is reported to have confessed to the murders in 1502 when he himself was under sentence of death for treason. This information was gained under torture however and must, therefore, be suspect. Why then should Richard of Gloucester need to murder the princes? Having had them declared illegitimate they no longer stood in his way. We know that much disinformation regarding Richard was spread by his successor Henry Tudor in an effort to strengthen his own right to the crown.

Another theory is that the princes were spirited abroad. It is known that their mother left sanctuary at Westminster with her other children and came to Richard. Would she have done this if she believed that he had killed her two sons?

What is known is that in 1674, some workmen, repairing a stone staircase in the middle tower, dug up a box containing two small human skeletons. These were thrown on to a rubbish heap, but later collected and placed in an urn which King Charles ordered to be interred in Westminster Abbey. In 1933, the bones were taken out and examined and were confirmed as those of two young humans, one a little older than the other. Our current monarch has refused permission for the bones to be further examined.

Richard III

Richard was born on the 2nd October 1452 at Fotheringay Castle, the fourth surviving son of Richard Plantagenet, 3rd Duke of York, and Cecilly Neville. Being the youngest son, he had little expectation of becoming king and spent much of his early childhood at Middleham Castle in Wensleydale under the guidance of his uncle Richard Neville, 16th Earl of Warwick. He was just 8 years old when his father and older brother Edmund were killed at the battle of Wakefield.

As a child he was rather sickly and developed rickets, causing a curvature of the spine and resulting in one shoulder being higher than the other, a not uncommon condition of the age. Thomas More refers to Richard's crooked walk and withered arm, but again, much of his writings were influenced by the Tudor desire to blacken Richard's name and he probably made the condition sound worse than it was. Shakespeare makes much of this in his play and portrays Richard as a rather hunchbacked shambling character in addition to being cast as a blackhearted murderer.

In reality Richard grew to be stocky, strong and aggressive fighting man, good at jousting and was a loyal commander on his brother's behalf throughout Edward's reign. notably at the battles of Barnet and Tewksbury. He could be very intense in his anger and contempories note his nervous habits of biting his bottom lip when thinking and half drawing and replacing his dagger repeatedly when frustrated.

It was during his youth at Middleham that he met Francis Lovell and formed a friendship that would last his life. It was here too that he first met Warwick's daughter Anne whom he would later marry. His elder brother George, Duke of Clarence had other ideas however. George had married Anne's elder sister Isabella and greatly wanted to retain full control of the old Duke of Warwick's estate. Richard's marriage to Anne would mean that the estate would be divided between the two brothers. The story goes that Clarence hid Anne as a servant in a chophouse in London, but was found by Richard and moved to safety in Westminster. The couple were married on 12th July 1472 and a year later, Anne gave birth to a son, Edward of Middleham who died on the 9th April 1484, shortly after being created Prince of Wales.

It is often supposed that Richard's marriage to Anne was one of convenience to gain a share in the Neville estate, but it is clear that the couple were devastated by the boy's death; they were often seen afterwards, walking together and clinging to each other's hand. Anne herself, always frail, died shortly afterwards. Richard did have two further, though illegitimate, children by a Katherine Haute. A son, John of Gloucester and a daughter Katherine, neither of whom seem to have left descendants.

Following his Brother George's murder in 1478, Richard was by now the most powerful of nobles. He had been created Duke of Gloucester and was also the King's Commander of the north. The brothers decided on the recapture of Berwick on Tweed, the Scottish border town that had constantly changed hands in the past and was currently held by the Scots. Edward was to bring an army northward to link up with Richard's forces, but by now, the king's health was in decline and the proposed joint venture was cancelled. Richard carried on alone and the town was successfully retaken.

With the constant struggle for influence over the king between him and the Woodvilles, Richard stayed away from court and spent his time on his northern estates. It was here that he received news of the king's death. His household immediately went into mourning and he rode with a body of knights to York where he arranged a requiem mass for the dead king and exhorted all the nobility to swear the oath of fealty to the new king, he himself being the first.

Upon learning of King Edward's death in April 1483, Richard immediately made plans to secure his position and to ensure that the rapacious Woodvilles would not benefit from their control of the new king. The king's retinue, with his Woodville relatives, Lord Rivers, Sir Richard Grey and Thomas Vaughan, plus a large force of knights was traveling south to London when they were intercepted by Richard at Northampton. The young King Edward was not with the main body, having gone ahead to Stony Stratford, a move by the Woodvilles to distance him from his uncle of Gloucester. With all outward show of affability and goodwill, Richard ensured that the Woodvilles could not travel on to join the king, but kept them close overnight at Northampton, even, it is said, sending dishes from his own table to assure them of his warmth towards them. In one swift stroke the next day, all three were arrested on charges of treason and sent to Richard's stronghold of Pontefract in the north. Surprisingly the escort accepted this change of leadership without demur and the party moved on, unlike the young king who protested loudly at the detention of his uncles. The royal party, led by Richard , Henry Stafford, Duke of Buckingham, plus the large retinue of troops, entered London with much pomp and ceremony. The townspeople were pleased that Richard was in control as they largely mistrusted the Woodvilles, although some rumors spread that Richard was intent on usurping the throne for himself. Richard went to some length to deny the accusations. He stated that his only desire was to ensure the safe keeping of the new king and accused the Woodvilles of plotting to take the throne themselves.

A great Council was convened to determine the governance of the country during the king's minority and two solutions emerged. One that Richard should be allowed to rule as Regent alone and the other that he be made chief among a council of ministers. This latter course was agreed, it being noted that Regents never laid down their office, save reluctantly or from armed compulsion. This decision had little effect however on Richard's later actions. All who favored the queen's family voted for this option, fearing that, if Richard where to rule alone, they who had a hand in Clarence's murder would be killed or ejected from their estates. Although no copy of King Edward's will exists, Richard insisted that it named him as Lord Protector in the king's minority while parliament made him Chief Councillor.

Richard now had all the reigns of power to ensure that the Woodvilles could no longer represent a threat. The Queen Dowager, seeing which way events were heading, fled with her daughters and younger son Richard to sanctuary in Westminster, taking with her however, a large part of the royal treasure amassed by her husband. Her brother, Thomas Woodville fled with her, also taking with him a share of the treasure. Edward Woodville, another brother of the queen, acting in his role as Commander of the King's Fleet, took to sea with his fleet of 20 ships and also took part of the old king's fortune with him. The wily Richard had the ships followed and bribes made to the various captains to ensure their return to London. Woodville, with only two ships remaining, sailed to Brittany to join the exiled Henry Tudor, another claimant to the throne.

Richard reinforced his claims of Woodville plotting when four wagons of weapons were discovered near London, bearing the Woodville arms. Supporters of the Woodvilles claimed that the arms had been assembled in readiness for waging war against the Scots, but as it was Richard himself who had most recently fought in the north, the claim looks doubtful and it is possible that they were being stored for just the Woodville uprising that Richard opposed. What was in Richard's mind now? He had control of the king; he had contained his main Woodville rivals and had control of the Council. He knew however, that his role as Protector could only last until the young king reached his majority. What would happen then? Would power be simply handed back to the hated Woodvilles?. History had many lessons regarding royal minorities; many still remembered the turmoil of the reign of the feeble Henry VI and Richard would have kept in mind the fate of another Protector, his uncle Humphrey of Gloucester, reputedly murdered when others gained control of a young king's mind.

Richard lodged the young king in the Tower which was at the time, a royal residence as well as a fortress "for his safety" and the business of the realm continued with royal writs now being issued under the seal of Edward V and countersigned by Richard with his motto "Loyeaulte me lie", until suddenly stopping on the 8th of June. On the 16th June, postponement of the coronation, scheduled for 22nd June was announced and a new date set for the 9th November.

A number of events now occurred that seems to have changed Richard. He discovered that Lord Hastings and John Morton the Bishop of Ely had been plotting with the Dowager Queen to challenge his authority and on the 8th June, Robert Stillington, the Bishop of Bath and Wells, had made a startling revelation in a council meeting (at which Richard was not present) to the effect that Edward V was illegitimate and could not, therefore, be a lawful king. It is likely that Hastings and Morton, seeing Richard's hand in this announcement, joined the queen's faction to stop Richard taking the throne. Richard did write to the city of York, requesting that troops be sent to him "to assist us against the queen, her bloody adherents and affinity" and London's streets were soon full of armed men in Gloucester's livery. Stillington maintained that Edward IV had a marriage precontract with Eleanour Butler; such a precontract would mean that his subsequent marriage to Elisabeth Woodville was invalid and that any offspring thereof would be illegitimate. This gave Richard clear line of sight to the throne. How much of this had been orchestrated by him we can never know, but within a short time he had the other remaining son of Edward IV, the young Richard of York, removed from sanctuary and lodged with the young king in the Tower "to keep him company". This request being backed up by troops surrounding his Westminster retreat.

Much has been written regarding Stillington's allegations and it has long been assumed that they were merely devices to clear Richard's path to the throne, but it should be remembered that, if true, under medieval law, Richard was the lawful heir to the crown. Henry Tudor's attempts later to suppress the laws and judgments on the subject, largely to help legitimize his own marriage to the prince's sister Elizabeth, resulted in chroniclers largely ignoring these important events or attempting garbled versions of the facts.

The ever suspicious Richard was determined to destroy any of the old king's adherents and looked for treason in all men. He settled on Hastings, the Chamberlain, John Morton, the Bishop of Ely and Thomas Rotheram. It was reported to Richard that these three frequently foregathered in each others houses and he became convinced that they were plotting against him, which was true. He arranged an elaborate plan whereby the three were instructed to attend a council meeting in the Tower and once admitted, Richard declared that there was a plot afoot to kill him and called in soldiers who he had kept in waiting nearby. Richard accused them of treason and also accused Elisabeth Woodville of witchcraft, stating that he had been cursed by her and was unable to sleep, eat or drink. He bared his withered arm and accused her of causing the infirmity. All three were arrested and Hastings was taken outside and executed.

These events caused much concern among the moderate nobles of the council. If Hastings could be so treated, so could they. There had been no semblance of a trial; Hastings was killed on the express order of Richard in direct denial of his rights under Magna Carta. There are some who would argue that Hastings was arrested on the 13th June, tried and executed on the 18th of June, but no proof now exists for this position. The populace too was restless with many believing that Richard was intent on usurping the crown.

Richard however, while still publicly proclaiming that he was merely righting old wrongs and protecting his young charge, while gradually removed all attendants who had waited on the king and withdrawing him and his brother into the inner apartments of the Tower, being seen less and less frequently until at length, ceasing to appear at all. The last of the king's old attendants, a Dr Argentin, reported that the lad was aware of his probable fate and, like a victim prepared for sacrifice, sought remission of his sins by daily confession and penance. Prince Edward and his brother were left to the care of Richard's man William Slaughter.

Richard held a series of secret meetings with a Ralph Shaa, half brother to London's Mayor and a noted theologian with a large following, during which he is said to have made clear his claims of his brother's bigamy and the young king's illegitimacy. Shaa duly preached a sermon at St Paul's in the presence of Richard "with a great guard of armed men". Shaa preached of Richard's mother, Duchess Cecily's adultery and naming Edward IV as a bastard. He urged the congregation to name Richard the true king. The ripples of the sermon spread throughout the land and caused much unrest, many ordinary folk feared for the lives of the young princes. Rumblings of rebellion were heard in the south and west of the country as well as London. In the north where Richard had most of his support, he reinforced it with bribes and rewards, buying loyalty and arresting opponents. On June 22nd 1483, Richard declared that he was taking the throne and on July 6th, was crowned at Westminster Abbey. It is said that, with the exception of three young Earls not old enough to attend, every peer of the realm was there, saying much for the power Richard now wielded.

Shortly after his coronation, he toured his old power base in the north, receiving a warm welcome in York and traveled on to see his son Edward invested as Prince of Wales. Richard was far from safe in his new position however, the unrest in the country among the supporters of Edward V, plus threats of invasion from the exiled Henry Tudor who claimed the throne through his ancestor John of Gaunt, plus the threat posed by supporters of the Dowager Queen and her daughters, caused him to lose trust in those who had helped him to his new position. Attempts were made by his enemies to rescue the queen and her daughters from their sanctuary, hoping that, should the worse happen and the young princes be killed, the daughters might provide at some future time, a king of Edward IVs line. Anticipating this, Richard had the sanctuary surrounded by the austere John Nesfield and his men, allowing no entry or exit without permission of the new king.

Events were now getting out of hand, throughout the south of England people were rising in protest at Richard's perceived favoring of the north at their expense, plus growing public concern at the disappearance of the princes. Richard would never be safe on his throne while the youngsters lived. Accordingly, it is said, he ordered Sir James Tyrell to visit Brackenbury, the Constable of the Tower, with a letter from Richard demanding that the Tower keys be handed over for one night. This accomplished, Tyrell appointed two henchmen, John Dighton and Miles Forest, to the task of murdering the princes. Creeping into their room in the night and smothering them to death with pillows. This done, they summoned Sir James to see the bodies before burying them at a stair foot deep under the Tower.

Rumour and unrest was rife and letters were sent to the exiled Earl of Richmond, Henry Tudor, to invade, assuring him of support in driving Richard from the throne, Richard's long time friend Henry Stafford, Duke of Buckingham, who had done so much to aid Richard in his elevation, now chose this time to change coats and join the rebels. He urged Henry Tudor to hasten to England and suggested marriage to Elisabeth, the eldest daughter of the late king, and together with her, take possession of the English throne. Buckingham promised armed support for Henry and began raising troops. Richard, through his many spies, got wind of the plotting and stationed loyal troops at strategic points in the West Country and on the Welsh borders to forestall any invasion plans. Bad weather in the channel forced Henry and his forces back to Brittanny. Without the promised invasion, Buckingham's support faded away. Buckingham was named a traitor and was now a hunted man. He exchanged his lavish clothes for peasant's rags and sought refuge in the lowly house of his servant Ralph Bannaster of Wem . Bannaster however, betrayed Buckingham who was taken to Salisbury and beheaded in the market square on 2nd November 1483. Richard with a large army moved on westward determined to destroy any armed opposition and by the time he had reached Exeter, the rebel leaders had fled. Richard with his usual cunning confiscated the estates of the rebels and redistributed them among his northern supporters to the great chagrin of the south. Richard, with his cronies Lovell, Ratcliffe and Catesby now ruled with little reference to parliament, thus causing a seditious rhyme to circulate, a copy of which was found fastened to the Cross in Cheap side, reading, "The Cat, the Rat and Lovell our dog, now rule all England under a Hog", a white boar being the motif on Richard's personal livery. Two Londoners, Collingwood and Turbeville were arrested for this and imprisoned. At the subsequent trial, Collingwood was found guilty and sentenced to be hanged, drawn and his bowels cast into the fire. This was so swiftly and expertly done that it is said that. When the butcher pulled out his heart he spoke and said "Jesus, Jesus"

At Christmas 1484, Richard learned from his spies overseas that Henry Tudor was preparing another invasion. The news pleased Richard for he realized that this could be the opportunity to rid himself at last of this final opposition. To fight however, he would need money and accordingly resurrected King Edward's practice of "benevolences" whereby he sent collectors throughout the country, examining the accounts of all and extracting taxes there from. This move further alienating him from the populace.

Following the death of his wife, he had began to pay much attention to his brother's eldest daughter, Elisabeth of York and rumors spread that he was to marry her and thus add more legitimacy to his claim to the crown. At this suggestion, even his closest confidantes Catesby and Ratcliffe were appalled. They made it clear that any such arrangement would alienate his support in the north and that even the Pope would refuse to condone a marriage of such close sanguinity. There was a measure of self interest in their protests as, should Elisabeth become queen, she could exact great revenge on those who had assisted in the reputed murder of her brothers. Their argument prevailed and in August, in the great Hall of St John's hospital, Richard denied that marriage had ever crossed his mind and threatening anyone repeating the allegation with imprisonment.

On the 7th August 1485, Henry Tudor landed at Milford Haven in Pembrokeshire with a small force. His Tudor heritage earned him some support in Wales and his force grew as he moved east. On hearing this, Richard was said to have rejoiced, writing to his supporters in every quarter that the hour of reckoning had come and he could finally rid himself of the last claimant to the throne and rule thereafter in tranquility. He sent out further letters demanding that all men of rank must now support him and that any man found not to have done so after the battle would lose not only his life, but his estates and titles too.

Richard's mistrust of those around him can be clearly seen when his seneschal, Lord Thomas Stanley, requested permission to return to his estates in Lancashire. Richard agreed, but insisted that Stanley's son, Lord Strange remained with the king as a hostage to ensure loyalty. Richard must have been all too aware of the conflicting loyalties facing Thomas Stanley, who had married Henry Tudor's widowed mother, Margaret Beaufort. Could Margaret persuade him to change sides and support the invasion?. Richard did not want to risk this and sent orders for Lord Stanley to meet him at Nottingham. Lord Stanley wrote to the king, begging to be excused and claiming that he had sweating sickness. Further, Lord Stanley's brother William was Lord Chamberlain of North Wales and in sole command of forces that might counter any advance by Henry Tudor. Richard realized the danger in the situation and, learning that the young Lord Strange had attempted to escape, had him questioned, revealing that the William Stanley and his henchman Sir John Savage had planned to join Henry Tudor all along, but that his father

Thomas remained loyal. Richard forced Strange to write to his father, explaining his plight and urging him to join the king without delay. He had both nobles declared traitors and moved northwards gathering forces as he went.

Henry Tudor gathered forces as he neared Welshpool and more Welshmen joined at a muster outside the town. He felt sufficiently strong to demand the surrender of Shrewsbury which, after a few days resistance, capitulated. With Wales largely pro Tudor, Richard summoned his forces to meet at Leicester, but not all answered the call. An extract from a letter written by the Duke of Norfolk to a John Paston, head of a family of Norfolk gentry reads "Wherefore I pray you meet me at Bury St Edmunds and that you bring with you such company of tall men as you may goodly make at my cost and charge besides, that which you have promised the king , and I pray, you ordain them with jackets of my livery and I shall content you at your meeting with me".There is no record of Paston having brought any men badged with Norfolk's white lion to the muster, but it is known that he was created Sheriff of Norfolk some two months later under Henry Tudor's rule, possibly a reward for his reticence?

Treachery was in the air and many nobles were choosing sides based on their reckoning of who would triumph in the forthcoming battle. Even those on their way to Leicester to join the king were not to be trusted with those such as Sir Thomas Bourchier and Sir Walter Hungerford slipping away at Stony Stratford to join the rebels.

Richard celebrated the Feast of the Assumption of Blessed Virgin Mary on August 15th, demonstrating his confidence at the time, but shortly afterwards learned of the mass defections in Wales, plus the surrender of Shrewsbury. By now he must have realized that he was not going to get the total support that he expected from the nobility. Norfolk continued raising troops but the Earl of Northumberland was proving less prompt, causing Richard to issue a summons for troops from York on 16th August.

Henry meanwhile, moved eastwards, keeping an escape route open into Wales. At Newport he was joined by Sir Gilbert Talbot, an important landowner, bringing with him 500 men. This was Henry's first major English contingent and must have heartened him. It is known that William Stanley met up with Henry Tudor at Stafford where he explained that his brother Thomas could not declare for Henry until the last possible moment without condemning Lord Strange, his son, to death. Lord Stanley with his forces reached Litchfield on August 17th, then moved eastwards, retreating in front of Henry to give the impression that he was making for Richard's muster at Leicester.

Richard left Nottingham on the 20th August and joined the muster at Leicester. His forces, reckoned by now to be between 10000 and 15000 strong and led by the Duke of Norfolk, and Earls of Northumberland, Surrey, Lincoln and Shrewsbury in what the Croyland Chronicle called "numbers greater than had ever seen before in England collected together on behalf of one person", moved through Peckleton and Kirkby Mallory. On the 21st, At Sutton Cheney, learning through his scouts that Henry was nearing White Moors, he positioned his troops up on the commanding ground of Ambion Hill, west of Sutton Cheney and close to the village of Market Bosworth.

Henry meanwhile, had arrived at Litchfield on the 20th. His forces camped somewhere between Litchfield and Tamworth that night. Henry himself disappeared from the camp overnight, possibly to prepare his mind for the coming fight. The historian

Polydor Vergil states that Henry merely got lost and spent the night incognito in a nearby town, rejoining his worried troops in the morning, excusing himself by saying that he had gone to meet certain influential friends and had received "some good news".

Vergil goes on to state that Henry traveled to Atherstone on the 21st, to where William and Thomas Stanley were camped "taking one another by th'hand and yielding mutual salutation, each man was glad for the good state of th'others, and all their minds were moved to great joy". Henry was further heartened when a number of Richard's captains deserting the king, arrived with their troops to join the rebels.

Richard's forces spent the night on Ambion Hill and, as the sun rose at 5.15 on the 22nd August 1485. , he marshaled them and brought them down from the height to better array them for the battle. He disposed them in two divisions, the van ward being commanded by the Duke of Norfolk and Brackenbury , with the Earl of

278

Northumberland in the rear. Archers were placed in front of Norfolk's troops. Richard placed himself and his bodyguards behind Norfolk.

It must have been a daunting sight for Tudor's men as they moved forward, seeing the might arrayed against them. Henry Tudor divided his force of 5000 in three divisions, the main centre under the experienced Earl of Oxford, plus two small flanking units under Sir John Savage on the left and Sir Gilbert Talbot on the right. An area of marshland protected his force on the right and He himself, with a small contingent of horsemen and some infantry, placed themselves some distance behind the main battle. The Stanley's meanwhile, had arrived with their force of 3000, but stood off some way to the south. Henry sent word to Lord Stanley to come and join the ranks, but Stanley replied that he would move once Henry's forces were deployed, not a very reassuring answer at that moment!.

There are a number of versions of the course of the battle, Molinet, a Burgundian historian states that Richard's artillery engaged the front of the rebels, causing them to edge to the left exposing a gap between them and the marsh , while others talk of Richard's hand gunners opening the battle . Vergil's version seems the more likely. He states that Henry's centre advanced and was met with a volley of arrows from Norfolk's archers, causing the troops to bunch up and expose some ground between them and the marsh. This move also presented their backs to Stanley's forces and if he were to aid Richard, now was the time. Norfolk's troops also advanced and the two sides met with a great crash of arms. From Richard's viewpoint he could see the gap and if he were to send his cavalry in, he could roll up Henry's right wing in a pincer movement between them and Norfolk's men. Richard however, had other ideas. Through the gap he could see the banners and standards of Henry and his entourage. If he could reach them and kill Henry his problems would be over. Without hesitation he charged forward, followed by his small band of retainers, aiming direct for Henry. So fierce was his assault that he tore through those surrounding Henry, slashing and cutting until he came to Henry's standard bearer William Brandon, felling him with a blow. He next attacked a John Cheney, described as a man of great fortitude, who also fell beneath the king's onslaught. Behind

Richard, his followers were fighting desperately against the foot soldiers who were trying to protect Henry. So fierce was the fighting that Richard's own standard bearer, Sir Percival Thirlwell was beaten down and had both legs hacked off, but Richard's small force came ever closer to where Henry Tudor stood. It was at this moment that the treacherous Stanley's chose to intervene, streaming in from the south and striking the king's forces on their left flank. Stanley had chosen his moment well. He knew that Richard would not forgive his failure to act earlier and also knew that Henry, now in deep trouble, would be suitably grateful for this timely intervention. Panic spread through Richard's men and many turned and fled, suffering much slaughter in their flight. Many others surrendered, including Northumberland's division which had taken no part in the battle, either because he had not had time to deploy or, as Vergil suggests, he was keeping his options open. The speed of the surrender accounts for the relatively small number of deaths during the battle. Vergil estimates that royalist losses were 1000, while Henry Tudor's amounted to no more than 100, but Molinet suggests 300 deaths on either side...

Richard meanwhile, with his army disintegrating around him was now surrounded, many of his knights had been unhorsed and were fighting on foot, his followers urged Richard to escape but he replied "God forbid that I yield one step. This day I will die as a king or win". With his horse bogged down in the marshy ground, Richard bravely struck at his enemies until at last he was pulled from his horse and hacked to death. While history has been cruel to Richard, there is no doubt of his bravery and fortitude when facing his death.

Virgil states that, following the battle, Henry "got himself to a near hill" where he commanded his troops to tend the wounded and bury the dead. He praised the nobility and gentlemen with his immortal thanks, promising that he "would be mindful of their benefits". The troops replied with great shouts of " God save King Henry" and Lord Stanley placed the golden coronet, so recently on the helm of Richard, on Henry's head.

Richard's naked body was slung across a horse, with one of his heralds being forced to ride it and taken to Leicester and left on show for two days for all to see at the church of St Mary, following which he was buried without ceremony at Grey Friars near St Martins church. Some years later Henry VII gave a sum of ten pounds and one shilling for the cost of a tomb for Richard, but at the dissolution of the monasteries it was plundered and his bones lost. Recent excavations have revealed Richard's remains under a Leicester car park, once the site of a monastery.

Richard's death ended the bloody dynastic War of the Roses and ushered in a new age. The uniting of York and Lancaster with Henry's marriage to Elizabeth secured the throne for the Tudors and finally brought peace to England

ACKNOWLEDGEMENTS

The Anglo Saxon Chronicles .Translated by Anne Savage.
Salamander Books
Illustrated Chronicles of Mathew Paris. Translated by Richard
Vaughan. Alan Sutton Publishing
Whos's Who in Early Medieval England. Christopher
Tyerman. Shepheard-WalwynPublishers
Who's Who in Late Medieval England. Michael Hicks.
Shepheard-Walwyn Publishers
The Hundred Years War. Robin Neillands, Published by
Routledge
Kings, Queens, Bones and Bastards. David Hillman. Sutton
Publishing Group
Ruling England. Richard Huscroft.   Pearson Education Ltd
Crecy 1346. David Nicolle. Osprey Publishing
Poitiers 1356. David Nicolle. Osprey Publishing
British Battles. Ken and Denise Guest. Harper Collins
Publishers Ltd
The Death of Kings. Clifford Brewer. T.D F.R.C.S.   Abson
Books, London
The Mystery of the Princes. Audrey Williamson.   Alan
Sutton Publishing
War Walks.   Richard Holmes.   BBC Worldwide Ltd
The Wars of the Roses. J.R.Lander.   Alan Sutton Publishing
Hastings to Culloden . Peter Young and John Adair. Sutton
Publishing